INSIDE

Panama

INSIDE

Panama

**Tom Barry and John Lindsay-Poland with
Marco Gandásegui and Peter Simonson**

Resource Center Press
Albuquerque, New Mexico

Acknowledgments

Inside Panama would not have been possible without the contributions of a number of individuals and organizations. Within the Resource Center, Chris Givler designed and produced the book. Josette Griffiths and Rachel Hays provided research assistance. Beth Sims proofed and edited the text. Debra Preusch coordinated this project.

We are grateful to the Fellowship of Reconciliation and the Panamanian organizations Peace and Justice Service (SERPAJ) and the Panamanian Center of Social Studies and Action (CEASPA) for their crucial research contributions. The Resource Center would also like to thank Charlotte Elton, George Priestley, and Richard Millett for their insightful and detailed comments on the manuscript.

Contents

Part 4: Society and Environment

Contents

Figures

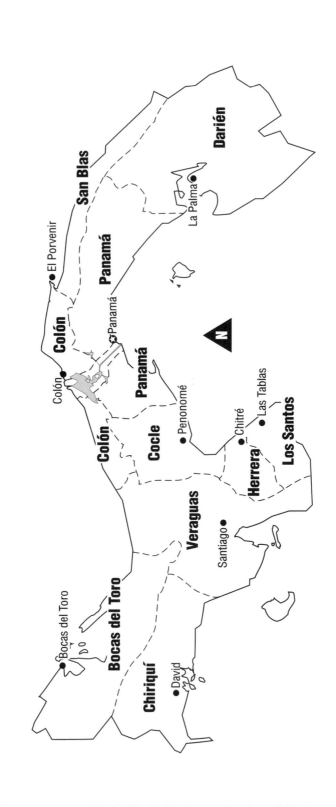

Introduction

Panama, the southernmost country in the Central American isthmus, stands apart from its neighbors. Although geographically it is clearly a Central American nation, Panama historically has not been included in such regional bodies as the Central American Common Market. Neither has it been considered a South American nation despite once having been a province of Colombia.

Despite its differences, Panama shares with most of its Central American neighbors a history bloodied by U.S. military intervention and shaped by foreign investment and trade. The enclave economies of the United Fruit banana plantations, the U.S. Canal Zone, and the Colón Free Trade Zone have largely defined the political, economic, and social structures of Panama. No other country in the region has been so thoroughly dominated by the United States—so much so that it has often taken the character of a U.S. protectorate.

Even more than this close relationship with the United States, Panama's special character comes from its role as an international crossroads. Panama was a territory of transit long before the Panama Canal was finished in 1914. King Charles V of Spain dreamed in 1534 of cutting a canal across Panama not long after the Spanish colonized this tropical land. Portobelo, a sea port on the Caribbean coast, was one of the major trading centers of the New World. In the nineteenth century the U.S.-built railroad took the forty-niners across the isthmus on their way to the hills of gold in California. Unlike elsewhere in Central America, the Panamanian elite were not a landed oligarchy but a business sector tied to international trade and services.

Over the past five centuries, peoples from all continents came together in Panama to create a society and political system guided more by pragmatism than by ideology. This pragmatism has shaped the responses and activities of the country's leading political and economic figures, who have developed a keen understanding of Panama's distinctive position straddling the Atlantic and the Pacific. Historically, the men who shaped Panama's political and economic history believed it impossible to define an independent course precisely because of the country's strategic geopolitical position. Rather, they have negotiated Panama's autonomy *vis-à-vis* the great powers.

Panama, about the size of South Carolina, stands out as the country in the region with the highest per capita income, highest foreign investment, and most highly developed economic infrastructure. Nearly 90 percent of its 2.5 million inhabitants are literate and 83 percent have access to potable water—indicators that compare very favorably with most Central American nations. Similarly, its 2 percent annual population growth and population density of 33 people per square kilometer offer a brighter picture for social and economic development than elsewhere in the region.

It is, however, a country of extreme contrasts. The shimmering office buildings and banks of Panama City face squalid slums. Looking out from the penthouse apartments of these skyscrapers you can also see where the concrete and electric wires stop and the dense tropical forests begin. More than 40 percent of country's population live in the Panama City-Colón corridor that parallels the canal. Traveling west from Panama City along the Pacific toward Costa Rica, one enters Panama's heartland. In the rural towns and villages that border the southern shore, one encounters an area rich in tradition and full of cultural expression. Forty-five percent of Panamanians live in rural areas.

Reaching east toward South America is a long strip of rainforest and swamps known as the Darién Gap. Like most of the country's Caribbean seaboard, except the city of Colón and United Fruit's banana plantations in the Bocas del Toro region, the Darién Gap is largely roadless and sparsely inhabited. Although rapidly becoming deforested and colonized, there are no immediate prospects for completing the Inter-American Highway between Panama and Colombia. In recent years, however, this remote region has become a refuge and staging area for drug traffickers and Colombian guerrillas.

There are those who say that the name Panama comes from an indigenous word meaning "land of many fish." Others insist that it stems from the indigenous phrase *panna mai*: When Spanish *conquistadores* asked the indians where they could find gold, they were answered with the phrase meaning "far away."[1] Located in the tropical zone, Panama has a uniformly hot and humid climate that cools off somewhat in the western highlands. The rainy season runs from April to November, although no month is entirely free of rain. More than 500 waterways crisscross Panama but only two rivers are navigable.

Introduction

Nationalism and anti-U.S. sentiments have been a constant feature of Panamanian society since independence in 1903. In 1964, 21 Panamanians lost their lives to U.S. bullets in a protest to win the right to fly the Panamanian flag at schools in the Canal Zone. But there is also, especially among the middle and upper classes, a pattern of dependent behavior and identification with all things with a USA label—from consumer products and cultural values to language and politics. It was no surprise to see many middle-class Panamanians out in the streets waving U.S. flags after the December 1989 invasion. It will also be no surprise to see the undercurrent of nationalism and resentment of the United States surge again in the future.

In the 1990s Panama has joined the other countries in the region in the path toward demilitarization and the consolidation of political democracies. Although still largely defined by its position as an international crossroads and its more integral ties to U.S. foreign policy interests, Panama has in recent years increasingly become part of regional integration efforts in Central America. Like the other small countries of the region, Panama confronts the challenges posed by economic globalization. However, the most pressing question facing Panama's leaders and the society in general is the scheduled transfer of the Panama Canal and of U.S. military and other facilities by the last day of this century. How Panama and the United States view this planned transfer remains a matter of much debate.

Although Panama shares with its regional neighbors the dilemmas posed by structural adjustment and U.S. intervention, it also enjoys some unique advantages. A nexus of world trade and finance, Panama displays comparatively well-developed systems of public service and infrastructure; levels of health and education are some of the highest in Central America (behind only Costa Rica). After the political upheaval of the 1989 U.S. invasion and the elimination of their military forces, Panamanians also have a greater sense of urgency about the development of democratic conditions in their country. In the last several years there has been a resurgence of debate, involvement, and energy surrounding Panama's social and political future that is unmatched in the country's recent history. This is as it should be. Panamanians will have to capitalize on the new political space opened up by the end of military rule if economic recovery is to continue and levels of poverty and unemployment are to be reduced.

Part 1

Government and Politics

© John Lindsay-Poland

Dictators and Democrats

Panamanians waited only four years before restoring to government the Democratic Revolutionary Party (PRD)—the political party that had been closely associated with the Manuel Noriega regime that U.S. military forces ousted from power in 1989. The May 1994 election of PRD presidential candidate Ernesto Pérez Balladares also displaced Guillermo Endara, a president installed in office by the U.S. military during the invasion.

Endara's swearing in on a U.S. military base in Panama in December 1989 marked the first time since 1968 that Panama's government was not beholden to Panama's military. The new civilian government, while breaking the two-decade tradition of military rule, renewed another more deeply rooted tradition in Panama—U.S. military intervention in the country's domestic politics.

A wealthy lawyer and businessman, Endara led the Democratic Civic Opposition Alliance (ADOC) that had won the May 1989 presidential election by a two-to-one margin according to most foreign and domestic election monitors but was denied victory by General Noriega. However, the vote for Endara and the ADOC coalition was more a protest vote against Noriega than an expression of support for this elite political coalition.

Amidst ensuing international condemnation of the fraudulent and violent nature of the election, the regime canceled the results of the election. The United States insisted that Erick Delvalle, ousted in February 1988, was still the legitimate president of Panama. In September 1989, when the former presidential term expired, Noriega selected Francisco Rodríguez as provisional president, while Washington declared that Endara should have been inaugurated as the country's new president. The December 1989 invasion toppled the Noriega regime, opening the way for Endara and the ADOC coalition to take the reins of government.

When Endara took the oath of office, Panamanians celebrated the end to twenty-one years of military rule. But it would be wrong to equate civilian rule in Panama with stability and progress. From 1903 to 1968—the year soldiers took control of government—Panama saw a series of aristocratic civilian governments, few of which made a serious effort to assert Panamanian sovereignty or to institute serious social reforms. Social and political control depended on close collaboration with the U.S. military and the country's own National Guard. The Endara government represented a fresh start. With its antimilitary credentials and its commitment to formal democracy, the Endara administration represented a clear break from the army-controlled governments of the past two decades, although the increased influence of the United States and the oligarchy were more traditional features of Panamanian government.

Legal Structure of Government

According to the 1972 constitution, executive power in Panama is held by a president directly elected every five years (next general election scheduled for May 1999) and assisted by two elected vice presidents and an appointed cabinet composed of twelve ministers.[1] Legislative power is vested in a unicameral Legislative Assembly that consists of seventy-two deputies, organized into fifteen specialized commissions.[2] The government's judiciary branch comprises the Supreme Court, subordinate tribunals, and district and municipal courts. The nine members appointed by the president to the Supreme Court are charged not only with constitutional law-making but also with mediating disputes between the executive and legislative branches.

Another important instrument of government is the Election Tribunal, an autonomous institution with representatives from the legislative, executive, and judicial branches. The constitution divides the country into forty electoral circuits, half of which elect one, and the other half two or more legislators. The country is also organized into nine provinces, each with a governor appointed by the president, and Panama has one semiautonomous indigenous territory. Each province is further divided into districts and municipalities. Mayors of the country's sixty-six municipal districts and representatives of the 511 smaller *corregimientos* are elected by direct vote.

Although Panama's constitution dates back to 1972, it underwent two reforms in 1978 and 1983, and it is the fourth such document to guide government since 1904. The 1978 reform removed an article that granted the National Guard power to coordinate the three government branches. In 1983 the National Guard was replaced with the

Panama Defense Forces (PDF). After the 1989 U.S. invasion, the PDF was dismantled, and the Public Force and the National Police were created.

Beginning in 1968 there developed an extensive structure of government participation in the economy and society. This includes dozens of (often highly corrupt) state enterprises and sectoral institutions, including a cement company, a racetrack, a sugar corporation, the telecommunications company, and a national lottery, as well as such institutions as the national university, the agricultural development bank, and the tourism bureau. Many of these entities were operated in inefficient, politically motivated, and corrupt ways. Although plans for privatization began in the mid-1980s, only recently have some of the parastatal institutions begun to be dismantled.

One of the most important of Panama's state institutions is the Social Security Institute, which was created by Arnulfo Arias in the 1940s. Covering over half the population, Panama's social security system provides health services and financial benefits in cases of illness, accident, and pregnancy. It also pays funeral expenses and assists widows and orphans. Retiring workers receive monthly pensions ranging from $145 to $1000. Since the early 1980s structural adjustment programs promoted by the World Bank, International Monetary Fund, and the U.S. Agency for International Development (AID) have whittled away at social security services as well as the rest of the expansive public sector.

Washington and Panama City

The United States has played an important historic role in the governance of Panama. Since the mid-1850s the United States has intervened militarily more than twenty times, sometimes to protect its own interests, other times to repress political dissent, and more recently to depose one government and install another (See U.S.-Panama Relations).

The Panamanian independence movement for example, can be traced deep into the past century, but it was Washington that made nationhood possible when it decided to build the Panama Canal. As Omar Torrijos often remarked, however, the United States too often behaved like a midwife who keeps the baby in return for her services.[3]

Even before Panamanian independence and the building of the canal, the United States had been in the habit of sending in troops to protect U.S. lives and interests. Between 1856 and 1903 the U.S. military intervened in Panama at least ten times. This custom of intervention became a right with the signing of the 1903 Hay-Bunau

Varilla Treaty. This first canal treaty gave the United States the right to intervene militarily to "maintain public order necessary" for the construction and operation of the canal. It also gave the United States the power to act in the Canal Zone "as if it were the sovereign of the territory." A year later the country's new constitution established the United States as the guardian of Panamanian independence and sovereignty. The constitution gave Washington the right to intervene "in any part of Panama to reestablish public peace and constitutional order." [4]

From independence to 1936 Panama was treated as an unofficial protectorate of the United States. Adjustments were made in the dependency relationship that year when Presidents Franklin D. Roosevelt and Harmodio Arias Madrid signed a revised canal treaty that abrogated the U.S. right to intervene in the country's internal affairs. [5] The treaty also gave Panamanians increased access to the business of the Canal Zone—which previously had been exclusively in the hands of U.S. entrepreneurs. Pressured by Panamanian business interests, another treaty revision was signed in 1955 which opened up increased commercial access to the Canal Zone. The canal and the surrounding zone, however, remained outside the Panamanian government's control.

As elsewhere in the region, direct U.S. military intervention in Panama's internal affairs diminished after 1936, and especially after the militarization of the Panamanian National Police in 1943 (when World War II came, Panama was obliged to ally itself with the United States, and 130 U.S. military sites were established throughout Panama). In 1964 U.S. troops were called in to control the riots that erupted after Balboa High School students and their parents (Zonians) tried to stop the raising of the Panamanian flag by Panamanian high school students. For the most part, though, the National Guard, created in 1953, maintained order without the need for U.S. troops.

Washington also exercised its influence in Panama through the oligarchy. The narrowly based oligarchy, whose members rotated in government until the mid-1930s, looked to the United States for its blessing of presidential candidates. In several cases, the oligarchy called for U.S. intervention to settle political disputes or to crush the popular movement. In 1944 a U.S. official noted that "there has never been a successful change of government in Panama but that American authorities have been consulted beforehand." [6]

Anti-U.S. sentiment abated after the 1977 signing of new canal treaties that eliminated the Canal Zone and provided for transfer of the canal and U.S. bases to Panama by the year 2000. But during the 1980s the presence of the U.S. Southern Command (SouthCom) in Panama and perceived violation of the treaties continued to fuel

Panamanian nationalism. The structural adjustment program imposed upon the Panamanian government by the World Bank and International Monetary Fund and strongly supported by Washington gave rise to renewed nationalist sentiment among the popular sectors.

For most of the 1980s U.S. attention was focused elsewhere in Central America, principally on Nicaragua and El Salvador. Washington feared that any U.S. challenge to Noriega might destabilize the internal political situation in Panama, obstruct the expanded use of U.S. military bases for operations in Nicaragua and El Salvador, and undermine collaborative military and intelligence operations with the country's military forces. Immediately after the 1984 presidential election Washington hailed Panama's "successful transition" to democratic rule despite the patent fraudulence of the election. Secretary of State George Shultz traveled to the inauguration of Nicolás Ardito Barletta to demonstrate U.S. support for the new president. When political dissident and "freedom fighter" Hugo Spadafora was killed a year later, Washington remained conspicuously silent.[7]

In 1987, however, Washington reversed its Panama foreign policy and set out to topple the country's strongman. A combination of international (disintegration of the Soviet bloc) and national factors (increasing focus on the drug war, rising emphasis on democratization, and President Bush's own political needs) were among the reasons behind this shift (See U.S.-Panama Relations).

To pressure Noriega to step down, Washington applied harsh economic sanctions, lent support to the political opposition, and attempted to isolate Panama diplomatically. Having failed to topple the Noriega regime through nonmilitary means, Washington launched a full-scale military invasion on December 20, 1989 involving more than 27,000 troops (including 13,600 already in the country). The invasion succeeded in "decapitating" the Noriega government by ridding the country of Noriega and the PDF, but it also seriously disrupted the infrastructure of government and politics.

For twenty-one years the Panamanian military had been the guiding institution in government. Not only had the PDF served as the country's army but also as its police. The PDF (until 1983 called the National Guard) had succeeded during the 1970s in shaping a national coalition around the politics of nationalism and populism. It had brought important sectors of the national bourgeoisie into the coalition through its support and promotion of local industries and had opened the economy up to a new financial elite. By the mid-1980s, however, the unifying principles of populism and nationalism had lost most of their power as the economy declined and Panamanians became ever more frustrated with the military's strong arm and corrupt tactics.

After the 1989 invasion, populism and nationalism, which had served for more than two decades to stabilize Panamanian politics and society, lay shattered. By so egregiously violating the 1977 treaties' prohibition of U.S. intervention in the country's internal political affairs,the invasion reopened an old wound. Not only did the future control of the canal area once again become an unresolved issue but the country's very sovereignty also became an open question.

Oligarchy

Before 1968 politics in Panama were dominated by the country's small oligarchy—a grouping of a couple dozen families that are known disparagingly as *rabiblancos* (white tails).[8] For the most part this elite represented the service and commercial sector associated with the transit operations of the canal. Less powerful were the large landowners and cattle ranchers.

Political parties in Panama have served as clubs of the oligarchy.[9] The two main political clubs of the 1800s were the Liberal and Conservative Parties of Colombia. Even after independence these two elite political groups continued to compete for office. Having no serious political differences with the Liberals, Panamanian Conservatives disbanded in 1912 and integrated themselves into one or another Liberal Party faction.

When elections approached, various offshoots of the Liberal Party formed to support individual candidates. More than a half-dozen different versions of the Liberal Party governed between 1903 and 1968. There was little real difference between any of the competing factions. Parties were based on personalities and promised favors rather than contrasting political platforms.[10]

The oligarchy ruled at the pleasure of the U.S. authorities and relied on the might of the U.S. military to maintain the peace. "The overwhelming dominance of American governments over Panama distorted political life both between the rulers and the ruled and within the elite itself," observed one U.S. academic. "Relieved of the burden of consolidating its rule over the population, the Panamanian elite failed to develop effective, long-term institutions of political accommodation and cooptation."[11]

When the National Guard took control over the government in 1968, the oligarchy lacked a unifying vision of economic progress and modernization. Although breaking the dominance of the oligarchy, the regime of Omar Torrijos did not represent a class-based attack on the private sector. Instead it set about establishing a new economic alliance with the industrial and financial sectors, bypassing the interests of some of the more traditional oligarchic sectors. Many representatives of the private sector were brought into the Torrijos government as cabinet ministers and Torrijos worked closely with business leaders in developing the international financial center, expanding the Colón Free Zone, and developing the country's industrial and agricultural production capacity.

Since 1964 the National Council of Private Enterprise (CONEP) has served as the private sector's principal lobbying organization. CONEP was formed by the Chamber of Commerce, the Panamanian Association of Panamanian Business Executives (APEDE), and other business organizations to function as a type of ministry without portfolio to be consulted by the government prior to the enactment of laws that would affect the private sector.[12] Until 1968 CONEP functioned as planned, but during the early years of the Torrijos regime CONEP lost its privileged place in economic policymaking. After 1968 the association focused on defeating or reversing Torrijos populist initiatives. CONEP played a key role, for example, in revising the Labor Code in 1976 and in blocking the proposed educational reform in 1979.

Torrijos succeeded in establishing a close alliance with the industrial bourgeoisie and those financial interests associated with the country's international services economy. After the death of Torrijos in July 1981 in a mysterious plane crash, representatives of the traditional parties were brought back into the government's political alliance for the 1984 elections. Joining the National Democratic Union (UNADE) were the Liberal and Republican parties, the business-oriented and military-created Panamanian Labor Party (PALA), and the Revolutionary Democratic Party (PRD). The choice of Ardito Barletta, while opposed by the *torrijista* factions of the PRD, was the choice of Noriega and widely supported by the business community. Ironically, in 1985 Noriega pressured Barletta to abandon the presidency after he demanded a thorough investigation into the assassination of political leader Dr. Hugo Spadafora. Barletta's replacement with misfit Vice President Erick Arturo Delvalle, a multimillionaire with interests in sugar, race horses, and television, also illustrated the close working relationship that existed between the government and oligarchy.

Beginning in mid-1987 the country's dominant economic forces began grouping around the National Civic Crusade and later the Democratic Opposition Alliance (ADOC). The Civic Crusade brought together dozens of civic groups, business organizations, and professional associations. Three opposition political parties also were closely associated with the Civic Crusade: Christian Democratic

Party (PDC), Authentic Panameñista Party (PPA), and the National Liberal Republican Movement (MOLIRENA). By 1988 it had become clear that the country's powerful financial sector, which for so long had supported the military government, had moved into the opposition. It was not, however, the oligarchs who were the main activists of the Civic Crusade. Its most active supporters were found among the country's merchant class, landowners, middle classes, and small-business entrepreneurs.

Elements of the oligarchy closely involved in the military business complex, like the Duque family, favored continuing the alliance with the National Guard. Likewise, although not supporters of Nori-

---

Arnulfo Arias Madrid: Wild Card in Panamanian Politics

Next to Omar Torrijos, Arnulfo Arias Madrid was Panama's most imposing politician. It was Arias (1901-1988) who first seized upon nationalism and populism as a winning political formula in Panama. Beginning in the 1930s Arnulfo and his brother Harmodio Arias presented a nagging challenge to the country's political establishment. While disputing the political stronghold of the Liberal Party, the Arias brothers never challenged the economic privileges of the oligarchy.

Arnulfo Arias, soon eclipsing his older brother, took politics out of the clubhouse. With his populist and nationalistic rhetoric, Arias established a popular base for politics in Panama. He tapped the long-breeding Panamanian resentment over U.S. control, while also calling for basic social reforms. Arnulfo Arias founded the *panameñista* movement which gathered popular support among small landholders and others resentful of the oligarchy's exclusionary politics. Although he espoused a populist program, Arias was more closely committed to the interests of the oligarchy than he was to the popular sectors. In particular he represented the more backward elements of Panamanian capitalism, for example: the landed elite, small entrepreneurs, and real estate interests.

He operated in many ways like a traditional *patrón*. Arias occasionally acted and spoke on behalf of the interests of the popular sectors and helped modernize the Panamanian government. But he never stood behind the kind of structural reforms needed to alter the country's narrow class structure or to integrate the popular sectors into the political process as full participants. Arias served as president three times and was deposed each time by changing alliances of the traditional political elite, the National Guard, and the U.S. embassy. The charismatic figure was also denied the presidency in two fraudulent elections—the latest one being in 1984.

Until his death Arias remained the country's most popular politician. For many years he successfully tapped the paranoia and deep resentment that Panamanians harbored as a result of having their country oc-

ega, the financial sector did not immediately throw its support behind the U.S.-supported Civic Crusade. Washington's attempts since the early 1980s to break down the country's bank secrecy laws had been strongly rejected by the banking community and were widely regarded as being part of a U.S. campaign to undermine Panamanian sovereignty. The Civic Crusade's initial backing of U.S. economic sanctions angered large sectors of the Panamanian elite and obstructed the construction of a unified upper-class alliance against Noriega.

There was, however, wide agreement among the oligarchy and those supporting the Civic Crusade that Noriega must go and the

cupied and often directly controlled by foreigners. During his brief stint as president in 1941, Arias decreed that all advertising be in Spanish. In his xenophobic zeal, Arias also appealed to widespread racism among Panamanians against Caribbean blacks and other immigrants.

Like Arias, Torrijos also propagated the politics of populism and nationalism. But unlike Arias, Torrijos actually made a break from the oligarchy—something that Arias, a wealthy coffee grower himself, never attempted. In the 1980s Arias, ever the political opportunist, dropped his anti-U.S. rhetoric. Instead he focused his vitriol on the Panamanian military and succeeded in capturing the country's swelling antimilitarist sentiment. He disdained the Civic Crusade's dependency on Washington and was running as an independent presidential candidate on the ticket of his own Authentic Panameñista Party (PPA) when he died in 1988.

For almost half a century Arias injected a kind of messianic appeal into Panamanian politics. Before 1968 this zeal was directed against the country's traditional political parties and later against those associated with the military. In the end, however, *panameñismo* was based more on personality than on a political platform. His charisma and populist rhetoric obscured the PPA's elitist character and lack of a popular based party infrastructure. After Arias died, the PPA split into two factions (with the encouragement and manipulation of the Noriega government) with one side staying in the 1989 election as an independent party and the other faction, led by Guillermo Endara, joining the U.S.-backed political ADOC coalition.

In the 1994 elections, the *arnulfista* faction of ADOC dropped Endara and rallied behind Arias' widow Mireya Moscoso de Gruber. Moscoso ran a close second to the PRD's Pérez Balladares in the presidential elections.

Arias was inaugurated president in 1940, 1949, and 1968. He was denied the presidency in the fraudulent elections of 1964 and 1984.
SOURCE: Milciades Pinzón Rodríguez, "Arnulfo Arias Madrid: Populismo y Mesianismo," *Diálogo Social*, September 1988.

PDF be returned to their barracks. All sectors of the oligarchy—except those directly linked with the PDF in business transactions—wanted the military to step down from its central role in government and resume its pre-1968 role as the armed guarantor of political stability and elite rule. With the installation of the Endara government, the *rabiblancos* again assumed direct control over the country's economic and political development, though heavily dependent on the U.S. and international financial institutions.

Military

The U.S. military invasion brought to an end a period of Panamanian history (1968-89) in which the military exercised direct or indirect control over government in Panama. More than armed might backed up those decades of military rule. The principles and practices of *torrijismo* allowed the military to govern without resorting to the widespread repression and human rights violations common to most other military-run governments in the hemisphere. By the late 1980s, however, *torrijismo* was little more than the empty rhetoric used to justify continued corrupt rule by the PDF and its puppet politicians. The dissolution of the PDF in December 1989 left a gaping hole in Panamanian government. This recalled the first years of Panamanian nationhood when the country's military was dissolved by the United States, which itself then assumed responsibility for maintaining internal order and defending the newly independent country.

For three decades following independence in 1903, the Panamanian police were kept at this lowly and largely subservient status. The police, mainly from *mestizo* rural origins, were labeled *cholos* (half-breeds).[13] As a result of the revised canal treaty in 1936, Washington relinquished its right to intervene militarily in the country's internal affairs. President Harmodio Arias appointed José Antonio Remón Cantera to be chief of police in 1943, and under Remón's reign the prestige and the power of the National Police Forces steadily increased.

By the mid-1940s the national police was a power in its own right and had become the chief arbiter of power in the political arena.[14] Under Remón the police brokered disputes among the oligarchy and colluded with certain factions. In 1952 Remón stepped down as police chief and ran successfully for president as the head of a new conservative political coalition called the National Patriotic Committee (CPN). The police (called the National Guard after 1953) did not participate directly in government but increasingly served in its repressive capacity as the guarantor of oligarchic rule. A faction of the Liberal Party joined with the CPN to sweep the 1956 election, and

The Civic Crusade

The National Civic Crusade emerged in June 1987 following the denunciations of Col. Roberto Díaz Herrera, former military chief-of-staff. The Crusade was created to give political form to the spontaneous demonstrations that erupted in the wake of Díaz Herrera's charges against Noriega. Following his dismissal, Díaz Herrera charged the government with electoral fraud, claiming that Noriega conspired with the U.S. Southern Command to kill Torrijos and was responsible for the murder of Hugh Spadafora. After the invasion the National Civic Crusade was assured a leading role in developing policy and in creating a new institutional framework for the Panamanian political elite.

The Crusade, an umbrella group of some two hundred mostly business and professional organizations, led protests and strikes against the Noriega regime. But it failed to demonstrate the resolve and popular support necessary to challenge seriously the increasingly brutal Noriega government. Sponsored by wealthy businessmen and professionals disaffected by the regime, the Civic Crusade never made a serious effort to incorporate the popular sectors into the coalition. For the most part activists were middle-class citizens, and the organization could not overcome its rabiblanco image. The credibility of the Civic Crusade was also seriously undermined by its close identification with the U.S. State Department and the U.S. campaign of economic destabilization. The Civic Crusade dropped its original nonpartisan posture when it joined the ADOC political coalition to campaign in the 1989 elections.

Describing the class character of the Civic Crusade, a May 4, 1989 *New York Times* report observed: "When the regime cracked down, often brutally, many stopped taking part in the protests, sending their maids. Many would not even risk damaging their pots and pans when banging on kitchenware became an opposition symbol. Instead, they played tapes of the sound on cassette recorders. Some complained to human rights monitors when riot troops scratched the finish on protesters' luxury cars."

In 1992, based on a campaign to "recover moral principles," members of the Crusade organized a new political party, the Civil Renovation Party (PRC). Corporate lawyer Tomás Herrera became its leader and later the new party's presidential candidate. In January 1994 Herrera stepped down and the party supported former Comptroller Ruben D. Carles' bid under the MOLIRENA banner for the presidency. Herrera joined the ticket as second vice-president candidate.

The lack of organization and political contacts at a grassroots level minimized the electoral chances of the PRC. The civic movement that had begun as an explosive political campaign against Noriega in the late 1980s fizzled in the early 1990s.

SOURCE: *Coyuntura 94*, N°5, Panama, April 1994.

two National Liberal party candidates—Roberto Chiari (1960-1964) and Marco Robles (1964-1968)—held presidential office in the 1960s.

Although the economy was expanding, Panama in the late 1960s was facing a hegemonic crisis.[15] The traditional political parties were badly divided and counted on little support among the popular sectors which had become increasingly restive. The election of maverick politician Arnulfo Arias in 1968 was unhappily received by the National Guard and the traditional Liberal parties. The National Guard saw Arias as a threat to the power and privileges it had been accumulating through close relations with the oligarchy. Having heard that Arias planned to restructure the guard and remove many of its officers, the National Guard ousted the president.

In the jousting for dominance following 1968, Omar Torrijos emerged as the dominant figure. Torrijos, a son of middle-class educators in rural Panama, became the National Guard's third commander-in-chief and the first not linked familially to the oligarchy.[16] Under the provisions of the 1972 constitution, Torrijos became head of government. In 1978 Aristides Royo was elected by the National Assembly to become the country's figurehead president. Until his death in 1981, Torrijos was the center of political and military power in Panama. With many of the paternal characteristics of a traditional *caudillo*, Torrijos ruled Panama with a strong but considerate hand. Years after his death many Panamanians still had photos of Torrijos hanging in a place of honor on their living room walls.

Raising high the banners of nationalism and populism, Torrijos proceeded to restructure Panamanian government and politics. The traditional political parties and the Legislative Assembly were abolished. At least through the mid-1970s the National Guard functioned as an autonomous political force that ruled the country with the consultation and assistance of leaders of the private and popular sectors. Progressives and communists were brought into government mainly in the ministries of education, labor, health, agricultural development, and foreign policy. Representatives of the business sector were appointed to positions in planning, finance, and commerce and industry.

For the first time, government institutions were opened up to participation by *mestizos*, blacks, and those with lower-class origins. Calling himself *"cholo* Omar," Torrijos won wide popular support from formerly disenfranchised sectors of the population.

Another characteristic of the Torrijos regime and subsequent governments in Panama is what some have called the "military-business complex."[17] Although he broke the stronghold of the oligarchy on government, Torrijos encouraged the participation and cooperation of the industrial and financial sectors of the economic elite in his government. In return the National Guard leadership corps enriched themselves with favors and bribes offered by the private sector. The extensive network of state enterprises that was developed during the Torrijos regime also offered a new source of wealth for ambitious officers. The Transit Corporation and Colón Free Zone were especially lucrative targets for National Guard corruption. Because of their involvement in gambling, prostitution, and vice businesses, National Guard officers have been called the "mafia chiefs" of Panama.[18]

The 1972 constitution inscribed the new-found power of the National Guard into the law of the land. Previously the National Guard was subject to the civilian government, but the new constitution stipulated that "the three governmental branches are obligated to act in harmonious collaboration with the public force [National Guard]." Among the important new government institutions were the National Assembly of Community Representatives, the National Legislative Council, Legislating Commission, and local community boards under the direction of the General Directorate for Community Development (DIGEDECOM). The new institutions, especially the community boards and the National Assembly, permitted popular sectors to participate in government for the first time. But legislative and executive power was concentrated in the hands of General Torrijos.

For many Panamanian political analysts the Torrijos regime never fully committed itself to the popular sectors. Rather it was a "government of pacification" that by coopting the popular sectors allowed the economic elite to enrich themselves without fear of social upheaval and political unrest.[19] Leftist critics of the regime also charged that even the nationalism of *torrijismo* has been much overrated. The 1977 Canal Treaties, for example, continued to compromise the country's sovereignty and Torrijos' promotion of Panama as a platform of transnational services further increased the country's state of economic dependency.

Although the National Guard was in fact the country's main political institution, few guardsmen actually held government posts. One exception to this rule was Rubén Darío Paredes who served as Minister of Agricultural Development in 1975.[20] Torrijos' fellow officers were not brought into the government apparatus, but more than thirty of his friends and family members were given key positions within his government—one reason explaining the extraordinary stability of the regime.[21] Another element in the Torrijos regime and subsequent military-controlled governments was the participation of such dedicated technocrats as Ardito Barletta who became Planning Minister and in 1984 rose to the presidency.

Responding to local and international pressure, Torrijos in 1978 took steps to return Panama to civilian rule. An official party, the

Democratic Revolutionary Party, was created to compete in local elections scheduled for 1980 and the presidential election set for 1984. The PRD was conceived as a centrist political party that would administer the Panamanian state with the politics of pragmatism and cooption much like the corporatist Institutional Revolutionary Party (PRI) of Mexico.

The PRD, however, quickly proved incapable of this challenge. In the 1980 elections for the Legislative Council the party faced a strong antimilitarist challenge from the Christian Democratic Party and reconstituted Liberal factions. Arnulfo Arias and his *panameñista* movement also challenged the legitimacy of the National Guard-PRD controlled state.[22] While the popular sectors did not break with the government, the gap between the regime's populist rhetoric and its private-sector oriented policies was widening.

The populism and nationalism of *torrijismo* effectively disappeared from government with the death of Torrijos. After 1981 the Panamanian government became steadily more conservative. In contrast to the 1970s when the National Guard prided itself for its role in establishing a more independent foreign policy, the guard leadership between 1981 and 1987 allowed U.S. military forces to use Panama as a base for intervention in Central America.

Three National Guard officers—Manuel Noriega, Rubén Darío Paredes, and Roberto Díaz Herrera—became contenders for political and military leadership after Torrijos' death. Apparently the three agreed to alternate in power. As National Guard commander, Paredes challenged the independence of the PRD and in July 1982 removed Torrijos' hand-picked president, Aristides Royo, and replaced him with Ricardo De La Espriella. Paredes meanwhile also began to extend his power base by trying to bring disaffected elements of the private sector, mainly the agricultural oligarchy, into a new political alliance. But when Paredes retired from the guard to run for president, Noriega did not support his bid, leaving Paredes marginalized and extremely bitter. As the new National Guard commander, Noriega engineered to have Ardito Barletta run for president as part of a five-party coalition.

The fraudulent nature of democracy in Panama became obvious to all who wanted to see in September 1984 when Nicolás Ardito Barletta was inaugurated president after the country's first national election in sixteen years. Once again Arnulfo Arias was denied the presidency despite an apparent electoral victory. Nevertheless, U.S. Secretary of State George Shultz attended the inauguration of his protegé, Ardito Barletta. Noriega eventually deposed Ardito Barletto after the president acquiesced to popular pressure to investigate the

Spadafora affair. He was replaced with Erick Arturo Delvalle who for three years proved a faithful servant of Noriega.

In June 1987 Díaz Herrera publicly revealed the sources of the 1984 electoral fraud, claiming that the conspiracy had been conceived in his own home. The ensuing public protest prompted the Delvalle government to declare martial law. Under pressure from the United States Delvalle tried in February 1988 to replace Noriega as PDF commander. Instead it was Delvalle who was forced to step down. In his place, Noriega appointed Manuel Solís Palma to finish out the five-year term started by Ardito Barletta. In September 1989 Noriega's puppet legislative assembly appointed Comptroller General Francisco Rodríguez to be provisional president.[23] In December 1989 Noriega was declared head of government by the newly appointed National Assembly.[24]

Government Comes Full Circle

Omar Torrijos had launched a government of "new politics" in Panama distinguished by the military's central role not only in maintaining the stability of the state but also in setting its domestic and foreign policies. By establishing the PRD, Torrijos hoped to create a political infrastructure to continue the policies of *torrijismo*. These can be summarized as follows: a nonaligned foreign policy with a strong nationalist flavor, populist reforms that gave formerly disenfranchised sectors access to government and allowed them to participate more fully in economic growth, expanded state intervention in the economy, and an alliance with the modernizing sector of the private elite (mainly industry and the international service sectors).

Only the shell of the new politics was left by early 1980s. The military's earlier success in stabilizing the state, giving the economy new direction, and incorporating the popular sectors had given way to a crisis of state. Symptomatic of this crisis was the quick turnover of Panamanian presidents from 1982 to 1989: Royo, De La Espriella, Ardito Barletta, Delvalle, Solís Palma, and Rodríguez. At each step the civilian government became more a puppet of the military. Finally the facade of a civilian government was thrown aside in December 1989 when the resurrected National Assembly of Community Representatives, largely composed of PRD functionaries, declared Noriega head of government.

Government had come full circle by the end of the decade. Once again the commander of the military was also the country's top figure in government. To legitimize this new military government, Noriega, like Torrijos before him, identified himself with the politics of nationalism and populism. Noriega's credentials as a populist and nationalist leader were, however, even less convincing. His recent history, joint military maneuvers with U.S. forces, increasing repression of workers, and his support for unpopular austerity measures all undermined Noriega's ability to portray himself as a leader in the *torrijista* tradition.

Popular Sectors

Before 1968 the working classes and the popular movements of unions, peasant organizations, students, leftist parties, and community organizations had been effectively excluded from the political system. When the popular movements seemed to be gathering too much strength, they were repressed either by local or U.S. security forces. The oligarchic parties paid little attention to the demands of the popular sectors, preferring instead to administer politics and the economy in the traditional exclusionary fashion.

A constant threat to the inertia of the oligarchy was the *panameñista* movement of Arnulfo Arias, a populist leader who received support among the lower classes for his support of social reforms. Although Arias did push through significant reforms during his brief moments in power, he made no effort to incorporate the popular sectors into the political system. In contrast, Torrijos, also a populist, adopted a series of measures that for the first time brought workers and peasants into the circles of political power.

Once having secured his dominant place within the National Guard, Torrijos established an alliance with the communist People's Party. As the country's most militant defender of worker and peasant rights, the People's Party was the organization most capable of mobilizing popular support for the new regime. In exchange for the party's collaboration, Torrijos brought worker and peasant activists into the new political structures established by his regime.

In the countryside, Torrijos revived the country's agrarian reform by promoting *asentamientos campesinos* (settlements of landless peasants) on lands secured by the government. The People's Party, whose student branch had already been drawn into an alliance with the government, was given a leading role in the National Confederation of Peasant Settlements (CONAC).[25] Besides representing the interests of the peasant settlements, CONAC, established in the 1970s, also served as a consultative body about peasant affairs and a focus for pro-Torrijos mobilizing.

Torrijos singled out the labor sector for his most concerted efforts to build popular support for his government.[26] The pro-union Labor Code of 1972 and the formation of the National Council of Workers (CONATO) were the main initiatives to incorporate unions into the new government alliance sponsored by the National Guard. Previously repressed and isolated, the labor movement was given official recognition and support. The newly established Ministry of Labor was obligated by the Labor Code "to promote the establishment of unions in the areas or sectors where they are lacking." Union leaders, particularly those from the leftist and more militant National Council of Panamanian Workers (CNTP), were consulted about labor and other government policies and appointed to government positions.

The Torrijos regime also attempted to defuse potential unrest among the marginal communities by incorporating them into government structures. A good example of this policy was the regime's initiatives in the explosive shantytown of San Miguelito. Located northeast of Panama City, San Miguelito was the focus of much progressive community organizing by Catholic priests. The government made San Miguelito a special autonomous municipality separate from Panama City. This opened the way for greater political and economic participation on the part of the squatters of San Miguelito.[27]

Popular access to political power was institutionalized through a new system of political representation authorized by the 1972 constitution. Torrijos disbanded the Legislative Assembly and abolished the traditional political parties. In their place, he established the National Assembly of Community Representatives on the national level and a network of community boards on the local level, with one board for each one of the 505 *corregimientos*, or local political districts. At each level of the hierarchy, popular representatives were to have a role in government along with appointed government officials.[28]

By the mid-1970s the strong commitment to popular political participation demonstrated by Torrijos during his first years in power had faded substantially. The regime had successfully coopted most of the popular sectors by giving them unprecedented political access and government recognition. But the economic downturn, increased private-sector pressure, and bureaucratic resistance combined to undermine the kind of inclusionary initiatives previously demonstrated by the government, especially from 1970 to 1974.

CONAC was defunded and land distribution to the *asentamientos* was sharply reduced. The government turned against labor, acceding to pressure from the private sector to revise the Labor Code in 1976, and CONATO was kept powerless by ideological and turf battles. The National Assembly of Community Representatives was more of a sounding board than a legislative branch of government.[29] It was consistently denied decision-making power and often treated patronizingly by the government ministries. The community boards frequently found themselves powerless in the face of the appointed *corregidores* and local economic elites. They were also frustrated in their economic initiatives by lack of cooperation by and assistance from the government ministries on which they depended for funding and technical help.

Although the reformism of *torrijismo* had lost momentum by the mid-1970s and was moribund by 1981, the military-controlled governments of the 1980s were able to dip into this historic political alliance with the popular sectors. Collaboration with the Torrijos regime had coopted and pacified most popular leaders and popular organizations. When faced with the U.S. destabilization campaign, Noriega was able to tap these coopted sectors to support the ruling coalition. CONATO, for example, supported the government's COLINA coalition in the 1989 presidential election in return for promises of government appointments and a greater share of representation in the National Assembly. But at the national university, banners and graffiti proclaiming "Neither *rabiblancos* nor the dictatorship" expressed a popular rejection of both the government and the U.S.-backed opposition.

The 1989 Election and Anti-Noriega Coalition

By installing the new government of Guillermo Endara in 1989, the United States assumed its historic role as a leading protagonist in the internal politics of Panama. The Endara-headed ADOC coalition had won the May 1989 presidential election by a two-to-one margin according to most foreign and domestic election monitors but was denied victory by General Noriega.

The new administration installed after the U.S. invasion in December 1989 was that of the Democratic Opposition Alliance, a grouping of three political parties and various civic organizations. President Guillermo Endara was a founding member of the Authentic Panameñista Party (PPA), a conservative populist party headed by Arnulfo Arias until his death in 1988. Endara's first vice president was Ricardo Arias Calderón, president of the Christian Democratic Party (PDC). As his second vice president Endara selected Guillermo Ford of MOLIRENA, a fusion of the traditional Liberal Party factions of the oligarchy.

Although the ADOC political coalition clearly received more votes than the government coalition in the May 1989 elections, none of the three parties represented in the coalition could point to a strong popular base and party infrastructure. "The vote is not for individual candidates," explained Alfredo Maduro, president of the Chamber of Commerce, "It is for Noriega or change."[30]

Traditionally in Panamanian politics there has been no strong party infrastructure that remains in place between elections. Parties and political coalitions often disintegrate after elections and emerge again with new names with the opening of a new political campaign. A further weakness of Panamanian politics is the lack of detailed political platforms. In 1968 the National Guard had brushed aside the country's political parties and substituted its own authority and populist ideology. With the military gone as the society's strongest institution, the responsibility of governing once again fell upon the country's weak political parties.

Government After the Invasion

Ushered into office by U.S. troops, Guillermo Endara's government had little to offer the Panamanian people aside from a return to the politics of pre-Torrijos Panama and an agenda dictated by its U.S. benefactors and the country's business elite. Endara's first official communication was sent by a U.S. government fax machine, his cabinet members were chauffeured in U.S. embassy vehicles, and the new government was unable to occupy the presidential palace because it had been taken over by the U.S. military command.

The postinvasion government hoped to fill the void left by the collapse of the Noriega dictatorship. Although initially counting on the good will of Panamanians elated to see Noriega gone, the Endara government did not face an easy future. Having come together hastily, as a broad alliance of business, civic, and political groups with the goal of deposing Noriega, the coalition had never ironed out a common political platform. Personal and political differences among the three parties were manifest from the very start. A little more than a year into Endara's presidency, the largest member of the governing coalition, the Christian Democrat Party (PDC), withdrew from the ADOC following the President's firing of five PDC ministers.

As if developing fractures in the ADOC were not enough, Endara's ability to hold government together was also threatened by growing reports of presidential corruption. The U.S. Drug Enforcement Administration (DEA) accused Endara's law firm of dealings with several companies belonging to a pair of Cuban-American drug traffickers, and the U.S. press revealed Endara's links to a bank that was suspected of laundering drug money. Rising narcotics activity and revelations of high-level government involvement in the drug trade provoked attorney general Rogelio Cruz to declare that "there is corruption at all levels."[31] After launching a barrage of accusations that implicated the furthest reaches of Endara's government, Cruz himself was placed under house arrest. The Supreme Court accused the attorney general of freeing up bank accounts that the DEA suspected belonged to drug traffickers.[32]

Compounding the reports of corruption, Endara's popularity plummeted in response to neoliberal measures that the government instituted under pressure from the United States and multilateral lenders together with Panama's own financial sector. The removal of Noriega, the end of economic sanctions, and U.S. promises of $1 billion for recovery led to high expectations which the Endara administration was incapable of fulfilling. Although the popular sectors were largely disorganized and without a clear agenda, students, labor groups, doctors, and teachers did occasionally take to the streets to protest austerity measures, privatization of state-owned enterprises, and cuts in social security, health, and education. As the protests intensified, police repression stepped up to control the outbursts. Developments took a strange twist in early 1992 when President Endara announced that police forces had uncovered a conspiracy within the military to overthrow the government. Revelation of the alleged "Kill the Fat Man" coup was met with widespread skepticism; some local analysts speculated that Endara was seeking to create an excuse for the police to escalate the level of aggression needed to discourage popular protest.

The public's discontent with the postinvasion president culminated near the end of 1992 when Endara asked Panamanians to vote on a package of proposed constitutional reforms. Although the referendum included a proposal to abolish the military and eliminate the concept of national defense from the constitution, the reforms were voted down two-to-one. Voter abstention was extremely high. The government tried to brush off the defeat as a mere rejection of the reform package, but analysts largely agreed that the results constituted a punishment vote for the Endara government.

As a final reminder of the corruption that was running wild through the government's ranks, in the summer of 1993 the Panamanian press revealed that officials of the Panama consulate in Spain had helped to divert weapons bound for the Panamanian police force to the Bosnian army. A violation of the United Nations arms embargo, the weapons deal also involved partners of a law firm owned by Guillermo Endara. Although a special government commission failed to turn up evidence conclusively linking officials outside of the consulate to the arms trade, deputy Olimpo Saenz, president of the Foreign Relations Commission, concluded that the commission's report "cast doubt over the entire Panamanian government."

By the time of the 1994 elections Guillermo Endara was predictably absent from the list of presidential candidates. The ADOC had decomposed into its constituent parties, and Endara's Arnulfista

Party had selected as its candidate Mireya Moscoso de Gruber, widow of three-time president Arnulfo Arias Madrid. Another of the coalition members, MOLIRENA, backed former state comptroller Rubén Darío Carles. Perhaps the most noteworthy addition to the electoral fray, however, was legendary Salsa star Rubén Blades, founder of the Papa Egoró Movement (an indigenous reference to Mother Earth).

Despite surprising popularity in early opinion polls, the musician-turned-politician Blades failed to attract sufficient votes for what would have been a storybook ending to the elections. Instead the PRD, risen from the ashes of the 1989 political and military crisis, stole the electoral show. Ernesto Pérez Balladares, an economist and businessman, won the public's confidence with his "people to the power" campaign that recalled the populism of Omar Torrijos, while he successfully distanced his party from the legacy of *caudillo* Manuel Noriega. The PRD victory was especially impressive given attempts by other parties to link Pérez Balladares with Noriega. As election day neared, the committee to elect Rubén Carles ran a television announcement that displayed a photograph of Pérez Balladares, looking bewildered but smiling, in a hearty embrace with strongman Manuel Noriega—Pérez Balladares had served as campaign manager for Noriega's COLINA slate in 1989. Ironically, in four short years many Panamanians had come full circle—from disgust and frustration with the ex-general's party to rejuvenated faith in the PRD's populist pretensions. However, the victory of Pérez Balladares, with 33 percent of the vote, was hardly overwhelming.

Political Specters and the 1994 Elections

Some insight into why many Panamanians so quickly returned to the PRD after its former subservience to the military can be found in the observation of one onlooker to the 1994 elections: "The people chose between the dead: Omar or Arnulfo."[33] Indeed the political icons of Omar Torrijos and Arnulfo Arias have divided the population politically since the late 1960s—and the 1994 political showdown was no different. One-third of the participating electorate voted for a presidential candidate whose campaign rhetoric drew heavily on Torrijos' populist legacy and a political party that Torrijos founded in 1978. Ernesto "El Toro" Pérez Balladares—so-called because of his imposing physique—promised Panamanians an end to government corruption and a new modernizing agenda to combat poverty. Although the new president supported the scheduled 1999 transfer of the Panama Canal into Panama's hands, he also announced his willingness to renegotiate U.S. military presence in the canal area.

The dominant member of the United Peoples Alliance, the PRD collected 30 seats in the Legislative Assembly. The other coalition members, the Panama Labor Party (PALA) and the Liberal Republican Party (LIBRE-PLR), obtained a total of three deputy posts.[34] Soon after the election, the Solidarity Party, which won four seats, gave its support to the ruling coalition, thereby giving it a slim majority in the 72-seat Legislative Assembly.

Mireya Moscoso de Gruber, presidential candidate for the Arnulfista Party (PA), was a close second to PRD candidate Pérez Balladares with 29 percent of the votes. Moscoso replaced Guillermo Endara as the leader of a reincarnated version of her husband Arnulfo Arias' Authentic Panamanian Party that joined with the Christian Democratic Party (PDC), the Civic Crusade, and the National Liberal Republican Movement (MOLIRENA) in 1984 to form the antigovernment ADOC. In her campaign, Moscoso vowed to fulfill the canal treaties with the United States, broaden opportunities for foreign investment, and improve health and education programs around the country. The *arnulfistas* gained fourteen seats in the Legislative Assembly. The National Liberal Party (PLN) and the Authentic Liberal Party (PLA), also members of the Democratic Alliance, each gained three deputy positions.

Analysts attributed the PRD's victory over its traditional *arnulfista* rival to greater wealth and better organization. During her campaign, Mireya Moscoso participated in few public debates or television campaigns. The Arnulfista Party also had to contend with the stigma attached to their previous leader Guillermo Endara after the president's prolonged fall from public grace.

The 1994 elections did, however, show some signs that the classic stand-off between the dominating *arnulfista* and *torrijista* factions is changing. Both Rubén Blades of the Papa Egoró Movement and Rubén Darío Carles of the MOLIRENA Party connected with significant portions of the Panamanian electorate. Blades campaigned on promises to institute a government unencumbered by political debts and free of commitments to established interests. The platform appealed to young urban professional males but generated little interest in the rural areas. The Salsa star remained ahead or close on Pérez Balladares' heels throughout most of the campaign, only to drop off suddenly for the election, winning about 17 percent of the vote. Analysts attributed Blades' loss to rumors of his communist sympathies and the fact that Blades did not live in Panama until the campaign began. Accusations also surfaced that Blades' party was hierarchically run, refusing input from its constituency and party leaders outside the executive committee. Still, Blades did well to attract so many votes in an electoral system dominated by two traditional parties. The Papa Egoró Movement gained six seats in the Legislative Assembly.

The third pillar of the 1989 ADOC alliance, MOLIRENA formed in 1984 as a coalition of traditional oligarchic political parties not associated with the preinvasion PRD government. A conservative party, MOLIRENA brought together the factions of the Liberal, National, and Republican Parties that stood outside the government's own political coalition. MOLIRENA and its representative Guillermo Ford were the driving force behind the neoliberal economic policy of the Endara government—a policy synthesized by Vice President Ford: "Panama will be a country that is 100 percent private property." MOLIRENA's 1994 candidate, Rubén Carles, primarily appealed to a wealthy sector of Panamanian society and placed fourth in the elections with 16 percent of the vote. MOLIRENA gained four seats in the Legislative Assembly. MOLIRENA led the Project Change electoral coalition, which also included the Civic Renewal Party (PRC) and the National Renewal Movement (MORENA).

Hushed, but not entirely silent during the election was the Christian Democratic Party that split from the ADOC in the early going of Endara's term in office. One of the most conservative Christian Democratic parties in the region, the PDC has closely associated itself with U.S. policy and strategy in Panama. The PDC's base is found among the middle class, professionals, and the financial community. Although once committed to the interests of the poor majority and to forging a new and more broadly based politics of national development, the PDC has dropped democratic elements of its ideology to embrace a private-sector oriented approach to economic development and a political direction that is closely associated with the U.S. State Department. The PDC emerged from the 1989 crisis as a major political player—owning a majority of the national legislators and the ministries of Government and Justice, Education, and Housing and Public Works. The 1994 candidate Eduardo Vallarino Arjona, on the other hand, gathered only 2.5 percent of the presidential votes, and the PDC captured only one seat in the Legislative Assembly.

Inaugurated on September 1, 1994, Pérez Balladares quickly demonstrated his political skills and sympathies. Within his first six months, he improved relations with the United States, established a more coherent policy framework, and won good marks in opinion polls conducted after his first month in office. Although his economic program differed little from that of his predecessor, he pursued it with greater skill—achieving, for example, a consensus on the controversial issue of the privatization of state telecommunications by giving the trade union a share in the sell-off. President Pérez Balladares announced that his administration would focus on three main areas in his first year: improving the climate for foreign investment, cracking down on organized and street crime, and tackling poverty.[35] At first, the only organized political opposition he faced was from elements within the PRD that opposed constitutional reforms, budget proposals, and some of the government's privatization measures. By early 1995, however, the new president also confronted more organized opposition from a new opposition alliance called the Democratic Opposition Coordinator, which included the PA, MOLIRENA, PDC, PRC, PLA, PLN, and MORENA. Some of the nation's most powerful unions, including construction workers (SUNTRACS) and banana workers (SITRACHILCO), also opposed the president's proposed labor code reforms, calling a successful 24-hour strike in May 1995.

As the first elections in recent history that were free of military pressure or interference, the 1994 political contest was a landmark event for Panama's history books. The elections were open, nonviolent, and hotly contested—an important step toward recovering national esteem after the shame caused by the Noriega years and the U.S. invasion.

Part 2

Security Forces and Human Rights

© Heriberto Valdés

Changing of the Guard

With the December 1989 invasion, the U.S. military resumed its historic role as the chief arbiter and guarantor of political power in Panama. The Panama Defense Forces (PDF) and the country's civil defense put up some resistance but within a few days were brought under U.S. control. In 48 hours the Battalion 2000 and the Machos de Monte Brigade—the PDF's two specially trained military divisions— were destroyed. Loose battalions from the San Miguelito district and in Colón put up some resistance for an additional 24 hours. The U.S. military apparently expected more resistance, but it did not anticipate the *saqueo* (looting) of the city following the invasion.

Suddenly, after twenty-one years in which the military had served as the country's central institution, Panama's army ceased to exist. It was replaced by a new police organization labeled the Panama Public Force (FP). The newly constituted security force, composed of many former PDF members, gradually assumed control of most of the country's police functions.

Most Panamanians were glad to be rid of the PDF, which had grown increasingly repressive and corrupt. But the dissolution of the PDF left a serious gap of authority in the country. As the country began its reconstruction efforts, it faced the challenge of creating a sovereign and ordered country without resorting to U.S. troops. There was also the question of the future of the Panama Canal now that the country was unable to protect the canal from military threats with its own forces. In the shaping of the new Panama, Panamanians have had to come to terms with what the PDF was and what kinds of military and police forces should emerge from its ashes.

Expanding Political and Military Role

The military and police forces of Panama have long operated under the tutelage of Washington. The United States disbanded the country's small army in 1904 and its police force some ten years later, taking control over internal and external security matters until the mid-1930s, when the end to the U.S. protectorate status was negotiated.[1]

During World War II the national police were militarized by the United States. With the location of the U.S. Southern Command (SouthCom) in the Canal Zone in 1948, this militarization and training by the U.S. military accelerated. In 1953, the year that former police chief José Antonio Remón Cantera became Panama's president, the national police force was modernized under U.S. direction and the National Guard created. As part of its new effort to foster hemispheric security, the Pentagon established close links with the National Guard, establishing a strong foundation of counterinsurgency and national security doctrine within its officer corps.[2] Imbued with a national security doctrine that targeted left-of-center social activists as the main threats to domestic stability, the National Guard commonly repressed popular organizing both in the cities and in the countryside.[3]

As the old oligarchic order crumbled, Panama faced a crisis of legitimacy in the 1960s. With the political parties in disarray and no plan for economic modernization in sight, Col. Omar Torrijos toppled the Arias government in 1968 and established a populist military dictatorship. Although the Liberal factions of the political elite had just lost an election to the Conservatives, they were unconvinced, at least at first, that a military coup was the appropriate solution to Panama's dual crisis of the government's lack of political legitimacy and the country's failure to modernize its economy. By 1970, however, both the Liberals and the U.S. State Department were supporting the direction taken by Torrijos, especially after Torrijos decided to establish a cabinet of technocrats to formulate a package of political and economic reforms.

The Torrijos coup made the National Guard the country's main political institution, and until the early 1980s the National Guard functioned as the country's leading political party, its only significant parliament, and its director of economic development. Breaking the links of oligarchic control over the National Guard and Panama's politics and economy, Panama's charismatic strongman proceeded to convert the National Guard into the country's sponsor and protector of populist reforms—ranging from agrarian reform to the institution of a progressive Labor Code.[4] Torrijos also promoted the National Guard as the guardian of nationalist values and led the drive to update and revise the canal treaties.

Another distinctive change in the National Guard under Torrijos was its new openness to blacks and other minorities. By giving ethnic minorities, especially blacks, increased access to the officer corps of the National Guard, Torrijos ensured widespread support among those sectors for his populist dictatorship. The Torrijos era (1968-81) was the prototypical "soft dictatorship."

The 1972 Political Constitution gave the military enough power to shape all State institutions. The National Guard, according to the constitution, became the fourth state power along with the executive, legislative and judicial branches. Torrijos, the National Guard's Commander-in-Chief, was authorized by the constitution to serve as Head of Government for six years. In addition to the powers commonly belonging to president, Torrijos also assumed powers associated with a legislature such as making laws and approving national budgets. What is more, the Head of Government appointed all cabinet members, all members of the powerful legislative commission, all the Supreme Court Justices, provincial governors, and city mayors. At the same time he was given direct control over all law enforcement agencies. These special powers granted to Torrijos were supposed to last only until 1978.

After the September 1977 signing of the canal treaties between President Carter and General Torrijos, Panama began its process of democratization. Torrijos announced the National Guard would abandon its "protective" role and return to the barracks. Political power would be transferred to civilian institutions in late 1978, the date scheduled for the swearing in of a civilian president—Torrijos' hand-picked successor, Aristides Royo. The Torrijos regime also announced that general elections would be organized on the basis of universal suffrage in 1984.

The National Guard gave itself a period of six years to consolidate Panama's democratic institutions. But after ten years of a military dictatorship with a strong populist base, the democratization process faced many obstacles. Torrijos himself assumed responsibility for directing Panama down the road toward democracy. But a mysterious plane crash put an end to Torrijos and his political program on July 31, 1981.

Most of Torrijos' political program was buried along with the remains of this popular Panamanian strongman. The National Guard reversed its 1978 promise to abandon politics. Moreover, the Panama Canal Treaties gave the country's security forces a new vision of their role by making them co-responsible for defending the canal. With the aid of the United States and counsel from other quarters, the PDF was born in September 1983.

With the death of Torrijos, Col. Florencio Flores became commander-in-chief, a position that was later assumed by Gen. Rubén Darío Paredes. When Paredes stepped down to run for president in 1983, Gen. Manuel Antonio Noriega became commander-in-chief. A month after he assumed that position, the National Guard was restructured under Law 20. Aside from modernizing the structure of the police and military forces, Law 20 also instituted PDF control over many aspects of Panamanian public life, including the immigration department, civil aeronautics administration, railroads, traffic department, and the passport bureau.[5]

The internal structure and objectives of the security forces were redefined under General Noriega's leadership, the country's foreign policy shifted away from its previous self-determined posture, and the relationship with illegal drug trafficking intensified. While Torrijos was adamant in developing the National Guard through new sectoral alliances, Noriega believed that the PDF had established the necessary platform for a long-term national program without the need to launch new populist initiatives.[6]

Under Noriega the PDF was targeted for U.S. grants and loans that permitted the institution to create a military infrastructure. Several military units were organized to coordinate with the United States in the defense of the Panama Canal. Battalion 2000 was given the conventional task of preparing for Panama's future responsibility in the defense of the canal. The Machos de Monte (razorback) Brigade was the unit prepared for unconventional warfare. Both units used U.S. military textbooks and practiced periodic maneuvers with U.S. troops.

While the National Guard emphasized multilateralism as its foremost weapon in the field of international affairs, the PDF was satisfied to rely on bilateral talks with the U.S. government. Together with his general staff, Noriega wrongly concluded that Washington was heavily dependent on Panama's military to maintain domestic stability and to serve as its associate on a regional basis. With this strategy in mind, Noriega believed he could negotiate on equal footing with Washington.

The 1983-1986 period was a time of optimism in U.S.-Panama relations, but this sweet honeymoon soon soured. By treating President Ardito Barletta (who had the personal support of U.S. Secretary of State George Shultz) as his underling and unceremoniously dismissing Barletta in 1985 when his orders were disobeyed, Noriega and the PDF angered the Reagan administration. Another rising source of tension was Noriega's close relations with drug traffickers. Although apparently supportive of U.S. covert activities involving illicit drug activities (particularly the arms-for-drugs deals that involved the

Nicaraguan contras, Israel, and Iran), his own reckless involvement with the narcotics trade set him up for later indictments.[7]

In 1987, the year that Noriega finally fell out of favor with the United States, Washington began encouraging dissident factions within the PDF to oust Noriega. Abortive coup attempts in March 1988 and October 1989 seriously depleted the PDF's officer corps, which had also been weakened by the forced retirement of many high officers suspected of harboring anti-Noriega sympathies. More than two years of diplomatic negotiations between the White House and the PDF leadership ended in December 1989 with the U.S. invasion. By the end of the third day the PDF was no more and Noriega was a hunted man.[8]

PDF: Army That Once Was

The PDF emerged as a result of a 1983 restructuring of the country's police and military forces. Until this restructuring, the National Guard was the country's only armed force and had both police and military functions. Until the U.S. invasion, all the country's military and police forces were subject to the authority of the PDF's commander-in-chief. Subordinated to the commander-in-chief were members of the *estado mayor* (general staff), whose members included the chief-of-staff, deputy chief of the Air Force, and deputy chief of Ground Forces.[9] Similar to the U.S. Army, the PDF's general staff included five divisions: Personnel, Intelligence, Operations, Logistics, and Civic Action.

The PDF had four branches, the largest of which was the 11,000-member National Guard, and various police forces, including the Police Force, National Traffic Directorate, National Department of Investigations (DENI), and the Immigration Department.[10] The Navy, with 400 members, functioned more like a coast guard, while the Air Force with 500 members had four combat planes. The 4,400-member Army included the newly created Panama Canal Defense Force.

The country's twelve military zones corresponded to the country's provincial divisions, although Panama City had three military zones. There was also a military zone in the San Blas Indian Reserve (*comarca*). Different combat or internal security units were based at the different military zones. The PDF had eight infantry companies, sometimes referred to as combat companies and bearing such nicknames as the Tigers, Red Devils, Cholos, and Pumas. The Machos del Monte expeditionary company was based at the Río Hato base on the Pacific coast. Other special units included the Public Order Company (Dobermans) and the Presidential Guard.[11] After the 1983 restructuring, two new combat battalions—Battalion 2000 (established to defend the canal) and the Battalion Peace (headquartered in Chiri-quí)—were formed in preparation for the year 2000 when Panama is scheduled to assume complete control of canal and national defense.

Because there has been no military academy in Panama, officer candidates received their training outside the country. Some like Noriega himself were schooled in Peru or in other Latin American countries, including El Salvador and Somoza's Nicaragua. Others received instruction through U.S. military training programs at the School of the Americas in the Canal Zone and after 1984 in Ft. Benning, Georgia. At the time of the school's relocation to Georgia, Panama was the third-largest user of it in terms of total number of graduates since the school's founding in 1946.[12] Other U.S. military training was continued until 1987 at the Panama Canal Area Military Schools. The School of the Americas was occupied by the PDF's José Domingo Espinar training center. Although the country still did not have its own officer training school, it did operate the Tomás Herrera Institute, a secondary school. Most PDF officers, however, received no formal officer training.

It was the nationalist and reformist legacy of *torrijismo* that gave the National Guard and later the PDF their credibility and sense of purpose. But institutional corruption, the death of Torrijos, and new involvement in canal defense all contributed to the altered state of the country's security forces in the 1980s. Instead of pursuing the goal of bolstering national sovereignty and spurring economic development by recovering the canal and the Canal Zone, the National Guard-PDF became focused on the new objective of protecting it in conjunction with the U.S. military. The role of the security forces in promoting economic development was overshadowed by the ambition of building a national military institution with the technology and training necessary to canal defense.[13]

In the 1980s the PDF became an increasingly corrupt institution that often put itself above law, morality, and government. Payoffs by businesses for special treatment were commonplace, it raked in large sums in multinational business deals, and skimmed off profits from the international drug trade and arms smuggling. The PDF also had direct economic interests, through a national bank created in 1989. The PDF described the bank as a private entity that functioned as a branch of the Defense Forces Benevolent Society.

Planning a Barracks Mutiny

Recognizing the central place the PDF played in Panama, Washington in mid-1987 began encouraging dissident elements within the PDF to mount a coup to oust Noriega. George Shultz, secretary of state during the Reagan administration, called the PDF "a strong and honorable force that has a significant role to play, and we want to see it play that." The Bush administration also placed its hopes for the ouster of Noriega on Noriega's own troops.

Following a coup attempt by disgruntled officers in March 1988, Noriega cleaned house, retiring some officers and strengthening links with other middle- and high-level officers. Another coup attempt was launched on October 3, 1989 led by Major Moisés Giroldi who had been thought to be close to Noriega, but it was effectively crushed by Noriega and loyal forces. It was later reported that there may have been two coup attempts underway—one led by mid-level officers and the other by a faction of military intelligence.[14] Officially, 77 died in that unsuccessful coup attempt. The ad-hoc group, Pro-Liberation Committee for Detained Military Personnel, claimed the numbers of killed and arrested were much higher than reported by the PDF. Following the invasion participants in the attempted coup held in military prisons were released.

Paramilitary Groups

Panama has not been plagued by the same kind of death squad terrorism seen in Guatemala, Honduras, and El Salvador. The ideological alliances and working relationships between the security forces and the right wing that have produced death squads in other Central American countries do not exist in Panama. Within the PDF, however, there have existed special units like the F-7, which is believed to have been responsible for anti-opposition violence during the 1984 election campaign. The successor to F-7, the F-8 terror squad, was widely accused of the death squad-like killing of rightist opposition figure Hugo Spadafora and the beating of Mauro Zuñiga, head of the Coordinating Board for National Civilian Organizations.[15]

In 1987 military harassment and repression of the political opposition increased. The Dignity Battalions, formed in 1988 as military-sponsored civil defense units to defend the country against U.S. intervention, were partly responsible for the harassment and beatings of the opposition movement. These voluntary paramilitary units were trained by retired PDF officers and were often accompanied by active-duty military officers. The Committees for the Defense of the Country and Dignity (CODEPA-DI) were also formed by the military. These were groups of civil servants in each government institution who were trained and armed for defense.

During the May 1989 election violence, it was reported that PDF members changed their uniforms for the T-shirts of the Dignity Battalions. The Strategic Military Council (CEM), created by Noriega as a parallel high command, was widely believed to have played a major role in coordinating paramilitary violence against the Civic Crusade.[16] Nonetheless, the U.S. invasion met only spotted resistance from the country's civil defense units.

Public Force

Created by the Endara administration to fill the public security gap left by the dissolution of the PDF after the 1989 U.S. invasion, the FP was conceived of as a small and efficient police agency capable of border control, the prevention of drug trafficking, and sea and air vigilance.

Operating under the supervision of the Ministry of Government and Justice, the FP is a collection of several divisions. These include the National Police (PN), National Air Service (SAN), and National Maritime Service (SMN). The air and marine services, which are extremely small and ill-equipped, are largely ineffective. SAN, which has a half dozen small airplanes and no helicopter, coordinates with the DEA as does its maritime counterpart. The SMN has only a half dozen small boats that can be easily outdistanced by the drug traffickers who negotiate Panama's 3000 kilometers of coast line. Since the formation of the FP, the National Police, which employs over ten thousand persons, has been charged with fighting crime, patrolling the border, gathering intelligence, coordinating canal defense with the U.S. military, penitentiary duties, and other "special" activities. Among the latter, the PN has cooperated with U.S. armed forces to combat drug trafficking, particularly in the Darién jungle.

The PN has allegedly been the source of different conspiracies to overthrow the Panamanian government. Police officials were behind the alleged 1992 "Kill the Fat Man" plot to murder President Endara and kidnap the two vice-presidents. In January 1995 ten PN officers were arrested for spearheading a similar conspiracy to assassinate President Pérez Balladares and other government officials. The executions were to have been followed by a take-over of police barracks in Panama City and Chiriquí and the formation of a civilian-military junta to assume government. Many speculated that the officers were simply frontmen for an organized group of prominent business and political figures. Others felt the plots were manufactured by the government to distract the public from social and political controversies. The government, however, never made public any of its evidence against the alleged conspirators, and those arrested were released after several weeks.

The Institutional Protection Service (SPI), another police unit set up shortly after the 1989 invasion, was initially charged with protecting the country's democratic institutions from insurgent acts by Noriega sympathizers and previous PDF associates. Under Endara, the SPI became a specialized police unit that was better equipped than the PF and placed under the president's direct command. The Presidential Palace, where Endara worked and lived, was surrounded by the SPI police and several surrounding blocks were declared off limits to ordinary citizens. As part of an effort to change the image of the presidency, Pérez Balladares ordered that the iron gates in front of the palace be torn down. Additionally, he proposed to the legislative assembly that the SPI remain the official security agency for the president and executive officials but be transferred from the president's direct control to the authority of the Ministry of Government and Justice and included as part of the FP.

Yet another police agency created after the U.S. invasion was the Judicial Technical Police (PTJ), an auxiliary judicial force that works with the Attorney General's office but answers to the Supreme Court. It replaced the National Department of Investigations of the PDF. The PTJ largely deals with drug-related crime and shares close cooperative ties with the DEA in Panama. Long the target of corruption charges, the organization is under investigation by the Attorney General for its participation in drug trafficking, car-theft rings, kidnappings, homicides, and extortion. In the period between 1991 and 1994 concerns over police involvement in drug-related activities prevented the U.S. Congress from approving the Mutual Legal Assistance Treaty with Panama. The agreement, which guarantees that the United States and Panama share classified information concerning illegal drug-related activities, was finally ratified in April 1995.

President Pérez Balladares announced that he would allow the PTJ more power to combat local crime and that he would push for the PTJ to be fully accountable to the Attorney General's office. Pérez Balladares also expressed his wish that the PTJ emulate the United States' FBI, although the Supreme Court of Justice rejected this proposal.

The postinvasion government placed the Customs Police under the authority of the Ministry of the Treasury while the Migration Office became the responsibility of the Ministry of Justice. Both law enforcement agencies had been dependencies of the PDF in the 1980s. Although this move from military to civilian control has brought some improvements, the two agencies have been repeatedly accused of corruption and fraud. The Customs Police controls borders, harbors, and airports, although during both the Noriega and Endara years the agency was involved in drug enforcement activities. According to official data, the Customs office seized millions of dollars worth of drugs during this period.

In addition to the legitimate functions of legal immigration, the Migration Office has commonly provided visas for foreign nationals who use Panama as a platform from which to enter the United States. This is the case of Cubans, Dominicans, Chinese, and other foreign nationals who purchase visas in Panama. According to a former Migration Director, during the Endara government more than fifteen thousand visas were issued to Chinese citizens.

Because most of the original members of the FP were former PDF officers, the Panamanian police have operated under military-like structures and regulations. Its officers, being former PDF members, are commonly graduates of foreign military academies. Since 1990 the PN along with the PTJ have received training and funding through the International Criminal Investigative Training Assistance Program (ICITAP), a police training project managed by the U.S. Departments of Justice and State.

Finally, the Panama Canal Commission employs approximately 300 police officers in its Canal Protective Service. These officers are deployed primarily near the canal's locks to prevent sabotage and vandalism.

The Military Question

The question of the role of the military in Panamanian society has long been debated. In the 1980s, as the PDF moved away from the army's earlier populist pretensions and as it became more corrupt and repressive, antimilitary sentiment intensified in Panama. But questions about the function of a military are complicated in Panama by the belief, partly born of the Torrijos experience, that an army ensures a certain degree of sovereignty in face of the United States, especially with respect to defending the canal.

The Political Constitution of 1972 incorporated the National Guard as the institution responsible for the country's public security and national defense. Although the PDF was created to replace the National Guard, the Constitution was never amended to reflect this change. Only after the 1989 U.S. invasion of Panama has more debate arisen concerning the need to modify the Constitution *vis-à-vis* the role of the military in Panama.

The debate since 1989 has gone around in circles over one issue: Should a military, as a formal institution, have any role at all in Panama's political life? Many of those who opposed the PDF and General Noriega in the late 1980s favor the elimination of any sort of Panamanian military force, primarily because of its tendency for domination of economic life and corruption. Other groups argue that Panama must have its own armed forces to defend its sovereignty and the Panama Canal. Without an armed force to defend the canal, some have argued, Panama will be unable to fulfill its joint responsibility to defend the canal as outlined in the Torrijos-Carter Treaty, thus ensuring a continued U.S. military presence.

Proposals to create divisions of the FP capable of defending the country against attack and protecting the Panama Canal have generated much disagreement about how to impede the revival of militarism in Panama. Any combination of military and police functions in one institution, some argue, would repeat the mistakes of the past by leading to the militarization of police and governmental functions. For others, the key to stopping militarization is to ensure civilian control over all the police forces.

In 1992 President Guillermo Endara held a national referendum to approve a package of constitutional amendments that included the formal abolition of the army and legal language needed for the formal constitution of the existing FP. The rejection of the proposals, along with dozens of other policy changes, by 67 percent of the voters (with 64 percent of the electorate abstaining) was apparently more a reflection of popular discontent with the Endara administration than a gauge of public opinion about the future role of a police force and a military in Panama.

The proposed amendments did not die. In addition to a public referendum, constitutional amendments can be enacted if passed by two successive Legislative Assemblies (with each assembly having a five year term). Three months before his term ended and immediately after the May 1994 presidential elections, Endara asked the Legislative Assembly to review the proposed constitutional changes. With support from president-elect Pérez Balladares, the assembly members approved a proposal to abolish the military before concluding their 1989-94 term. Later, a modified version of this proposal was also approved by the new legislature. While the reform made the police the only legally armed group in the country, it allowed for the formation of temporary citizen militias in the event that national independence and the territorial integrity of the state are threatened.

In mid-1995 the debate over the proper roles of police and military institutions resurfaced following a new government proposal to amend the constitution and give authorization to a reorganized FP. The proposed amendment establishes the president as the chief of the FP, which will also include the presidential security force known as the Institutional Protection Service. Most controversial is the proposed mission of the FP, which will include defending the national sovereignty, territory, and constitution as well as protecting the canal area.[17]

This continuing debate reflects Panama's singular circumstances. Among those objecting to the integration of police and military functions and calling for the creation of a new army are nationalists, anti-imperialists, and leftists. While some Panamanians see this delegation of traditional military functions to the police as a step away from the militarization of the past when the police were subject to the military, others contend that militarism will result from this mixing of public security and national defense. The police force could be the refuge of militarism in Panama, just as police functions were militarized within the National Guard and PDF. A better alternative, according to critics, would be the creation of an institutionally distinct army that could guarantee national sovereignty and satisfy Panama's defense obligations under the canal treaties. They say that without a professional army, the country would need to rely on the U.S. military for canal defense, thereby forfeiting national sovereignty. However, many observers—including U.S. military officers and canal workers—say that the canal is militarily indefensible, particularly against a terrorist attack. "One bomb in Gatun Lake, and it's finished," said one canal worker representative.[18]

The left-of-center Service for Peace and Justice in Panama (SERPAJ) criticized the proposal to abolish the army as "legitimizing by omission the U.S. military presence" in that it would support U.S. contentions that Panama is not fulfilling its treaty obligations, thereby opening the way for a renegotiation of the Panama Canal Treaties and establishing a rationale to postpone the closure of U.S. military bases.[19]

That argument was rejected by those who insisted that a democratically elected civilian government is the best guarantee against militarism and that civilian control over the FP will ensure that public security and national defense functions are properly defined and monitored. Camilo Brenes of the Christian Democratic Party said, "Latin American history has shown that armies have not served to defend countries but, rather, in the majority of cases have been used to rule them despotically."[20]

Human Rights

It was not until the kidnapping and decapitation of Dr. Hugo Spadafora in 1985 that the human rights situation in Panama became a matter of great national and international concern. In 1987 the Inter-American Commission on Human Rights of the OAS accused ten soldiers and officers of the PDF of the crime, and in 1989 called for "an exhaustive investigation" into the assassination of Spadafora. Many Panamanians believed Noriega ordered the assassination after Spadafora publicly accused the general of drug trafficking activities. Others suspected the CIA also had a hand in the murder to prevent the former contra supporter from revealing the involvement of the contras in illicit arms and drugs deals.

The mutilation and murder of Spadafora sparked internal criticism within the National Guard and popular protests. From June through August 1987, after the revelations of Colonel Díaz Herrera, there were large demonstrations marking the anniversary of Spadafora's death and the fraudulent elections, in which protesters also complained about other human rights violations by the PDF. The protests were brutally crushed by the "Dobermans," the PDF's anti-riot squads. Human rights violations by the security forces and associated paramilitary groups increased in the late 1980s, although serious abuses, such as torture, killings, and disappearances, were rare. Harassment of journalists and government control over the media became common. Threats and attacks on the media continued into the Endara administration, with the National Journalists Academy recording 25 incidents of aggression from 1990 to 1993.[21]

The Spadafora murder case came to an unlikely head late in 1993 when a jury acquitted seven of the ten accused PDF soldiers claiming there was a "lack of evidence" to prosecute them for the assassination. Noriega and two other high-level officials were found guilty of the murder. The initial acquittals prompted several protest marches throughout the country, including one led by First Lady Ana Mae

Díaz de Endara in the town where the verdict was issued. Antiriot police broke up the protest with tear gas.

The PTJ has been linked to such illicit activities as drug trafficking, carjacking, homicides, and kidnappings. In 1994 the attorney general's office described the PTJ as a "nest of corruption and inefficiency."[22] The office has also been accused of constitutional violations including abuse of authority, withholding evidence, and the personal use of confiscated money and narcotics.

Since 1989 there has been a marked improvement in political rights—a fact underlined by the peaceful and fraud-free 1994 elections. But Panamanians continue to suffer from many human rights violations, as a 1994 report by SERPAJ made clear.[23] Among other abuses, the report cited the continued persecution of journalists and decried rampant overcrowding in jails. Children are often incarcerated in the same facilities as adults and many detainees are not given opportunities for legal audience.

Violent suppression of demonstrations, arbitrary short-term detentions, sexual abuses of detainees, and sharp limitations of freedom of press and expression constitute the most common violations of civil and human rights in Panama. In May 1993 and again in April 1995, anti-riot police fired on demonstrations by Ngobe people in western Panama, leading in the first instance to the death of an Ngobe activist. A protest in Colón for greater employment in July 1992 also resulted in the killing of an unarmed woman by the PN. Panamanian homosexuals and transvestites report that they are brutally persecuted by the armed forces and that the government does little to assist them.

In their 1994 reports, both the Popular Coordinator of Human Rights in Panama (CONADEHUPA) and the Panamanian Committee for Human Rights (CPDH) leveled scathing criticisms at the U.S. military for failing to assist Panama's transition to democracy in the wake of the 1989 invasion. The CPDH also charged that the economic, social, and cultural rights of Panama's lower income groups have been consistently violated because "the state has implemented policies which intentionally or unconsciously do not attend to the necessities of the most impoverished." In 1995 a mission from the United Nation's Economic and Social Council visited Panama to document the country's housing shortage and resulting human rights problems.

In the aftermath of the invasion, there were charges that the new government and the U.S. military were violating the human rights of those suspected of having supported the Noriega government. Many members of the Noriega regime were held in "preventive detention" for years. Nevertheless, in the last months of his presidency, Guillermo

Endara pardoned hundreds of members of the Manuel Noriega regime who were jailed for political crimes. Many of the people released were connected to incoming president Pérez Balladares' PRD party.

Following the 1989 invasion crime rose dramatically, especially in Panama City, prompting police authorities to adopt increasingly aggressive methods of deterrence. On the day of his inauguration, President Pérez Balladares instructed the police to step up their efforts to combat street crime. During the first stage of the "Energy with Courtesy" Operation, police concentrated on ferreting out "suspicious persons," particularly adolescents who were out after dark engaged in "scandalous" activities. In the second stage of the operation, the PN combined with members of the PTJ to address Panama City's rising gang problems. Although police efforts temporarily reduced the incidence of crime and were met with widespread public support, numerous complaints were filed claiming the police used excessive force and violated human rights. According to the U.S. State Department's human rights report for 1994, Panama's "principal human rights problems continued to be prolonged pretrial detention, an inefficient and often corrupt criminal justice system, and overcrowded, oppressive prisons." In the first three months of 1995, reported crime rose 9.3 percent to 176 crimes per day.[24]

Part 3

Economy

© Maryknoll Photo Library

State of the Economy

Panama began the 1990s with an economy badly shaken by U.S. economic sanctions (1987-89) and smarting from the devastation and looting that accompanied the December 1989 invasion. The gross national product had dropped dramatically—about 25 percent since mid-1987. Percapita income had been pushed back to the levels of the early 1980s. Government revenues were down about 44 percent—which had caused a similar drop in public services and investment. Industrial output had declined by 40 percent, and the tourism sector had slumped to 25 percent of capacity.

With credit so scarce, the construction industry ground to a standstill. Foreign-exchange revenues were down 50 percent, and debt payments had been suspended by the Noriega government. Official unemployment in early 1990 was at 22 percent but most observers set the real figure at 25 percent with another 25 percent being underemployed. The population living in poverty had risen from 33 to 40 percent by early 1990.[1]

Most conventional economic indicators indicate that Panama has made a successful recovery. Led by a boom in the construction industry and bolstered by high rates of growth in the financial sector and Colón Free Zone, Panama has experienced relatively high rates of economic growth since 1990. After an initial postinvasion spurt in GDP growth in 1990-91, the rate dropped to 5 percent in 1994 (Figure 3a). The 1990-94 average annual economic growth rate was an impressive 6 percent.

Low interest rates and enviably low inflation have strengthened the Panamanian economy. But the economic indicators also reveal some sources of instability. Although rising imports are an indication of economic health, the stagnant position of exports is causing an alarming increase in the trade deficit (Figure 3b). This $1 billion plus trade deficit is partially offset by the service income in the current account from the increased trade activity in the Colón Free Zone, the continuing recovery of the international banking center, and higher canal tolls. In addition to the huge trade deficit, other worrisome economic signs include a large foreign debt, the government's own widening fiscal deficit, the apparent end of the construction boom, and the end of the U.S. economic recovery assistance program.

Panama enjoys the highest percapita income in the region, and it ranks 68 in the UN's Human Development Index of 173 countries.[2] These statistics and rankings, however, obscure the degree to which wealth is concentrated in Panama. Panama has the second worst income distribution in the hemisphere, behind Brazil. The bottom 20 percent of Panama's population receive only 2 percent of national income, while the top 5 percent receive 18 percent.[3]

Panama's economic prospects are to a large degree associated with the success and failings of the country's neoliberal economic re-

Figure 3a

Change in Panama's GDP, 1983-1993

Percentage change from previous year

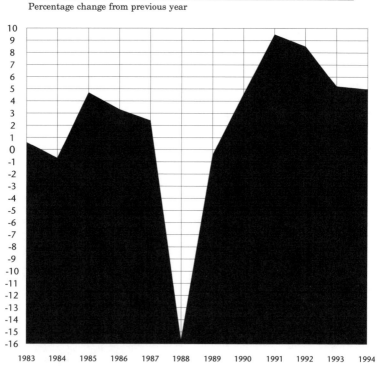

SOURCE: Economist Intelligence Unit, *EIU Country Report: Panama*, 1995; United Nations, *UN Statistical Yearbook, 1992-1993*.

Figure 3b

Change in Panama's Exports and Imports, 1983-1993

In mllions of U.S. $

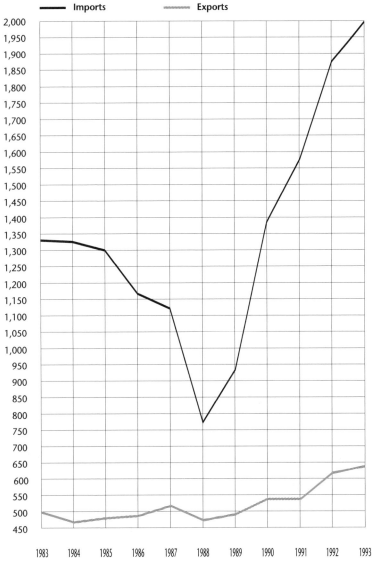

SOURCE: Inter-American Development Bank, 1991, 1994.

forms and the ability of its service sectors to gain an advantageous position in the increasingly liberalized global economy. Also important will be progress of the government's Inter-Oceanic Region Authority (ARI), the autonomous agency established to develop the assets of the Panama Canal area that have been transferred or will be transferred by the year 2000.

The Transit Economy

Since the sixteenth century the Panamanian economy has relied on commerce and service activities stemming from the canal and other transit operations linking the Caribbean Sea and Pacific Ocean. Unlike in most other Latin American nations, where the dominant class historically took the form of a land-based bourgeoisie, Panama's elite issued from a wealthy community of merchants.[4] Between 1550 and 1750 the narrow land bridge between Central and South America developed as a key transfer point for gold bullion shipments arriving from mines on the western coast of South America in route to the Spanish mainland. The Spanish colonial government populated the territory with fortified cities, markets, and army outposts.[5]

A British sea assault that laid to waste the northern port town of Portobelo in 1739 sent the merchant class into temporary decline and prompted the settlement of the Panamanian countryside. In the following decades an agrarian elite emerged in rural Panama, whose power was rooted in extensive cattle ranches and agricultural estates. Although the wealthy landowning community continues to exercise some influence in contemporary political and economic affairs, it has never stood at the center of national power or shared the degree of preeminence enjoyed by the urban business class.[6]

Panama's economy received a major shot in the arm in the mid-1800s when gold was discovered in California and a group of New York investors financed the construction of a railroad spanning the narrow isthmus region.[7] Still a part of Colombia, the territory soon became the primary crossing for gold and industrial goods moving between the eastern United States and growing port cities in California and the western coast. Secession from the South American nation in 1903 opened the way for U.S. negotiations to construct the Panama Canal—a project which lasted from 1904 to 1914. National independence and canal-based trade solidified Panama's class structure for years to come—the urban business elite wielded a national political monopoly, but economic power resided with the foreign capitalists who regulated the ebb and flow of goods and finances through the Canal Zone. The country's oligarchy—known as the *rabiblancos*—have also traditionally been closely tied to foreign investment and trade.

The addition of the U.S. Southern Command during World War II added to the vectors of foreign influence bearing upon the small Central American country.

Being at the center of world trade, Panama had long relied on imported food and manufactured goods to meet its internal needs. It was not until after World War II that local investors began placing their accumulated capital into industrial and agroindustrial projects. Panama adopted an import-substitution model of development that fueled impressive new private investment by local capitalists and foreign corporations. Although the new industrialization did put an array of locally produced goods on store shelves, it did nothing to broaden the market of consumers who could afford these products.

In the 1950s and 1960s, a time when the economy was expanding at unprecedented rates, most Panamanians continued to live and work in misery. Increasing landlessness and rural-urban migration were just one sign of the structural weakness and injustice of the Panamanian economy.[8] The country lacked an economic modernization plan and a political system that incorporated the middle and lower classes into the governing process. With the oligarchy floundering and divided, the National Guard in 1968 moved to take the country's economic and political agenda into its own hands.

Military-Led Reformism and Rising Debt

Torrijos and the National Guard set Panama on the path of political reform and economic development. Breaking the political knot, the Torrijos regime adopted a populist approach to economic development. Through a series of reforms, Torrijos brought peasants and workers into an alliance with the state and the private sector with the goal of capitalist modernization.

A reinforced agrarian reform, a new Labor Code, and the incorporation of formerly neglected sectors into the government were among the steps taken by Torrijos to broaden the benefits of economic development and to expand the domestic market. Rejecting the politics of class confrontation, Torrijos called his populist program a "revolution of growing aspirations" of the lower classes.[9]

Populist reforms established a stable social base. From this base, the Torrijos regime launched an economic modernization project that included public sector productive investments (sugar, tourism, and credit, for example), infrastructure construction (hydroelectric dams, ports, and roads), the promotion of a new international banking center, and the renovation of the transnational service sector. From the beginning, the economic project of the Torrijos regime met opposition from the hidebound oligarchy. But in its effort to consolidate the internal market and to broaden the country's role as a transnational service platform, the modernization project succeeded in forging a new economic elite that was closely allied with the state. The success of the international banking center also gave rise to a financial sector that was closely tied to international capital.[10]

Torrijos was by no means a leftist revolutionary. He did shake up the country's economy and politics, but it was never his aim to displace the private sector from its central role in production and distribution. The general espoused the politics and economics of class collaboration. Always careful not to alienate the oligarchy, Torrijos tried to negotiate a middle way, a third path. "Neither with the left, nor with the right, but with Panama" was his favorite posture when faced with tense social situations.[11] As George Priestley noted, "Non-confrontation and class cooperation were the watchwords, even in the face of resentment on the part of the groups concerned."[12]

When the National Guard took power in 1968, the economy was sailing along at an 8 percent rate of annual growth. World recession and rising oil prices were among the main factors causing this fast economic pace to slow down by 1974. The private sector, however, blamed the downturn on the populist bent of the Torrijos regime, and it began a campaign to rein in *torrijismo* and establish its preeminence in the ruling alliance. As a result of this pressure and Torrijos' own efforts to draw the oligarchy into the campaign to revise the canal treaties, the government shifted away from the popular sectors by the mid-1970s. The CONAC peasant confederation was defunded in 1974. The focus of agrarian policies moved from distribution to production, the Labor Code was revised, and the regime backed away from its earlier promises to incorporate popular sectors into national policymaking.[13]

During the 1970s the government did maintain its commitment to expanding government social services, especially health and education. It also continued to insist that a large public investment budget was necessary for an expanding economy. By the 1980s, however, these remaining features of *torrijismo* began to fade in the face of an incipient coalition of the country's financial elite with the multilateral banks, foreign private banks, and the U.S. Agency for International Development (AID). A second jump in oil prices in 1981-82, another downturn in world trade, the debt crisis, and pressure from the economic elite combined to cause the collapse of the Torrijos development model.

Public social services and the government's direct participation in the economy through more than three dozen state enterprises had been pushed forward in large part to strengthen the internal market. This development had been financed not by progressive taxation but by funds borrowed from international banks. The borrowing spree of the 1970s, encouraged by foreign private banks, resulted in the country having Latin America's largest percapita debt. In 1979 the International Monetary Fund (IMF) concluded that Panama had arrived "at a relationship between indebtedness and national income unprecedented in the Western Hemisphere."

By 1981 Panama could no longer keep up with the interest payments on its debt, let alone pay off the principal. The crisis in international accounts was paralleled by one in the government's own budget. Falling revenues and the burden of a large government payroll and social service sector had caused the budget deficit to widen to crisis proportions. Battered by the slowdown in canal traffic, escalating petroleum prices, and rising interest rates, the Panamanian economy toppled into crisis.[14]

Structural Adjustment and Neoliberalism

During the 1980s the military governments attempted to tackle the structural crisis with adjustment programs recommended by the World Bank and IMF and backed by the Inter-American Development Bank (IDB) and the U.S. Agency for International Development. Although never implemented to the degree advocated by international donors, the structural adjustment measures adopted by the Panamanian government in the 1980s represented a first attempt to reshape the country's economic model along neoliberal lines.[15]

Although these programs had some success in easing the balance-of-payments crisis and closing budget deficits, they failed to spur significant new economic growth. Debt repayments continued to drain the national treasury and this decapitalization obstructed economic recovery. The government moved to liberalize the economy and promote exports, but domestic industries blocked any major liberalization of foreign trade and export growth proved disappointing. Nontraditional agroexports did increase significantly but still constituted only a minor part of the country's export offering, and there was no sign that the industrial sector would at any time soon demonstrate a capacity for export production.

At the same time that the new economic model was failing to meet its initial promise, additional symptoms of the country's economic crisis surfaced. Unemployment was steadily rising, the country's once encouraging indices of health and education were falling, and the housing crisis was becoming more acute.[16] The combination of structural adjustment and deteriorating socioeconomic conditions heightened social protest and anti-government sentiment.

In the late 1980s the Noriega regime suspended debt-servicing payments which were soaking up about 40 percent of government revenues. By defaulting, Noriega was able, despite the U.S. embargo and declining tax revenues, to continue to meet most civilian and military payroll demands. But this was clearly a temporary solution to an increasingly grave financial crisis. With government revenues continuing to nose dive, the financial collapse of the Noriega regime was all but inevitable.[17] Rather than wait for the disintegration of the Noriega regime because of growing economic instability, Washington chose to launch a military invasion to oust the military leader, break the PDF, and install a new government in Panama.

The War of Economic Sanctions

The economic and political crisis arising from Panama's internal problems of the late 1980s, together with the U.S. campaign of economic destabilization derailed the plans and projections of the structural adjustment program. Starving the government of cash was the main strategy in the economic aggression unleashed by Reagan and escalated by Bush. A nation whose national currency is the dollar, Panama was particularly vulnerable to Washington's economic tactics. U.S. strategists expected that the government of Panama would quickly collapse when it found that it was unable to pay its bills or guarantee bank deposits. The sanctions were designed to sow political discontent with the Noriega-managed government by driving the economy into a deep recession.

One of the first signs of rising U.S. displeasure with the Noriega regime came in January 1986 when the National Security Council (NSC) recommended that Economic Support Funds (ESF) scheduled for Panama be transferred to Guatemala.[18] Instead of receiving the $46 million that AID had allocated, Panama in fiscal year 1987 received just $12 million—down from $33 million the year before and $74 million in 1985.[19]

The war of economic sanctions began after the June 1987 political crisis in Panama, when Colonel Roberto Díaz Herrera suddenly retired and then accused Noriega of rigging the 1984 elections and murdering Dr. Hugo Spadafora. Later in the month the U.S. Congress approved a resolution calling for Noriega to step down.

In August 1987 the State Department suspended aid to Panama. Allowed to continue were a few scholarship and training programs, aid to several local nongovernmental organizations, and regional and Washington-based funding for U.S. private organizations active in Panama. As it became clear that the Noriega regime was not going to be toppled easily, Congress and the White House imposed a series of escalating economic sanctions. In addition to restricting U.S. aid to Panama, Washington prohibited joint military exercises with the PDF, terminated the U.S. sugar quota for Panama, and required that U.S. representatives vote against any proposed loans to Panama from multilateral banks.[20]

The U.S. government then moved to destroy Panama's monetary system in a plan that was hatched after Noriega's indictment in Miami for drug trafficking on February 4, 1988.[21] The first step was the March 3, 1988 decision by the State Department to freeze the U.S. deposits of the Panamanian central bank. The next day the Panamanian government closed the country's banks to prevent a run on the banks and capital flight, demonstrating the seriousness of the escalating financial crisis in Panama.

Later in March, President Reagan rescinded Panama's preferential tariff treatment under the Generalized System of Preferences and the Caribbean Basin Economic Recovery Act. The U.S. government also suspended Panama Canal Commission payments to the Panamanian government in March. In April Reagan imposed sanctions under the authority of the International Emergency Economic Powers Act by declaring that the Panamanian government represented "an unusual and extraordinary threat to the national security." The same act had been used to justify the trade embargo against Nicaragua.

In the case of Panama, a total trade embargo could not be imposed because of the United States' own dependence on Panama Canal trade and because such a boycott would blatantly violate the 1977 Canal Treaties. Instead of a complete trade embargo, Washington sought to create a destabilizing cash crunch for the regime by freezing its dollar accounts and other interests in the United States and by prohibiting U.S. individuals, companies, and government agencies from making payments to the government. Escrow accounts managed by the U.S. Department of the Treasury and Department of State were set up to collect taxes and fees that normally would be paid to the Panamanian government.

When it became obvious that U.S. companies were evading the restrictions on paying taxes and fees to the government, Washington tightened the sanctions in 1989 to close loopholes. At the same time, however, Washington was forced to back down on blanket sanctions to enable U.S. government and military personnel to remain in the country. Late in the year the Bush administration again escalated the economic assault by announcing that ships registered in Panama would not be permitted to dock in the United States.

Barely able to meet its payroll, the Noriega regime had no extra funds to maintain the basic infrastructure. So cash-short was the government that it could not afford the fluoride for the country's water supply. With recession setting in, investors and entrepreneurs began pulling their capital out of the country. Many established businesses closed down, and the informal sector of the self-employed swelled as thousands of newly unemployed Panamanians went into the streets to scratch out a living. Other unemployed workers began returning to rural areas.[22]

Economic sanctions had the desired effect of pushing the economy into a tailspin. But the economy managed to stagger along—supported by the diversity of the commercial and services sectors, the wages paid to 12,000 employees of U.S. government agencies, steady income from the Colón Free Zone, and the largely unaffected agricultural sector. In its destabilization strategy Washington failed to anticipate the flexible response of Panamanians to the liquidity crisis through the increased use of checks and vouchers and the government's ability to use the sanctions to build nationalist resistance. Despite the blow dealt by the withdrawal of U.S. investments, Panama's business with Latin American and European corporations continued unabated. The crisis did have severe consequences for relations with Japanese companies, however. Japanese banks reduced their business to a bare minimum, and Japanese families living in Panama were evacuated as the financial and commercial crisis worsened in March 1988.

Initially the political opposition supported the sanctions in the belief that they would be only temporary. Indeed, it was the Civic Crusade (see Politics) which first urged Panamanians to close down their businesses and to withhold revenues. Many private enterprises, like supermarkets, attempted a lock out, but PDF troops forced them to open. As it became clear that toppling Noriega would not happen overnight, most sectors of the society and economy criticized the measures as unproductive or even counterproductive. Although it eventually tried to distance itself from U.S. sanctions, the Civic Crusade suffered from its inevitable association with the campaign of economic destabilization. For its part, the American Chamber of Commerce complained that the sanctions had succeeded only in "slowly strangling U.S. companies, Panamanian business persons, and the middle class."[23] The popular sectors—students, workers, and community organizations—were among the hardest hit by the country's economic decline but were largely unable to forge an independent popular response to the crisis.

Because of the country's close association with the United States, the impact of economic sanctions on Panama was especially grave when compared with other countries where sanctions have been enforced. A 1983 study published by the Institute for International Economics showed that in most cases of economic sanctions the cost to target countries as a percentage of the national product has been only a few percentage points. Of 18 cases between 1918 and 1982, only in three countries—Iran, Rhodesia, and Surinam—did the estimated damage from sanctions reach 10 percent.[24] After just one year, U.S. sanctions caused a more than 15 percent drop in Panama's total GDP.[25]

Internationally Washington received little support for the destabilization measures which violated international law and trade agreements and were an obvious breach of the 1977 Canal Treaties. The

Statement of Understanding appended to the treaty specifically clarifies that the U.S. prerogative to defend the canal against threats to its neutrality "does not mean, nor shall it be interpreted as the right of intervention of the U.S. in the internal affairs of Panama. U.S. action...shall never be directed against the territorial integrity or political independence of Panama."

Economic Recovery

By early 1990 Panama's internal markets were a shambles, debt payment arrears to international financial institutions surpassed $500 million, and the country faced one of the world's highest ratios of debt to gross national product.

In the aftermath of economic sanctions and the military invasion, the Bush administration provided $461 million in economic assistance to support Panama's economic recovery in the 1990-92 period. The aid was less than originally expected, did not compensate those individuals and businesses who suffered losses as a result of the invasion, and was conditioned by demands that the government implement a number of policy reforms.

Since 1990 economic growth has been consistently higher than in most countries in the hemisphere. Growth has been fueled by a construction boom, a steady expansion in the financial sector, and continuing dynamism in the import-export business of the Colón Free Zone. Under the guidance of the United States and multilateral financial institutions, the Endara government renewed Panama's commitment to structural adjustment, launching a "modernization" plan that aimed to reduce public sector spending, privatize state-owned agencies, slash tariffs on foreign trade, and promote export production—all of which represented an extension and deepening of previous structural adjustment measures.

In 1991 GDP growth soared to near 10 percent but has since leveled off and is expected to continue within the 4-5 percent range, perhaps less over the next several years. The neoliberal slant of government policies continued during the first year of the Pérez Balladares administration, although the new president negotiated the restructuring with considerably more political skill than his predecessor and expressed a stronger commitment to tackle the problem of deepening poverty in Panama. Planning Minister Guillermo Chapman in 1994 stressed the need for economic policy to combine "a dynamic vision toward modernization and the world market" with a social development program aimed to improve living conditions for the poorest sectors of the population. Other focal points of Chapman's economic program include plans to cut subsidies to industry, continue trade liberalization, increase foreign investment, maintain economic growth at 5 percent, and pursue membership in the North American Free Trade Agreement (NAFTA) and General Agreement on Tariffs and Trade (GATT). Acknowledging that the neoliberal posture of the new government was leading to rising popular dissatisfaction, the labor minister said the government intended to "pass the changes quickly and use the next four years recouping the political cost." [26] Supporting the new government's plan to address social concerns while at the same time boosting business prospects, the Inter-American Development Bank offered $750 million in low-interest loans to fund the so-called Chapman plan. IDB funds will be used to promote foreign investment and develop agriculture, industry, and mining in addition to underwriting new health, education, environmental, sanitation, and infrastructure projects.

In December 1992 Panama joined the System of Central American Integration (SICA) whose members also include Costa Rica, Honduras, El Salvador, Nicaragua, and Guatemala. But Pérez Balladares showed little interest in pursuing increased regional economic integration in Central America. Instead, his administration demonstrated more enthusiasm for increasing trade connections with South American nations. But the main focus of foreign economic relations was the attempt to situate Panama to take advantage of the increasing globalization of the world's economies. Regarding regional relations, President Pérez Balladares stated that Panama "respects the Central American integration process" but that the country "has found itself in a privileged geographical situation with the Interoceanic Canal, the International Banking Center, and a history of special relations with the United States, moreover having a stable currency. This indicates to us that the path points to the Free Trade Agreement (with the United States)." [27] In this regard, the new government recognized the importance of gaining membership in the World Trade Organization (WTO), which is the successor to GATT. Panama was accepted in early 1995 as an observer in the trading bloc of Andean nations, despite objections by Colombia that Panama is a source of contraband over their common jungle border.[28]

As a condition of Panama's entry into GATT, the United States demanded in late 1994 that Panama cut back tariffs on 420 different industrial and agricultural goods and remove barriers to a host of U.S. service industries, including consultancy, insurance, health, transport, and tourism. Japan and Australia also objected to Panama's petition for membership because of its excessively high tariffs on certain imports.

Luís Barraza, president of the Panamanian Industrialists Union (SIP), predicted that the proposed reductions of tariffs on foreign goods and services would result in "the disappearance of a large number of industries and the loss of thousands of jobs, without the security that GATT membership will bring new investors to replace what will be lost."[29] With respect to U.S. pressure for Panama to slash its import tariffs as a condition of gaining WTO membership, Barraza said that the United States would be permitted "to bring in its industries, inundate the market with inexpensive merchandise, and bring local industry to ruin."[30]

Pérez Balladares was forced to juggle international pressures for a more open domestic market and better protection of intellectual property rights with national concerns over the repercussions that a more open economy would have on domestic industry. The president won the approval of the country's industrial sector for his government's effort to join the WTO but not at the cost of capitulating to what are considered unreasonable U.S. demands.

To maintain a favorable standing with the international financial institutions, the Pérez Balladares government also needed to follow through with structural adjustment measures initiated by the postinvasion administration. The new government directed most of its initial measures in this regard toward privatizing state agencies. Pérez Balladares signed laws auctioning off 49 percent of shares in the state-owned National Telecommunications Institute (INTEL) and announced plans to end public ownership of the Hydraulic and Electrical Resources Institute. At the same time that the government privatized parastatal corporations, it was actively trying to attract new foreign investors—particularly from East Asia and Europe—in the tourism, mining, export production, banking, and commerce sectors as a way of boosting economic prospects.

Coming to office on the heels of widespread disapproval and distrust of the Endara government, Pérez Balladares faced the challenge of offering the country new leadership. Initially, at least, the new government was successful in formulating a more cohesive package of social and economic policies than his predecessor. Although privatization, deregulation, liberalization, and austerity measures generated some popular opposition, the government's initiatives to combat crime and poverty gave the Pérez Balladares government a respect and credibility that the Endara government never achieved. Yet if escalating concerns over joblessness and poverty are shunted aside in favor of adhering to a neoliberal agenda, Pérez Balladares will likely see high popular approval ratings slip, just as they did for his predecessor.

Services, Industry, and Finance

Well before the opening of the canal in 1914, Panama was one of the world's major crossroads. Since the earliest days of the Spanish Main, the thin strip of land binding the continents of North and South America has served as a crucial stop-over for diverse interhemispheric trade, from Inca gold to Japanese sports cars. Construction of the Panama Railroad in the mid-nineteenth century secured the territory's status as an international crossroads. In 1903, at the same time that Panama declared its independence, it also adopted the motto *Pro Mundi Beneficio* (For the World's Benefit). Like a major artery threading its way through the country's social and geographical heart, the canal supplies the lifeblood upon which Panama's commercial and service-oriented economy thrives.

The Panama Canal

The Panama Canal, foundation of a transnational service platform, is the country's most important source of income. Nearly 5 percent of all ocean-going world trade passes through the canal, with more than 70 percent originating in or destined for the United States. The United States sends 13 percent of its exports through the narrow water passage.[31]

Each year more than 12,000 ships—about 35 a day—slowly cruise through the canal, paying high fees to avoid making the long trip down and around Cape Horn. The average toll paid is $26,000 but the fees can be as high as $107,000 paid by the Queen Elizabeth II luxury liner in early 1988.

The Panama Canal Commission, administrative office for canal affairs, employs 800 U.S. citizens and more than 6,500 Panamanians.[32] About 6 percent of the country's national product comes directly from canal operations. The overall financial benefit to Panama of the canal (including wages, service contracts, treaty payments, etc.) has increased at a steady pace, rising from $320 million in 1987 to $384 million in 1993.[33] Indirect economic benefits from the Panama Canal—port services in Panama City and Colón and bunker sales to ships, for example—also represent an important economic contribution.

Panama Canal traffic reached new heights in the 1980s, and several proposals are on the drawing board to upgrade and expand canal facilities. Following more than ten years of investigation, the U.S.-Japan-Panama Commission for the Study of Panama Canal Alternatives recommended in 1993 a $6 billion project to construct a new set of locks to accommodate larger ships. The commission rejected a proposed $10-20 billion investment to construct a sea-level canal (i.e. one without locks). Japan continues to be interested in this possibility.

The United States has shown little enthusiasm for investing in the canal's future because of alternative routes competing for transcontinental transportation. The treaty stipulation that the canal has to be handed over to Panama "free of liens and debts" presents another obstacle to U.S. investment in canal improvement during the 1990s. Nevertheless Japan and most other Far East countries continue to view the canal as strategic to their trade interests and have kept a close eye on events unfolding in Panama.[34]

The United States grossed $419 million in 1994 in tolls paid by ships to the Panama Canal Commission.[35] For other services to vessels in transit the Commission received another $145 million.[36] These payments are made directly to the U.S. Treasury. A yearly budget is approved by the U.S. Congress for operations of the Panama Canal Commission.

The canal treaty also requires that the Canal Commission transfer a portion of the tolls to Panama. Since 1979 Panama has received on a yearly average $70 million from the U.S. government. In 1993-94, canal tolls rose by 7 percent and transit through the canal increased by 10 percent.

In late 1994 the Legislative Assembly passed a constitutional amendment creating an autonomous Panama Canal Authority to replace the current Panama Canal Commission in the year 2000. The same reform stated that the present toll system and all U.S. legislation regulating the operation of the canal would continue to be valid after the transfer to Panama. The idea motivating the reform was that a more autonomous institution would provide better continuity and prevent abrupt changes following the election of a new government. President Clinton proposed similar changes supporting the creation of an autonomous authority, but any measure thought to diminish U.S. authority over the canal was expected to meet opposition in the Republican congress in which there are strong opinions that the United States should retain dominant influence over canal operations even after the year 2000.

Managing the Canal Area

To manage the canal area facilities that are being gradually transferred to Panama, the Endara administration in 1993 established an autonomous government entity known as the Inter-Oceanic Region Authority (ARI). The difficult challenge facing ARI is to maintain the current levels of employment and purchases of goods and services generated by the canal area facilities and to develop a strategy to increase the canal area's contribution to the economy once all the facilities are under Panamanian control.

The legislation enacting ARI purportedly attempted to insulate its directors from political influence, in part by granting them five- and seven-year terms. But ARI's original board of nine included no women, environmentalists, or representatives of the University of Panama. The only labor representative, Mariano Mena, has strong ties to the centrist-conservative Christian Democratic Party.

ARI set out to create a master plan for the canal area that would guide zoning and reuse for areas transferred to Panama in 1979 and military areas that would be transferred between 1994 and 1999. Funded by a $8.4 million loan from the IDB, ARI signed off on the contract for the master plan with a consortium led by Nathan Associates, a U.S. consulting firm, in September 1994. But the contract was held up by the Pérez Balladares cabinet for more than nine months, while new legislation governing ARI was submitted and approved by the assembly. The appointment of ARI's third general manager in less than two years, former Panamanian president Nicolás Ardito Barletta, was announced in May 1995. Ardito Barletta was also vice-president of the World Bank, as well as the architect of Panama's most comprehensive economic plan while Planning Minister in 1979.

Using its mandate over the canal area, ARI initiated such projects as a container terminal on Telfers Island near Colón and the construction of a new transisthmus highway to complement the congested Panamá City-Colón road. In addition, ARI manages the long-term leases of housing and other buildings on properties transferred in 1979.

During the delay of its master plan, ARI has come under considerable pressure from a number of interests. These interests include Colón Free Zone traders eager to develop reverted lands for commerce and luxury bungalows, Kuna base workers interested in establishing businesses on former bases, and urban *precaristas* in need of a place to live. But because ARI's structure has scarce avenues for public participation of any kind, backroom and "old boy" networks are likely to have more influence on which initiatives are supported or tolerated and which meet with a cold shoulder or outright eviction.

Colón Free Zone Booms

Until the middle part of this century, Panama's service economy revolved almost exclusively around the canal. The increased canal traffic after World War II spurred further development of Panama as a transnational services platform. In 1948 the Colón Free Zone was established, in part to stave off the postwar depression in Colón. Located by the Atlantic entry to the canal, the Colón Free Zone was ideal for trade between the United States and South America and, today, forms the second largest free zone in the world after Hong Kong. More than 800 companies employ some 5,000 people in warehousing, regional distribution, manufacturing, and wholesale trade. The targeted market for these freeport operations is Latin America and the Caribbean. Companies from Japan, Taiwan, the United States, and Hong Kong are the main users of the zone. Business activity in the Colón Free Zone peaked in 1981 and slumped until 1985, reaching new heights in 1988-89 despite the national crisis. The Colón Free Zone registered 12 percent growth in 1994, but showed no growth in the first quarter of 1995.[37]

Companies located in the free zone do not pay import duties or taxes on inputs to production. However, they are required to pay the Panamanian government tariffs on all goods assembled and exported from the zone.[38] To start a new business, an operator must guarantee employment to at least ten Panamanians. With an unemployment rate triple the national average, Colón is in dire need of such opportunities, but a large number of free zone employees commute from Panama City. Half of the local working population earns less than $250 per month—insufficient to meet basic needs. Separated by a high barbed-wire fence from the depressed city of Colón, this enclave of international trade accounts for about 3 percent of the country's GDP.[39]

In the 1990-94 period free zone business more than doubled, showing a 17 percent annual rate of growth. In 1993 the Colón Free Zone was remodeled and expanded to increase its retail business. But this boom has failed to alter dismal socioeconomic conditions in this port city. In early 1995 the Movement of Unemployed Colón Residents (MODESCO) organized an impressive 78 kilometer protest march across the isthmus to demand that an unemployment agency be created in Colón and that each business operating in the city be required to employ at least one city resident. Victoria Figge, general manager of the free trade zone, acknowledged, "It is a cliché: The free zone is an island of wealth surrounded by a sea of poverty."[40]

International Banking Center

Avenida Central, recently converted into a partially pedestrian precinct, stretches from the old downtown district of Casco Viejo through the bustling retail district of discount stores and sidewalk sales to Panama City's banking district. Here is an enclave of towering glass skyscrapers, hotels, and banks from around the globe. The world's main financial centers are in London, New York, and Tokyo. What one finds along Calle 50, however, is what financial experts call an "artificial" banking center of offshore financial institutions through which the world's financiers and traders avoid taxes and where illicit profits are easily laundered and passed into other accounts. Transnational companies also use this financial center of 115 banks to finance their international operations.

It was the 1970 banking law that created the ideal conditions for an international offshore financial center. Besides allowing numbered accounts, the 1970 law stipulated that bank deposits were not to be taxed, that no reserves were to be required, and that profits would be exempted from local income tax. The other essential element in building the international banking center in Panama was the U.S. dollar being the country's unit of exchange. A dollar-based economy means that there is no danger of currency devaluation *vis-à-vis* the United States and the inflation rate also matches that of the United States.

The international finance center was thriving by the early 1980s with nearly $50 billion in deposits, but little of the profit from this banking complex stays in Panama.[41] The employment of more than 7,000 Panamanians is an important contribution of the banking center. Many indirect benefits also result from the presence of over one-hundred offshore banks. The Panamanian Tourist Institute, for instance, estimated that one in every four airport arrivals was related to the banking business.[42]

The political crisis of the late 1980s rocked Panama's banking center to its core, but the military ouster of Noriega was not the only source of trouble. Since 1982 the opening of offshore centers in Miami, among other places, and assaults on the country's bank secrecy laws by U.S. tax and drug enforcement agents contributed to the center's decline. From 1986 to 1989, bank deposits—foreign and domestic—dropped by two-thirds. In the past several years, however, the finan-

Figure 3c
Bank Deposits in Panama

In billions of U.S. $

	Domestic	Foreign	Total
1986	4.28	28.95	33.22
1989	2.82	8.71	11.53
1993	7.53	13.72	21.25

SOURCE: Panama Banking Commission, 1994.

cial sector has been booming, although total deposits still fall short of the levels enjoyed before the crisis of the late 1980s (Figure 3c).

Pressure from the United States to rescind strict bank secrecy laws which now keep the owners of the accounts out of the reach of U.S. Drug Enforcement and Internal Revenue Service agents is the chief obstacle to recovering full banker confidence in the international system. Panama's National Banking Commission denies U.S. charges that the laundering of drug money is central to the international banking center, noting that access to numbered accounts is attractive to a wide variety of financiers and investors.[43] Nonetheless, in 1991 Panama agreed to sign with the United States a Treaty of Mutual Legal Assistance that makes it obligatory for bank officers to hand over to U.S. authorities, upon their request, all information relating to money laundering. The treaty was not ratified by U.S. Congress until May 1995.

Paper Companies, Ship Registry, and a Pipeline

The registry of "paper" companies is another branch of the offshore industry in Panama. The flexibility and ease of the country's 1927 incorporation law, based on that of the State of Delaware, has resulted in an estimated 100,000 incorporations in Panama. Corporation registry in Panama facilitates bookkeeping sleights of hand that enable companies and individuals to avoid taxation in their countries of operation.

The easy incorporation law also explains why so many merchant ships fly the Panamanian flag. Panama tops all other countries in the "open" registry of the world's merchant fleet (known previously as flags of convenience). A surge in the registry of Japanese ships in the early 1980s made Panama first in the world followed by Liberia, which also has an open ship registry. With more than 12,000 ships—about 10 percent of the world's merchant ships—Panama has the largest phantom fleet in the world.[44]

According to *El Boletín*, a specialized maritime trade paper, Panama's paper shipping registry "has sustained an annual average growth (rate) of 5.1 percent...[faster] than the annual increase of 2.1 percent experienced by the world merchant fleet." At present there is legislation in the U.S. Congress that would give incentives to ship owners that remain under the U.S. registry. If not approved, it is likely that the number of ships using the Panamanian registry will further increase.[45]

In 1977 the Panama Petroterminal company added a major oil transshipment facility to Panama's transnational service economy. This joint venture—60 percent owned by U.S. investors and 40 by the

Panamanian government—was specifically formed to assist the cross-isthmus transport of oil from Alaska's North Slope.[46] The problem was that the super tankers carrying the oil could not fit through the canal locks. As a temporary solution, the new company arranged the transfer of the oil to smaller ships that could squeeze through the canal. The permanent solution was complete in 1982—a pipeline extending from Charco Azul on the Pacific (near Puerto Armuelles) to Chiriquí Grande Bay on the Atlantic side of the country.

During its early years about one-third of Alaska's North Slope annual production flowed through the pipe. Value added by the oil pipeline fell for the sixth consecutive year in 1994, at least in part because of the operation of a new oil pipeline on the U.S. west coast. To increase its utility, the pipeline company began to explore plans for constructing diversified docking facilities at the port terminals on the Atlantic and Pacific Coasts and to upgrade the connecting road to attract container and bulk cargo.

The pipeline, which is buried three feet below the earth, rivers, and lakes it traverses, remains a pressing ecological concern. Oil spills at the two terminals represent an environmental hazard and have caused damage to endangered turtle breeding grounds.[47]

Domestic Industry

Being an international crossroads, Panama has never developed a strong industrial sector of its own. Mining and manufacturing represent about 8 percent of the gross national product and employ about 10 percent of the workforce (Figure 3d and 3e).

It was not until after World War II that a local manufacturing sector began to emerge in Panama, mostly in the food-processing industries. Between 1946 and 1956 manufacturing expanded faster than any other economic sector. Import-substitution policies, which encouraged local manufacturing growth with protective tariffs and import quotas, sparked another spurt of industrial growth in the 1960s.[48] The country's domestic market grew quickly in the 1950s and 1960s but reached its limit in later years due to lack of political reform and the inefficiency of the local industrial sector. Today, the main components of Panama's manufacturing sector are food and beverage processing, textiles, petroleum products, chemicals, and construction materials. During the 1980s the manufacturing sector experienced negative growth. As part of the structural adjustment program imposed on Panama by international financial institutions and AID, tariff and quota barriers protecting the small manufacturing sector were removed and industries were encouraged to move to export-oriented production.

The relatively high labor and infrastructure (energy and transportation) costs of doing business in Panama limit the prospects for export-oriented manufacturing. After the invasion, Washington moved once again to integrate Panama into the Caribbean Basin Initiative (CBI), but expanding U.S. protectionism has largely counterbalanced the benefits from the export incentives offered by this regional program. In the late 1980s, for example, the U.S. textile industry acted to block increased imports of sweaters and other products into the U.S. market. Although U.S. export-oriented manufacturers did not invest in Panama during the 1980s, by the middle of the decade numerous Asian textile manufacturers began to establish assembly operations in Panama to take advantage of access to the U.S. market through the CBI.

In the last fifteen years, mining has become surrounded by controversy as government-endorsed mining ventures have encroached upon territories claimed by indigenous groups. Mineral extraction is especially intense in the Chiriquí, Bocas de Toro, and Veraguas provinces wherein lie territories claimed by the Ngobe Buglé group. "We live in this area," Felipe Morales, a Ngobe Buglé *cacique* asserted,

Figure 3d
GDP in Panama by Economic Sector, 1993

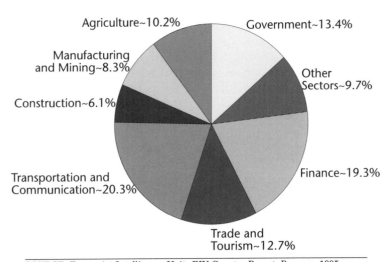

SOURCE: Economist Intelligence Unit, *EIU Country Report: Panama*, 1995.

"and we demand to know the extent of land that is going to be exploited by the mines."[49] Indigenous leaders argue that the only way to resolve the growing land-use conflict is for the government to approve a law of autonomy that would guarantee native groups a voice in the decision making and a share of the benefits associated with mineral extraction on their lands. The government will not bow easily to the demands of indigenous communities, however. An estimated $200 million is to be made from Panama's mineral reserves, the majority of which are found in regions claimed by indigenous groups.[50] At current rates of expansion, foreign exchange earnings from copper and gold mining in the Cerro Petaquilla may rival canal receipts within a few years.

In mid-1995 there were indications that Panama's new president intended to foster Panama's traditionally underdeveloped mining sector. To head the Ministry of Industry, Pérez Balladares named Nitzia de Villareal, a technocrat who for over a decade worked in the Mineral Department of the ministry. The Remance Mining Corporation, which mines gold in Veraguas, recently invested $4.5 million and has

Figure 3e
Employment in Panama by Economic Sector, 1993

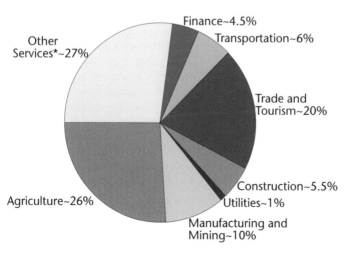

*Government, Social, and Personal Services

SOURCE: United Nations, *UN Statistical Yearbook, 1992-1993.*

250 miners on its payroll as part of its effort to increase its extracting capacity.

Agriculture

Outside of the Panama City-Colón corridor, Panama is essentially an agricultural country. Agriculture and cattle ranching provide employment to 26 percent of working Panamanians. Despite its contribution to employment and domestic food consumption, however, the agricultural sector plays a decreasing role in the economy. Its contribution to national production dropped from 19 percent in the late 1960s to only 10 percent in 1993. Agroindustry (food processing) adds another 4-5 percent.

The crisis in agriculture was particularly severe in the 1980s as export revenues declined, percapita food production fell and food imports increased. Among the main factors for this sectoral crisis were the structural-adjustment measures that deemphasized local food production, shrinking government support for farmers, inequities in land distribution, and low crop yields.[51] Over the last four decades many rural dwellers have left the countryside to seek a better living in the Panama City-Colón corridor. There has also been migration to the agricultural frontier areas opened up by new road construction: the Darién jungle, Colón Coast, Bocas del Toro, and along the pipeline road.

Neither terrain nor soil quality favors agriculture in Panama. Over three-quarters of the land is hilly, and only 37 percent of these hillside zones have good, deep soils—compared with 50 percent in neighboring Costa Rica or 76 percent in El Salvador.[52] Only about 30 percent of the country's land is suitable for cropping and pasture. Of this, 8 percent of the land is cultivated and 15 percent is in pasture—leaving a large agricultural frontier in Darién and other isolated regions, though most of these areas are tropical forests.[53]

Agricultural land is unevenly divided among the country's farmers, with one percent of the farms covering more than 33 percent of the farm land. Over 90 percent of the farms are small holdings, representing only a third of the agricultural land. Only 4 percent of the farms are categorized as commercial, while 35 percent report no cash income at all. Clear land titles are held by just 10 percent of the country's farmers. Most of the estates larger than 500 hectares are dedicated to cattle and milk production.[54]

Slash-and-burn cultivation, machetes, and planting sticks still distinguish the agricultural practices of the small farm sector. As a result crop yields are extremely low—half the average for corn and beans production in South America.[55] Nonetheless, small and medium farmers produce most of the country's foodstuffs. The production increases that have occurred over the last couple of decades have been more the result of expanding the land under production rather than improved production practices. It is only in the more organized export crops, such as bananas, sugar, and coffee, that there is substantial use of mechanization, fertilizers, and technical assistance.

The Government and the Farm Sector

In the early 1960s the government began to increase its intervention in the agricultural sector. Through Alliance for Progress programs, government technical assistance and loan programs were established. In 1963 an agrarian reform program was established with the intent to settle landless peasants on uncultivated lands, especially in the agricultural frontier. The program, stalled by oligarchic resistance and lack of government funds, only resettled some 3,100 landless families leaving over 25,000 applications for land pending and unheeded.

The 1968 coup and the ensuing populist program of the Torrijos regime resulted in a marked increase in government attention to rural problems. Agrarian reform efforts were resurrected, government-peasant alliances were created, the rural infrastructure was expanded, and the state became a major player in agricultural production.

During the early years of the Torrijos regime, agrarian reform and other programs targeting the peasant sector were driven by both political and economic imperatives. Torrijos saw the peasantry as an important base of political support for the government and its nationalistic foreign policy. Before Torrijos, the main political allegiances of the organized peasantry were with the communist People's Party and to a lesser extent with the nationalism and populism of Arnulfo Arias. Encouraged by the People's Party and having spent decades fighting the Chiriquí Land Company and the encroachments of the Canal Zone, the peasantry tended to be anti-imperialist. Torrijos set out to tap this anti-gringo sentiment in his own efforts to legitimize his government and assert Panamanian control over the canal. Alfredo Acuna, director of the Agrarian Reform Commission (CRA) in 1974, described the agrarian reform process as "a means of incorporating that broad sector of the Panamanian population into the patriotic struggle for the liberation of our people."[56]

As a way of realizing this political goal of the agrarian reform, Torrijos opened up his government to the People's Party and its rural leaders. At first distrustful of the National Guard junta that replaced the Arias presidency and unleashed a new round of repression, rural leaders later gained more confidence in the new regime with the removal of the avowed anticommunist Col. Boris Martínez and the new populist leadership of Torrijos.[57]

Recognizing that the Torrijos regime was reaching out to conservative and capitalist elements of society as well as progressive ones, the Peoples' Party decided to cast its support with the government in hopes that its influence would make the progressive elements dominant. The peasant leadership of the People's Party subsequently gained control of the newly created National Confederation of Peasant Settlements (CONAC), established in 1970.

Unlike the Peoples' Party, Torrijos did not regard the agrarian reform process as a challenge to traditional economic structures in rural Panama but simply as a way to increase food production while tapping underutilized land and labor. The emphasis was not expropriation of large private landholdings but distribution of unused estates and marginal lands through government auctions and land sales. Landowners were encouraged to substitute land for taxes or to accept government bonds in exchange for portions of their estates. To pacify peasant demands, the Chiriquí Land Company in the early 1970s lopped off several thousand acres of its vast enclave for the agrarian reform and later sold unused lands to the government and private purchasers.

By the mid-1970s the agrarian reform had slowed to a crawl. Large and medium-size producers complained that government funds would be better spent on more productive and commercially viable agricultural sectors. Under increasing pressure from the oligarchy, the government dropped its earlier commitment to land distribution and increasingly stressed productive investment. Without the full commitment of the government, the agrarian reform sector found itself wallowing in debt and without adequate technical assistance and credit.

The newly established Ministry of Agricultural Development (MIDA) and the Ministry of Planning and Economic Policy bypassed the peasant-controlled CONAC. Political clientelism, a torpid bureaucracy, and increased emphasis on commercial agriculture combined to undermine the agrarian-reform process and the government's commitment to the peasant settlements. By 1972 the pace of government land acquisition was already slowing down even though only 5,000 families on 200 *asentamientos rurales* had at that point benefited from the reform process.[58] This fell far short of the actual need and earlier government promises for extensive reform. The much touted agrarian reform of the Torrijos regime was no more effective than the program of the early 1960s, covering only 4 percent of the country's agricultural land, most of which was the most marginal land.[59]

A much stronger element in the rural program of the Torrijos regime was its commitment to extend rural infrastructure and build a dynamic state-owned farm sector. During the 1970s the government sponsored a construction boom of roads and bridges, hydroelectric plants, and rural electrification projects. The most dramatic state intervention occurred in the sugar industry with the creation of the giant La Victoria corporation. But without parallel advances in agricultural productivity and technical assistance, the agricultural sector did not experience the predicted boom.

Widening government deficits, rising foreign debt, corruption, and the structural adjustment measures of the 1980s brought the Torrijos-era agricultural policies to an end. In return for support from AID and the World Bank, the government agreed to eliminate its direct role in the agricultural sector, to promote agroexports, to rely on the free market to determine commodity prices, and to embrace the economic dictates of comparative advantage. The inclusion of the agricultural incentives policy as part of an important March 1986 law represented another move away from earlier peasant-oriented agricultural policies. Although the agricultural sector is certainly in need of serious reform to promote increased productivity, it remains to be seen if the free-market policies of the 1990s can lift the sector out of its stagnation.

Traditional and Nontraditional Agroexports

Bananas, the country's leading export, constitute about 40 percent of Panama's export offering (Figure 3f). Other leading agroexports are seafood, sugar, beef, and coffee.

The Chiriquí Land Company, owned by United Brands, is the country's largest banana producer and exporter. United Brands began carving out its Panamanian enclave in the early years of this century. By 1976 it owned over 200,000 acres. As part of the agrarian reform of the Torrijos era, the banana giant divested itself of most its estates—prefering to contract out more of its production—leaving it with 35,000 acres today. This opened up room for increased private and government banana production. The share of national production held by individual private producers is about 25 percent and that of the state-owned Atlantic Banana Corporation is 5 percent.[60] In addition to the Chiriquí Land Company, United Brands also owns the Fruit Processing Company and Polymer, which manufactures plastic products.

In 1993 the European Union (EU) imposed quotas on imports of Latin American bananas to protect banana production in the former British and French colonies of Africa and the Caribbean. Prices for the tropical fruit subsequently took a major tumble in the world market. Although the banana producing nations of Latin America banded together in the Union of Banana Exporting Countries (UPEB) to petition the EU for a nondiscriminatory quota system, their efforts met with minimal success. Despite the ruling by a special panel of the GATT that the European Union (EU) quota system violates provisions of the GATT treaty, in 1994 several of the UPEB countries—including Panama's neighbor to the north, Costa Rica—entered into unilateral agreements with the EU, effectively splitting the regional banana coalition. In 1994 Panama's banana exports rose significantly, with sales to the United States making up for reduced sales to Europe. According to the government's trade and industry ministry, good relations between labor and management boosted production in 1994. Although production was up, prices were down—probably the result of oversupply caused by the EU banana quota.

The second-largest agroexport business is the seafood (mainly shrimp) industry, in which Ralston-Purina is the major investor. Following seafood, sugar is the next most important agroexport. Panama became a major sugar-exporting nation in 1973 as a result of substantial government investment in the industry. At the center of the sugar industry is the state-owned La Victoria corporation, which until the recent privatization initiative, operated three sugar mills. Just at the time when the country's sugar export business was peaking,

Figure 3f

Panama's Principal Exports and Imports, 1993

In millions of U.S. $

Exports

Bananas	199.5
Seafood	57.0
Sugar	21.8
Total (including others)	507.6

Imports

Capital Goods	515.1
Oil	192.0
Food Products	182.3
Total (including others)	2,187.3

SOURCE: Economist Intelligence Unit, *EIU Country Report: Panama*, 1995.

world prices began their sharp decline. The increasing substitution of corn sweeteners for cane sugar also deflated Panamanian sugar exports.

Despite programs sponsored by AID and other international lending institutions, there has been only moderate success in diversifying Panama's agroexport offering. Such nontraditional agroexports as winter vegetables and fruit constitute an insignificant portion of the country's agroexport production.

In terms of comparative advantage in the international market, any expansion of Panama's agroexport sector, particularly of nontraditional exports, is hindered by the country's relatively high wages (about 90 cents an hour minimum wage, compared with several dollars per day minimum in many other countries of the Caribbean Basin) and worker benefit rates and the uncompetitive transportation and shipping costs from Panama to the U.S. market. Compared with many other countries in the Caribbean Basin region, Panama suffers from a lack of experience in nontraditional production and marketing. In the 1989-93 period nontraditional agroexports to the United States increased 11 percent, matching the region's average.[61] Although this growth is encouraging, nontraditional agroexports still constitute only a small percentage—3 percent—of total exports. The prospects of significant increases in traditional agroexport production also appear dim given generally low commodity prices and saturated markets.

Economic Challenges in the 1990s

More than most third world nations, Panama is better suited to develop its economy and improve socioeconomic conditions. By virtue of its strategic geographic position, Panama has a number of economic assets—including the Colón Free Zone, international banking center, transisthmian pipeline, canal area facilities, and the canal itself—that in addition to its agricultural, industrial, and mining sectors will help maintain economic stability. In addition, Panama counts on a better educated society, a less dense population, and a less devastated environment than many other small nonindustrialized nations.

Given the presence of many inefficient and corrupt parastatal corporations and the existence of many high tariffs that favor some powerful Panamanian interests but offer few benefits to the poor majority, structural adjustment certainly has a role to play in pushing the Panamanian economy forward. But liberalization and deregulation are hardly the answers for all the country's economic and social problems. These solutions do little to address such persistent problems as deepening poverty, intensifying social polarization, a heavy external debt burden, increasing unemployment, and a widening trade deficit.

According to the UN's Economic Commission on Latin America and the Caribbean, 36 percent of Panamanian households fell below the poverty line in 1991, including 14 percent that suffer extreme poverty (meaning without sufficient income to cover basic food needs). The incidence of poverty was lowest in the Panama City metropolitan area (32 percent) and increased in other urban areas (40 percent) and in rural Panama (43 percent). A study by the Isthmus Foundation for Social and Economic Studies (FIEES) found that nearly 50 percent of Panamanians fail to meet their basic consumption needs. According to the foundation's director José Galán, the fact that unemployment and poverty continued to rise between 1990 and 1994 despite a concurrent 23 percent increase in Panama's GDP "indicate[s] that economic growth is neither creating jobs nor meeting the needs of the majority of the population."[62]

Following major advances in meeting basic needs and broadening access to health, education, and utilities in the 1960s and 1970s, socioeconomic indicators dropped dramatically in the 1980s and have failed to bounce back in the 1990s. Nonetheless, they still are commonly higher than in other Central American nations, except Costa Rica and Belize.

The external debt, which rose to $6.7 billion in 1994, remains a major obstacle to economic stability. Panama's external debt roughly equals its annual GDP, the highest such ratio in Central America and one of the highest in the world. As part of its debt negotiations with foreign commercial banks, Panama announced that it was setting aside $800 million for debt payments in 1995—an amount representing about 20 percent of the government's total budget and 160 percent of what the country receives in foreign exchange from its export offering. Not only does a high debt ratio make Panama vulnerable to foreign pressures for policy reform, but it also means that there is less money for social services and infrastructure development.

Close association with the United States is both an economic blessing and curse for Panama. As the country's largest trading partner, the United States supplies Panama with more than one-third of its imports and purchases more than one-third of its exports. A strong U.S. economic presence is an accepted fact in Panama, and as unemployment remains high there is widespread sentiment that the United States should not withdraw from its military bases in the canal area because of the severe loss of jobs and sales income that would result.

There is no denying or altering the basic structure of the Panamanian economy and its extreme dependence on service income. But services, no matter how beneficial in generating foreign exchange, generally are less successful in providing jobs and spurring associated economic activity than the productive agriculture and industry sectors—which in Panama constitute approximately one-quarter of the country's GDP. The weakness of the productive economy is compounded by its failure to increase export production at a time when imports are exploding because of reduced tariff barriers.

The main economic challenge facing Panama for the balance of the 1990s is to take further advantage of its geographic position as a crossroads for international trade, transport, and finance. However, the economic advances that may result from such a strategy should be evaluated not simply in terms of growth rates or the percapita

GDP. To sustainably develop its economy, Panama will need to implement reforms designed to reduce the extreme economic polarization that currently exists and to formulate economic policies that result in productive work. In other words, policies that spur economic growth must be accompanied by ones that ensure social justice. Another critical part of the mix is a dose of nationalism and negotiation skills to keep international pressures from pushing aside broadly defined national interests.

Such an economic development strategy will require political leadership that recognizes the importance of popular participation and socioeconomic advancement while at the same time maintaining a strong grasp of trends in global trade and production. Panama's experience with both inward-looking populist economic development and outward-looking economic internationalism give it a good head start on formulating such a mixed development strategy.

Society and Environment

Popular Organizing

Activism by working-class Panamanians dates back to the Renters' Movement of 1925. These urban protests, which were closely associated with the labor movement and inspired by socialist and anarchist ideologies, established a militant legacy for popular activism. The movement adopted a more nationalist ideology following the 1964 demonstrations asserting Panamanian sovereignty in the Canal Zone.[1] But more than just changing the character of popular organizing, the events of 1964 altered politics in Panama by establishing the foundation of an alliance between organized social sectors and national policy. This nationalistic, populist alliance coalesced after the 1968 coup by Torrijos and dissolved by the late 1980s.

Despite their long tradition of political activism, popular organizations played a largely passive role in the political crisis of the late 1980s. At a time of rapidly worsening economic conditions and intensifying U.S. pressure, the popular sectors remained distant and without a political agenda. Ideological differences, leadership struggles, and the absence of a unifying political program all weakened the popular movement. The rank-and-file of the organized social sectors were no longer responsive to the popular leaders associated with Noriega. As an expression of their discontent with the regime, many moved closer to the Civic Crusade and the rightwing opposition. Most, however, did not share the conviction common within the Civic Crusade leadership that Noriega was Washington's responsibility. Expressing the widespread disillusionment following the invasion, Panamanian sociologist Raúl Leís observed, "The popular sectors, for the most part, have not been able to establish themselves as a popular movement (the dynamic and organized part of the popular sectors)....What we find is a people without a plan for political power."[2] Much of the rank and file of the labor and popular movements registered their displeasure with the Noriega regime by moving closer to the Civic Crusade and other conservative forces.

The U.S. invasion brought a violent close to an era of military-led populism in Panama. Although the alliance between government and the popular sectors had been disintegrating since the late 1970s, the promise of *torrijismo* continued to be used by the Noriega regime to keep the popular sectors off balance and compromised. With the installation of the Endara administration, the popular sectors and the left wing no longer hoped for support from the government and military. The longtime leaders of the popular sectors and left-wing parties were somewhat hampered by their previous association with the Noriega regime, while emerging leaders and organizations were faced with overcoming their lack of experience and history.

The deep disgust most Panamanians felt for Noriega was the immediate explanation for the initial enthusiastic support of the invasion. Many Panamanians had convinced themselves, as author Frederick Kempe observed, that ridding the country of Noriega was Washington's responsibility. They believed that Noriega was "America's 'Frankenstein,' and thus the *gringos* must destroy him." [3] In the wake of the Noriega period and the U.S. invasion, the state of popular organizing was affected by a generalized disenchantment in Panamanian society.

Participation in the 1994 elections and national pride in the free and fair character of those elections helped Panama to recover from the 1989-90 period. The recovery of the economy also helped revive national spirits, although persistent high employment and widespread poverty provide a reality check for those who insist that Panama is now headed in the correct political and economic direction.

For the popular sectors, the challenges ahead are manifold. Like their counterparts elsewhere in the region popular organizations need to build alliances among the diverse interests of different social sectors to ensure that their own agendas of social justice and broad economic development form part of the platforms of political parties and the policies of the state. In Panama, nationalism has long helped to give the popular movement a cohesive, unified purpose. But the self-serving, fraudulent nationalism of Noriega, together with the December 1989 invasion and occupation shattered the footings of Panamanian nationalism.

Recognizing the importance of pushing forward Panama's geographic advantages in the globalizing economy, since 1990, and especially since the start of the Pérez Balladares administration, the Panamanian government has redefined nationalism as the ways in which Panama can benefit the world—a variation of the traditional *pro-mundi beneficio* strategy. While not discounting the importance and beneficial impact of the nation's service economy, the inchoate popular movement in Panama faces the challenge of reviving a more self-determined and class-sensitive definition of national development.[4]

Pacifying Effects of Torrijismo

Some observers attribute the loss of political dynamism and militancy in the Panamanian majority to the success of *torrijismo*. The 1960s were a time of rapidly expanding political and nationalist consciousness on the part of workers, students, and peasants. But during the 1970s the popular sectors lost the initiative. In the 1970s the military regime co-opted popular organizations and divided them. It was the military which now carried the banner of national sovereignty, the recovery of the Canal Zone, agrarian reform, and educational reform. Only the student movement maintained its form, but that too has now been demobilized.

The Torrijos regime succeeded in pacifying and integrating most elements of the popular movement as part of its reformist effort to modernize the government and the economy. In the agrarian sector, the government sponsored colonization and land-distribution projects that targeted the most conflictive rural areas. Although only 5 percent of the peasant population benefited and the structure of land ownership remained much the same, Torrijos did manage to put a lid on rural unrest and win the support of formerly neglected peasant communities.

The Labor Code of 1972 increased employee rights and facilitated union organizing. One result was the integration of the labor movement into the government's broader modernization project. Union activists and leaders of other popular sectors were brought into government as members of various public sector commissions and committees—the result being the loss of their independence and militancy.

As part of its populist program, the government established hundreds of community "health committees" throughout the country. Health conditions did improve, but the government took measures to insure that local committees did not become a forum and catalyst for more independent political organizing. By establishing a new National Assembly based on the *corregimiento*, the Torrijos regime undermined the local power of the old *patrones* but only to substitute it with a system of political representation controlled by the central government. The reformism of the 1970s was not directed by the popular movement. Instead, the popular sectors formed the base of support for new political and economic projects.[5]

Although the reformist character of *torrijismo* did have the effect of integrating most popular elements into the government's own stabilization plan, there also existed a more combative and independent edge to the popular movement in the 1970s. Within the Catholic church, for example, base communities constituted an important force for social activism.

In the late 1980s several attempts to revitalize the popular movement brought together unions and other popular organizations, notably the United Popular Front (FUP). Different sectors raised specific demands related to their own concerns, but no overall political vision arose that could encompass the broader and long-term needs of the poor majority. The popular movement lacked a unifying political platform as well as the organizing and mobilizing capacity needed to back up its demands.

The *torrijista* grassroots organizations had vanished even before the 1989 invasion. General Noriega tried to revive *torrijismo* with some nationalist rhetoric just before the invasion, but his efforts were largely unsuccessful. Likewise, the few existing radical organizations failed to muster support from the fading *torrijista* base to build popular resistance to the invasion.

Organizing after the Invasion

After the U.S. invasion many social organizations associated with the government disbanded. Few had financial backing and their level of activity was restrained to small meetings and even smaller street rallies. Immediately after the U.S. invasion, the Student Revolutionary Movement (FER) called for a protest march on the 26th anniversary of the 1964 flag demonstrations. Later, as part of the National and Democratic Jornada, church, student, union, and community groups demonstrated against the U.S. military occupation.

Two popular organizations formed soon after the U.S. invasion: Family Members of the Soldiers Killed in Action and the National Network for the Right to Life (no relation to the movement constraining women's reproductive rights in the United States). Isabel Corro, leader of Family Members of the Soldiers Killed in Action, called for a silent march of mourning a month after the invasion in honor of those who sacrificed their lives in defense of the country. Throughout 1990 Corro convened a monthly March of Mourning in commemoration of those who fell during the U.S. invasion.

The National Network for the Right to Life brought together most of the labor, student, and peasant organizations that had survived the U.S. invasion. Led by the State Employees Federation (FENASEP) with nearly 100,000 members, the coalition claimed that the government had fired 20,000 employees, including 396 FENASEP organizers, and that the government had disbanded seventeen employee associations. In response to these government actions, the network in October 1990 held its first rally, which it claimed brought together 50,000 protesters. Spearheaded by dissatisfied labor groups, the network held a second massive demonstration of some 70,000 mainly workers several weeks later.

The December 20th March of Mourning in 1990 was the next massive demonstration of protest against the government and U.S. military occupation. The Family Members of the Soldiers Killed in Action soon merged with other family organizations representing civilian dead. Corro helped forge a broad coalition with the El Chorrillo War Refugees movement that became a principal voice for popular protest.[6]

The most dramatic challenge to the new Endara government came not from popular organizations but from a protest led by former Public Force Commander Colonel Eduardo Herrera who escaped from prison and gathered together a group of military officers to confront the Endara government. On December 5, 1990 Herrera led a protest march that proceeded from Police Headquarters towards the Legislative Assembly. Halfway to their destination the protesters, largely Public Force members, were intercepted and dispersed by U.S. military forces. Herrera was arrested and turned over to the Panamanian police.

President Endara, along with cabinet members, the press, and the progovernment political parties, labeled the protest an attempted coup and linked Herrera to a workers' rally held the same day. In the following crackdown, FENASEP leadership and 500 other workers were discharged. The Legislative Assembly enacted Law 25 that gave the executive branch extraordinary and retroactive powers to fire any public servant who, in the opinion of the cabinet, acted "against democracy or the constitutional powers."[7]

The Endara government's attempts to stifle popular dissent did not succeed in crushing popular organizing. Instead, a partnership developed between workers and other groups, especially Corro's vibrant organization. Joined by Panama City high school students, Corro's organization kept the popular movement alive by holding monthly rallies.

The popular movement attracted international attention when President George Bush came to Panama for a state visit on June 11, 1992. Panama City's mayor, Mayín Correa, had invited Bush, who was on his way to the Rio Environmental Summit, to visit the city. The day before his visit a U.S. soldier had been killed by machine gun fire from a passing car. Bush was given a grand reception by President Endara and dignitaries from around the country. As Correa officially welcomed the U.S. president in an open plaza meeting, several popular organizations held a rally nearby involving some two thousand protesters. The police teargassed the protesters to prevent their demonstration from bothering Endara and Bush and interrupting Mayor Correa's welcome speech. Winds quickly carried the tear gas in the direction of Porras Plaza, only two blocks away.[8] Mayor Correa, choking, did her best to continue praising President Bush, but Mrs. Bush urged her husband to abandon the Plaza with her. Chaos ensued as Bush left for a neighboring U.S. military base in his limousine, followed by Endara's entourage. Halfway there Endara's driver discovered Panama's president was not in the back seat. Returning to the plaza, the chauffer found Endara sitting alone.

The protest and the press attention that it attracted helped boost the popular movement. Afterwards, workers started to mobilize with more self-assurance, Corro's organizations were legitimized, and some unions started talking of conciliatory discussions between workers, the government, and business leaders. Worker's Confederation (CTRP) and Panama Industrialists Society (SIP) jointly condemned the government's economic policy. CTRP leader Aniano Pinzon stated that "no persecution, massive firing, or denial of union rights will intimidate organized workers."

In July 1992 the police shot and killed a participant in a demonstration against joblessness in Colón, but this failed to dissuade further demonstrations, particularly by the Movement of the Unemployed in Colón (MODESCO). In December 1992 and March 1993 the police intervened several times using tear gas and firearms to disburse rallies. President Endara promised scholarships and housing projects to appease the demonstrators, but his promises did little to diminish the grievances against his government.

Precarismo

Both historically and recently, urban land squatters known as *precaristas* have constituted one of the most militant sectors of the popular movement. Since the 1950s poor Panamanians have increasingly resorted to illegal land occupations. At first, *precarismo* was limited to the Panama City area, but beginning in the 1980s land occupations also occurred in Colón and Chiriquí. These squatter settlements are known variously as *barriadas brujas* (underground/unofficial areas), *barriadas de emergencia* (emergency settlements), and *asentamientos espóntaneos* (spontaneous settlements). They are a response to the country's deficit of 200,000 housing units.[9] Since the U.S. military invasion in 1989, *precarista* land takeovers have multiplied to an average of up to three occupations monthly.[10]

San Miguelito, a sprawling area on the outskirts of Panama City, is a product of this squatters' movement. An estimated 10 percent of the nation's population and 20 percent of Panama's urban residents live in these *barriadas*.[11] Although the *precaristas* represent a major sector of interest in Panama, they do not pursue a clear or coherent political agenda. Thousands of residents from one site, El Chorrillo, which was completely destroyed during the U.S. invasion, were relocated to Felipillo, an area forty kilometers east of downtown Panama City. Many of those who were resettled joined protests that demanded that the government launch programs to address the neighborhood's lack of running water, paved roads, schools, and health centers.

Residents of Colón, a city of 80,000 that lies fifty miles north of the capital, feel similarly abandoned by the government. Two movements, MODESCO and FRASCO, emerged since 1990 to struggle for better housing and jobs and to protest the government's improper use of development assistance. The social base and leadership of both of these movements consist largely of young, educated, Afro-Panamanians. Their efforts met with little success, and MODESCO and FRASCO have since lost much momentum.

One of the most active of the different squatter movements is found in Loma Coba, an area formerly under U.S. control a couple of miles west of the Panama Canal. Established as the result of a cooperative effort by homeless and Kuna people, the community of Loma Coba had conflicts with the Panamanian police, who unsuccessfully used dogs and tear gas to uproot the settlement. The residents obtained provisional title to the land in 1995.

A hopeful sign for the development of a more influential and focused popular movement was the presence of worker representatives running as candidates in 1994 for seats in the Assembly and *corregimientos* (smallest political division, similar to a parish or county).

If the country's social sectors are to defend the gains of the past and help shape the new democratic Panama, they will need to unite around a political vision. Otherwise, they will simply be reacting to government and business initiatives. Protests will flare up in reaction to some new injustice, then dissipate if any immediate solution is found. The government in Panama has a long tradition of providing populist solutions that rarely go to the root of the problem and are seldom accompanied by the tools to render them effective. Unlike the Endara government, which responded to popular demands with intransigence and sometimes with force, the Pérez Balladares administration has proved more skillful in winning popular allies, although the economic programs of the two presidents bear many similarities.

Workers and the Labor Movement

Unemployment in Panama has steadily declined from the high levels of the crisis years but the 12 percent rate is still quite high. As economic growth rates decline from the high rates of the 1990-93 period, Panama's economy will be hardpressed to employ the 25,000-30,000 new workers expected to enter the labor force annually during the remainder of the 1990s.[12] Owing to the high public external debt and the government's budget deficit, the public sector is unlikely to generate new jobs. In fact, downsizing and the privatization of state enterprises will likely reduce the number of workers employed by the public sector. In 1993, the private sector, including the self-employed, created 95 percent of the new jobs. Most new jobs, however, are temporary or are in the informal sector.

The private sector accounts for 43 percent of Panama's employed work force, while the public sector accounts for 17 percent, with another 2 percent employed in the canal area. The balance (38 percent) of working Panamanians are either self-employed, owners, or family workers, nearly half of whom are underemployed.[13] Approximately one-quarter of those employed in government ministries or state enterprises are organized into unions, while about 9 percent of the private sector work force is organized.

Labor organizing and workplace struggles have a century-old tradition in Panama, but before 1968 the labor movement always found itself at odds with the economic and political elite. Railroad workers were the first to organize and fight for better pay and conditions. The first labor strike was called on September 8, 1853 by workers at Taboga Island against a U.S.-owned railroad for better wages. When the French Canal company started operations in 1880 it was also a target of strikes, and after 1903 strikes and work stoppages hit the U.S. canal construction effort as well.[14]

Canal workers organized to protest discrimination, inhuman working conditions, and poor food and housing, as well as low and racist pay scales. During the years of the canal construction, the organizing efforts were supported by churches and mutual aid societies established by the largely Caribbean work force. Two such groups were the Colored Progressive Association and West Indian Protective League.[15]

Worker organizing by these associations culminated in a 1920 strike involving over 17,000 laborers—most of those who were being paid in silver (the management and whites were paid in gold). The Panamanian government intervened, demanding that U.S. authorities keep the strikers within the Canal Zone and then deporting two thousand black workers.[16] A year after the famous 1920 strike, the Panamanian Workers Federation was founded by several anarcho-syndicalists from Spain. This first labor federation soon split into two opposing political factions. The more leftist members, who had formed the Communist Group, rejected the federation's links with the AFL-CIO of the United States and in 1924 founded the General Workers Union. Members of the original Communist Group also later founded the Communist Party (known after 1943 as the People's Party) in 1930 and the Socialist Party in 1932.[17]

The General Workers Union was short-lived, but it played a leading role in the Renters' Strike of 1925, having organized the League of Renters. Once again the government responded with deportations and repression. To break the renters' strike, U.S. troops occupied Panama City and Colón. Following the strike, all labor organizing was suppressed by the government until World War II.

Both the U.S.-linked Workers Federation and the leftist General Workers Union disintegrated during the 1930s. But the labor organizations that formed in the 1940s and the 1950s maintained their predecessors' ideological proclivities and the resulting factional divisions.[18] With World War II came increased canal traffic and the emergence of a domestic import-substitution industry. As the economy changed, new labor organizations formed around the various trades. These unions, organized for the most part by the socialist and communist leaders of the 1920s, joined together in 1945 to form the Panamanian Union Federation (FSTRP). Over the next several decades, FSTRP was at the center of most of the country's labor and popular movements. (FSTRP became the National Central of Panamanian Workers, CNTP, in 1956.) Protests, strikes, and marches led by the FSTRP resulted in the enactment of price-control laws, renters' laws, and the country's first minimum-wage law. Representatives from the FSTRP also formed part of the Labor Code Commission, which approved the country's first Labor Code in 1947. Among the most militant elements within the FSTRP were the unions of seamstresses and tailors, who were led by Marta Matamoros, a labor heroine in Panama and a founding member of the FSTRP.

Along with its responsibilities in the labor movement, the FSTRP took up the banner of national sovereignty in the late 1940s and organized against the proposed Filos-Haines U.S. Bases Treaty, eventually rejected by the National Assembly. In the 1950s it protected squatters against government evictions and formed neighborhood associations in shanty towns.[19] For their dedication to popular causes, FSTRP leaders frequently became victims of police repression. President José Antonio Remón, who served as Chief of Police until he became president in 1952, outlawed communist organizations and banned the FSTRP and the progressive Federation of Panamanian Students (FEP). During the 1950s and 1960s many labor leaders were forced to work underground or leave the country.[20]

In contrast to the government's treatment of the FSTRP, the Panamanian Workers Federation (CTRP) formed in 1956 with the blessings of the government. This was the result of U.S. pressure on the Remón government to facilitate the creation of a U.S.-linked labor federation to counterbalance the leftist FSTRP. Once again, the country's labor movement was split between its leftist and conservative wings. From its beginning CTRP has counted on U.S. government financing and training channeled through the AFL-CIO and (after 1962) the American Institute for Free Labor Development (AIFLD).

The early 1960s were marked by intense worker struggles, particularly in the banana and sugar industries. For decades United Fruit had successfully crushed unionizing efforts with mass firings. "Rabble-rousers" and their families were loaded onto company trains and abandoned in isolated regions of the Chiriquí grasslands.[21] The general strike of 1960 paralyzed banana plantations in both provinces of Chiriquí and Bocas del Toro. The government and United Fruit worked together during several months to try and stop the labor movement. But the workers withstood the pressure and finally United Fruit agreed to increase salaries and create better working conditions. The country as a whole supported the banana workers and saw the victory as its own.[22]

The pre-1968 labor movement was characterized by its effort to win popular support. Subject to government repression and victimized by unfavorable labor laws, the unions were aware that the movement could only achieve its demands with popular support. Things changed dramatically after 1968. No longer was the labor movement on the margin. Torrijos gave union leaders preferential positions in his military government, something not all big business leaders had. In efforts to gain legitimacy for his new regime, Torrijos turned to the labor movement, hoping to make it part of his political base much as Juan Perón used Argentine labor to establish one-man rule.[23]

The enactment of the pro-union Labor Code of 1972 provided more than most unions had ever hoped for. Workers were guaranteed job security after two years, union dues were collected for all workers covered by labor agreements, and the rights to strike and to bargain collectively were upheld. The decidedly pro-labor tone of the new code was set forth in its first article: "The present Code governs relations between capital and labor, establishing special state protection in favor of the workers, so that the state may intervene with the purpose of providing remunerative employment to all those who lack it, ensuring every worker the necessary economic conditions for a decent standard of living."[24]

The 1972 code came at a time when the old oligarchy and traditional business were in disarray while the union movement was gaining unprecedented prestige. Both of the two main labor confederations—CTRP and CNTP—enjoyed close relations with the Torrijos government.[25] Besides granting workers new rights and guarantees, the 1972 code provided for the formation of the National Council of Organized Workers (CONATO) as a consultative organization of union representatives. While the Labor Code did protect private-sector workers, public-sector employees and rural workers were excluded. No corresponding Civil Service Code protects government employees, although specific legislation does govern labor relations in certain autonomous public-sector agencies.

During the 1970s the labor sector expanded rapidly, particularly the left-leaning CNTP. The Isthmian Workers Central (CIT) dominated by Christian Democrats split to form the Authentic Independent Workers Central (CATI). The powerful Construction Workers Union (SUNTRACS) and Panamanian Transport Workers Central (CPTT) also appeared on the scene at that time.

By the middle of the decade the private sector successfully pressured the government to revise the 1972 Labor Code. More than any other measure, the Labor Code had served to define the Torrijos government as reformist, populist, and pro-labor. Its revision in 1976 through Law 95 promoted by CONEP and other private sector organizations signaled a change in the political direction of the regime.

In advancing its support for Law 95, the business sector had argued that the economic downturn of the early 1970s was directly linked to the 1972 Labor Code, which they said discouraged new economic activity. Although the government's approval of Law 95 was a blow to the labor movement, it did force it to reorganize and unite to fight the growing political power of the country's dominant economic forces. By 1981 the tenuously unified labor movement was able to force the government to remove the most restrictive measures of Law 95, but it never regained the strong position it had enjoyed in the early 1970s.

The Labor Movement's Decline in the 1980s

As a result of the country's debt crisis in the 1980s, international financial institutions gained increased leverage over Panama's economic policy. In return for loans and renegotiations of debt servicing, the government was obligated to implement austerity policies, privatize state-run enterprises, and place higher priority on foreign investments—all of which worked against the labor movement.

Government and the business elite teamed up to prevent unionization in the international service sectors like the large banking center and the Colón Free Zone, which blocked the union movement's access to some of the more dynamic economic sectors. During the 1980s, labor struggles were mainly concentrated in the public sector. The National Federation of Public Workers (FENASEP), created in 1984, still represents more than half the country's public sector labor force. During the 1980s FENASEP led major mobilizations against the government's structural adjustment measures. Not protected by the country's Labor Code, FENASEP continues to struggle for the right to strike, unionize, and bargain collectively. Highly politicized, it has led the struggles against the government's proposed civil service bill and against privatization of state-owned enterprises.

Joining with the National Council of Organized Workers (CONATO) and the Coordinator of Panamanian Popular Organizations (COPP), FENASEP in 1988 demanded the departure of the U.S. Southern Command, suspension of foreign debt payments, nationalization of banks, and a foreign policy independent of Washington. In the late 1980s FENASEP called numerous public protests against government corruption and patronage, austerity measures, and the militarization of government enterprises like the Energy Institute (IRHE), the state's electrical power company.

When the Civic Crusade called for a general strike in early 1988, unions, for the most part, declined to join. Notable exceptions were the associations of teachers and medical workers. Expressing the sentiments of most unions, the CNTP's Manuel Meneses said, "Despite our differences with the Noriega government, we unite with it in opposing U.S. attacks on our sovereignty." The CNTP and other union federations like FENASEP denounced the proposed general strike as a lock-out strike that had little worker support.[26]

Postinvasion Challenges

The economic downturn that resulted from U.S.-Panama tensions in the 1980s was a severe blow to the labor movement and workers in general. Official unemployment rose to more than 20 percent, manufacturing plants closed down or went on half shifts, and government agencies cut back on employment. During and following the invasion, union leaders became targets for repression. Labor organizers who had been close to Noriega were arrested and imprisoned for short terms, and government and U.S. military suspicions about the sympathies of the unions forced the labor movement to maintain a low profile.

The union movement suffered a blow in early 1993 when the Supreme Court of Justice declared several Labor Code articles unconstitutional. The most important of these, article 373, viewed by more conservative groups as the central column of union power, made it mandatory for all workers to pay union dues. The unions had grown steadily after 1972 thanks to this article. Labor movement leaders said the Supreme Court decision was a violation of the International Labor Organization's (ILO) convention that protects the right to unionize.[27] The ruling still requires that workers benefiting from a collective bargaining agreement, whether or not members of the union, pay union dues.

Ironically, later in 1993 the United States lifted its "probation" on Panama after determining that Panama fulfilled provisions for labor rights in the U.S. Generalized System of Preferences (GSP). The AFL-CIO, responding to a petition from CTRP leader Aniano Pinzón, filed a claim against Panama's GSP benefits in 1991. Responding to domestic and U.S. pressure from labor unions, Panama restored the right to collective negotiation of labor contracts.[28]

Among the unions there was hope that the PRD's candidate Pérez Balladares would be more sympathetic to worker concerns than the Endara administration had been. The PRD candidate did call on the unions to help him search for economic solutions to the country's development problems, and his planning minister promised that there would be no structural adjustments that would hurt workers. Several labor leaders, the most prominent being CTRP leader Aniano Pinzón, openly aligned themselves with the PRD during the 1994 campaign.

Thus far, however, there has been little to distinguish the new administration's economic policies from that of its predecessor. Responding to worker concerns about high unemployment and low wages, Pérez Balladares said that attracting more foreign investment was the best alternative. Among his 12-member cabinet there are no labor representatives or officials that the unions trust. Other concerns are the government's proposal to reform the Labor Code and privatize more state enterprises.

In mid-1995 twenty-six Panamanian labor organizations claiming a combined membership of 70,000 threatened to strike if the government followed through with its promise to introduce a bill to reform the Labor Code. The unions carried out a successful one-day "warning strike" in May. Leading the anti-reform movement were two of the most influential unions in the country: the Chiriquí Land Company banana workers' union (SITRACHILCO) and SUNTRACS. They claimed that the government was following the dictates of the international finance organizations and that the proposed reforms removed protections against the arbitrary firing of workers. While not denying that there are indeed international pressures to change the Labor Code, President Pérez Balladares said that the reforms would be in the best interests of Panamanian workers who would gain by the increased employment from making the economy more efficient, competitive, and attractive to private investors. For its part, Panama's business community has strongly criticized the code as creating unjustifiably high costs for employers who have difficulty dismissing workers and must pay high severance costs. Furthermore, business owners say that the country's high minimum wage—the highest in Central America—also acts as a brake on increased private investment.

The weakening of union organizations goes hand in hand with the political and economic crisis of the 1980s—something that Panama has yet to overcome. Except for some thriving sectors such as construction, workers are not convinced of their own ability to stand up and negotiate with employers. Skyrocketing unemployment has created uncertainties among workers and their families. Although unemployment has decreased slowly since 1990, joblessness remains one of the greatest concerns of the unions and Panamanians in general.

The Panamanian labor movement, like other components of the country's popular movement, is weak, fragmented, and without a clear direction. Political upheaval, economic crisis, and neoliberal economic restructuring have all played a part in the weakening of Panamanian unions. Internal problems, including corruption, unresponsive hierarchies, and politicking, have also undermined the labor movement and prevented it from assuming a strong and independent role in the popular movement. From this weak position, the labor movement faces a series of new challenges. Not only is it confronted with the need to mount an alternative to the dominant neoliberal development model, but the labor movement also must take a strong stand in negotiations over revisions in the Labor Code, the reinstatement of summarily fired state employees, and the privatization of state enterprises. The successful May 1995 strike against Labor Code reform offered a glimpse of some labor groups' determination to meet these challenges.

Major Labor Organizations

National Council of Organized Workers (CONATO)

Established in 1973 in accordance with the Labor Code as a collaborative and consultative umbrella group for private sector labor confederations, CONATO has no authority over member unions. Initially established to coordinate the policies of the four major confederations, CONATO has since included many more labor centrals and independent unions. Although wracked by major ideological divisions, CONATO was able to gain some influence in putting forward labor's position since the U.S invasion. Under the Endara government the Ministry of Labor gave CONATO renewed importance.

Immediately after the U.S. invasion CONATO confronted the Endara government's labor policy. In 1990 Endara's proposed "National Strategy for Economic Development and Modernization" called for lowering salaries, cutting jobs, and eliminating key articles of the Labor Code. CONATO was able to defuse the harsher aspects of Endara's labor policy.[29] However, the lack of growth of Panama's manufacturing, agribusiness and other productive areas has cornered CONATO into a permanent defensive strategy. As a consequence it has become largely ineffective with little mobilizing capacity.

Worker's General Central of Panama (CGTP)

Affiliated with the Christian Democrat-affiliated Confederation of Latin American of Workers (CLAT) and the World Confederation of Labor (WCL), the CGTP was founded in 1990 under the auspices of Endara's Labor Ministry and the Christian Democrats following the fragmentation of the Isthmian Workers Central (CIT). Its leaders had close ties to the Civic Crusade in the late 1980s. The Central has a three-level structure: a National Congress, a Council of Delegates, and an Executive Committee that is renewed every two years.

Of the forty unions belonging to the CGTP, sixteen are based in agribusiness activities, eleven belong to the service sector, and ten to manufacturing. According to official documents, the CGTP considers itself a class-based organization. It organizes its activities around a "doctrine of social Christian humanism" and "the human person, liberty, social justice and solidarity." The CGTP played an important role during Endara's administration in establishing structures for dialogue between labor and management. Benefiting from its government connections, the CGTP secretary general was designated by the government to fill the labor seat on the Interoceanic Regional Authority Board (ARI).

National Central of Panamanian Workers (CNTP)

Founded in 1956 as an outgrowth of the FSTRP (1947), CNTP has a leftist orientation and is affiliated internationally with the World Federation of Trade Unions (WFTU) and the Permanent Congress of Trade Union Unity of Latin America (CPUSTAL). On a regional level, it is affiliated with the Central American Trade Union Committee (CUSCA). The CNTP represents about 8,000 workers and is composed of six federations and twenty local unions, including the National Federation of Food, Beverage, and Tobacco Workers, the National Telecommunications Institute Union (INTEL), the Institute for Electrification (IRHE) Union, and the National Union of Typesetters.

The CNTP administration also divides into three levels: the National Congress, the Confederate Council, and the National Executive Secretariat. Self-described as a class-oriented organization, the CNTP characterized postinvasion Panama as a militarily occupied country with a puppet government. The organization supports the Carter-Torrijos Canal Treaties that call for full U.S. troop evacuation by the year 2000. Several members of the CNTP's top leadership ran for legislative offices as PRD and Papa Egoró candidates during the May 1994 elections. Although still associated with the left, the CNTP has recently received support from the Christian Democratic Labor International and its Latin American branch, CLAT.

Workers Confederation of the Republic of Panama (CTRP)

Founded in 1956, CTRP is the country's largest confederation. Internationally, it is affiliated with the International Confederation of Free Trade Unions (ICFTU), Interamerican Regional Organization of Workers (ORIT), and in Central America with the Confederation of Central American Workers (CTCA). Funding and training for CTRP has come largely from the AFL-CIO and AIFLD. From 1985 through 1990, it was allocated a total of $1.3 million by AIFLD. CTRP includes eleven federations and sixty-five unions, the most important of which are Local 907 (Panamanian workers in U.S. Army installations), Federation of Workers of the Central Provinces (mainly sugar workers), Industrial Federation of Food, Beverage, and Hotel Workers (FITA-HBA), National Union of Bank Employees (SINABAN), and SITRACHILCO. Since the early 1980s CTRP has made an effort to become more politically active.

The wealthiest confederation, CTRP has exerted considerable influence through its AIFLD-sponsored education programs. According to the AIFLD plan for CTRP activities in 1985, CTRP had to seek to "influence economic, social, and political development of Panama through effective electoral and public opinion activities....If CTRP is to have more influence, it must become more politically active." [30] Shortly before the U.S. invasion AIFLD director Bill Doherty threatened to cut off all support unless the CTRP followed the U.S. foreign policy position and demonstrated against the Noriega regime.[31] Refusing to adopt the U.S. position, CTRP lost its monthly allotment from AIFLD.

On an ideological level, the CTRP believes that the labor struggle should aim at creating a democratic system of credit that would enable all citizens to finance small business enterprises. It also calls for a modern state that is efficient and aware of the needs of the poor. General Secretary Aniano Pinzón was an unsuccessful PRD legislative candidate in the May 1994 elections, and his leadership's legitimacy was challenged by other CTRP leaders in May 1995.

Isthmian Workers Central (CIT)

Founded in 1959, the CIT follows a strong Christian Democratic agenda. It is affiliated with the World Confederation of Labor (WCL) and CLAT. After the split in the 1970s that gave birth to the Authentic Workers Central (CATI) and later the creation of the CGTP, the CIT has lost most of its members. Nevertheless, the beleaguered organization continues to hang on as member of CONATO.

Authentic Workers Central (CATI)

Organized in 1976 after a split in the CIT, this is a militant organization that has had a Trotskyite orientation and which has only a minimal presence in Panama with its one thousand members.

Local 907

There are nearly 12,000 Panamanian employees and several hundred U.S. citizens working in the Panama Canal Area who are represented by local affiliates of the AFL-CIO.[32] Panamanian workers are distinguished by whether they work for the Panama Canal Commission or for one of the several military bases located along the canal. The Panama Canal Commission workers are grouped around unions such as the American Federation of State, County, and Municipal Employees (AFSCME), American Federation of Government Employees (AFGE), and the National Maritime Union (NMU). Local 907 of AFSCME represents over 5,000 workers at the U.S. bases and is the largest of the unions in the canal area. The relationship between canal workers and the U.S. government has often been marred by conflict, although recently the relationship has improved.

Despite the political and economic crisis of the late 1980s, labor relations in the canal area remained relatively peaceful. Employees at the Panama Canal Commission, as well as those on the bases, generally supported the Civic Crusade against the military government. Since the invasion these workers have expressed concern over their rights once the canal is turned over to Panama and the U.S. military evacuates the bases.

A coalition of employee organizations at the Panama Canal Commission advocated constitutional reform that would ensure a future canal administration that would be autonomous from the central government. The coalition is controlled by conservative activists linked to U.S.-Panamanian business interests that are lobbying for an internationally run Panama Canal.[33] Also wary of involvement by the Panamanian government, Local 907 has campaigned for the United States to continue its military installations in Panama. Ray Bishop, the coalition's leader until 1994, lobbied in Washington and Panama City for the renegotiation of the canal treaties. Bishop was unsuccessful in his 1994 bid for a seat in the Legislative Assembly on the MORENA party ticket, and his successor at Local 907, Arturo Thomas, has been more open to alternatives to keeping U.S. bases in Panama.

Labor Foundation (Fundación de Trabajo)

The Labor Foundation provides the primary forum for labor-management relations and includes representatives from the CTRP and the Industrialists' Association of Panama (SIP). The foundation's central objectives include creating a nonprofit, private employment agency, financing worker training programs, and addressing changes in the Labor Code. The Foundation's approach has been highly conservative, with the CTRP and SIP pushing their own interests rather than advocating for reform in current labor conditions.[34]

Education and Students

As a result of a higher percapita income and due to educational reforms implemented in the 1960s and 1970s, Panamanians have a high literacy rate and better access to educational institutions than citizens in most neighboring countries. In the mid-1990s the literacy rate was estimated at 88 percent. About 13 percent of the national budget is dedicated to education, down slightly from the Torrijos years but higher than most other countries in the region. With respect to education and health, Panamanians enjoy better conditions than those in most Latin American countries. There are, however, severe discrepancies between urban and rural areas, and especially between indigenous and nonindigenous peoples.

Panama has two state-financed universities, the University of Panama (UP) and the Technological University of Panama (UTP), along with several private universities. These include the Universidad Santa María La Antigua (USMA), a Catholic institution; Panama Canal College, associated with the U.S. Department of Defense Dependents Schools; Nova University; Universidad del Istmo; Universidad Latina; Columbus University; ULACIT; Universidad Interamericana; and a branch of Florida State University.

Founded in 1935, UP is the country's educational center. It has also served as a center for progressive political research and activism. In its attempt to maintain high educational standards, UP requires first-year students to pass an admissions test. In 1987 only 5 percent of those entering the university successfully passed the test, requiring the failing students to take a summer preparation course. Secondary school administrators complained that the test is too difficult, while UP officials said that the primary and secondary school systems are not providing high-quality education.[35]

A strong student movement developed in Panama with the foundation of the Panamanian Student Federation (FEP) in 1943. Unlike elsewhere in Latin America, the strongest force in this movement involved high school rather than university students. Panamanian high school students spearheaded the "Flag Demonstrations" of 1964 when twenty-one Panamanians were killed and four hundred wounded by U.S. soldiers stationed in the Canal Zone. Both high school and university students have played a leading role in pushing forward national sovereignty issues in Panama. In addition, university students were instrumental in lobbying the government to open up educational opportunities for the country's poor and rural population.

In 1973 the Marxist-influenced FEP took another turn and swore allegiance to Torrijos' new style of revolutionary government. Along with other popular movements, the FEP gave the military regime a needed boost to push through its economic reforms. The FEP's alliance with Torrijos bolstered the general but left the student movement without an independent direction. Other radical student organizations have moved in to replace the FEP. The FEP was joined by Guaycuhco, which later gave rise to the Workers Revolutionary Party-PRT and the Socialist Workers Party (PST). Among the leftist student movements to replace the FEP was the Revolutionary Student Front (FER), which is still active.

The State of Health

Health conditions in Panama compare favorably to most other Central American countries. Panama was subject to rigorous public health measures during canal construction to ensure the health and survival of canal workers, vastly reducing malaria and other diseases in the process. As elsewhere in the region, Panama saw steady improvement in health care in the 1970s that resulted in improving mortality rates and increased life expectancy. Panama's life expectancy at birth is 73 years (1994), compared to 65 years in Guatemala and 76 years in the United States. Infant mortality (during the first year) dropped from 105 per thousand births in 1960 to 21 per thousand in 1994.[36] Panama City has one of the few potable municipal water systems in capital cities of the region, a result of fresh water that feeds the canal.

A U.S.-financed study of health care in Panama prepared in the late 1950s made a series of recommendations about steps needed to improve the public-sector health care system. Many of the fifty-nine recommendations were eventually adopted by the government in the early 1960s. In 1963 the government published its first National Health Plan in conjunction with Alliance for Progress projects.

A renewed and expanded government commitment to improving the country's health care began with the 1968 military coup. The Torrijos regime launched a national campaign which included the formation of community "Health Committees" throughout the country. The government's new Ministry of Health promoted the grassroots work of the Health Committees, which sponsored latrine, water, popular education, and communal vegetable projects. The health committees also developed productive economic projects designed to cover the costs of new health centers.[37] The number of doctors doubled between 1970 and 1979 and the number of health care facilities jumped 70 percent.[38] In 1992 there were 12 physicians per 10,000 inhabitants (Figure 4a), which compares favorably with most Central American nations including Guatemala, where there are only 7 doctors per 10,000 inhabitants.[39]

The country's social security system also expanded rapidly in the 1970s, but since the late 1980s it has been in serious financial difficulty. The extension of health services coupled with corruption strained the social security system's ability to cover demand. Population doubled in the 1970s, but those covered by social security tripled. Some 6,000 banana workers of United Brands (formerly United Fruit)

Figure 4a
Education and Health in Statistics

Education

Mean years of schooling	
Male	6.9
Female	6.5
Adult literacy (over age 15)	
Male	88%
Female	88%
Adults age 15-19	95%
% enrolled in primary schools	100%
% enrolled in secondary schools	59%
% enrolled in higher institutions of learning	22%
Years to produce 6th grade student	7.3
% of national budget spent on education	11%
Public education expenditure as % of GDP	5%

Health

Life Expectancy	73
Infant mortality per 1000 live births	21
Fertility (children per woman)	3.0
Daily caloric supply (as % of daily requirements)	98%
% of one-year-olds fully immunized	87%
Physicians per 10,000 people	11.8
Access to safe water	83%
Access to health, sewage, and sanitation services	84%
% of national budget spent on health	7%
Public health expenditure as % of GDP	3%

SOURCES: United States Agency for International Development, 1994; Bread for the World Institute, 1994; *Europa World Year Book* vol. II, 1994.

were brought into the system, thereby relieving the company of its responsibility to provide health care benefits to its employees. Other strains on social security were the Noriega government's practice of dipping into its coffers to cover other government expenses and its own failure to contribute its obligated share to the system. The absence of a profitable investment policy has also weakened this important source of health care.[40] After the U.S. invasion the government and the Legislative Assembly passed a social security reform that forces workers to contribute more of their wages and to work more years before becoming eligible for retirement.

The country's health system was probably the hardest hit by postinvasion government policies. Most rural health centers set up in the 1970s were shut down by budget cuts. Health care is an issue that presents Pérez Balladares with a complex political challenge. Public health plans are fiercely opposed by the business elite, who want to shrink the public health system and expand private health care. Supporters of public health programs point out that half the population cannot pay for prescription drugs or a visit to the doctor.

A widening gap between rural and urban health conditions is another growing problem in Panama's health care system. The areas of the country of least population density (Darién and Bocas del Toro) are the areas with the lowest levels of health care and the lowest per capita income. The difference between rural and urban areas is sometimes extreme, as in the case of the largely Indian population at the Tabasara Sierra where the life expectancy in 1976 was only 38 years.[41] In remote rural areas the causes of death are largely preventable and transmittable illnesses related to poor diet, lack of access to medical care, and contaminated water supplies. In urban areas and more accessible rural areas, however, the most prevalent causes of death are cancer, accidents and other violent deaths, and heart failure, paralleling patterns found in the industrial world.[42]

As in most underdeveloped countries, fertility rates are significantly higher in rural than in urban areas of Panama. This trend seems to be changing. A decade ago urban women bore an average of 2.7 children while rural women had more than 5.[43] By 1992 the average for urban women had declined to 2.4 children and rural women were producing only 3.9 children.[44] Some 70 percent of married women report having used contraceptives, compared to only 45 percent in Guatemala.

In mid-1989 the Ministry of Health reported that Panama is among the countries most affected by Acquired Immune Deficiency Syndrome (AIDS). Between 1983 and 1994 the office recorded 788 confirmed cases of AIDS, 438 of whom died. More than 20,000 Panamanians are believed to be HIV positive.[45]

Communications Media

Historically the media in Panama has seldom strayed out of the hands of the country's oligarchy. Between 1968 and 1989, however, the military regime forged its own media empire, publishing its own newspapers and shutting down media considered too critical of the military or government. Immediately after taking power in October 1968, the National Guard closed several newspapers published by Pan American Publishing Company, which was owned by the Arias Guardia family. Two radio stations associated with Arnulfo Arias were also closed.

In 1969 the new military regime established an official government radio station called Radio Libertad, which later became Radio Nacional. The following year the government expropriated the Pan American Publishing Company and changed its name to Editora Renovación (ERSA). During the 1970s the private media was closely controlled, and in 1975 the Torrijos regime closed Radio Impacto for its intense criticism of the government. With the signing of the 1977 Canal Treaties, there was increased press freedom but the regime soon clamped down again. In 1979, for example, several radio commentators were banned because of their strong antigovernment opinions.

Despite pervasive government control, the independent press continued to push forward. The most important of the antigovernment papers that appeared in the 1980s was *La Prensa*. Upon becoming defense minister in 1982, General Paredes stepped up the repression against the opposition media, temporarily closing down several papers, including *La Prensa*. Besides the appearance of new dailies in the early 1980s, two new privately owned television stations (channels 5 and 13) began broadcasting, joining channels 2 and 4.

A new wave of repression of the media followed the June 1987 revelations by Col. Roberto Díaz Herrera. A state of emergency suspended freedom of the press, and the powerful Radio KW Continente was shut down by the military. As the crisis heated up, military repression of the press intensified. In February 1989, Noriega, infuriated by all the bad publicity, again closed several radio stations and newspapers including *La Prensa*. The ouster of Noriega in December 1989 caused a flourishing of media operations. The newspapers *La Prensa*, *El Siglo*, and *El Extra* were reopened, and *La Crítica* was returned to its previous owners.

Print Media

All the country's daily newspapers—*La Prensa*, *La Crítica*, *El Siglo*, *La Estrella de Panamá*, and *El Panamá América*—are published in Panama City and are poorly distributed outside the capital. The largest paper is *La Prensa*, a daily formerly owned by Roberto Eisenmann, one of the country's most powerful businessmen.[46] In the 1994 elections, the paper opposed the PRD and its line of candidates, supporting instead Rubén Darío Carles, one of the paper's directors. *El Siglo*, founded in 1985, is a sensationalistic tabloid owned by businessman Jaime Padilla Beliz that also endorsed Carles' bid for the presidency. *El Panamá América*, owned by the Arias Guardia family, did not support any specific candidate. Rather the paper's staff was split between two candidates, Mireya Moscoso de Gruber and Darío Carles. *La Estrella de Panamá*, which nearly closed down during the Noriega regime for lack of advertising, has consistently supported the government in power, but the paper broke with its tradition and stood firmly next to the PRD and its candidate Pérez Balladares in 1994. *La Estrella*, which has a much lower circulation than it once enjoyed, is owned by the Duque family, and its director is Tomás G. Altamirano Duque, elected first vice-president in May 1994.[47] During the first year of the Pérez Balladares administration, it was the only strongly progovernment daily, although none of the papers were especially hostile to the government's attempts to overcome the economic and political instability of the 1980s and early 1990s.

Three valuable sources of progressive analysis are the bimonthlies *Canal de Panamá Hoy* and *Premisas* (both published by the Center for Latin American Studies, CELA); the monthly *La Chiva* (published by the Panamanian Center for Research and Social Action, CEASPA); and the bimonthly SERPAJ *Boletín*.

Radio

As in the rest of Central America, radio is the most important communications media in Panama. Virtually all Panamanians have their one or two favorite radio stations among an impressive eighty-eight stations in the country (forty four in Panama City). Especially popular are the lively morning talk shows broadcast by most stations between 6 AM and 9 AM that discuss a variety of political issues.

Many radio stations were tied to the Noriega government. Radio Nacional, which broadcasts throughout the entire country, was directly owned by the government and was bombed shortly after the U.S. invasion in December 1989. At least four other radio stations were closed down by the Endara government.

The country's most powerful radio network is RPC, followed by Radio Mía, KW Continente, and Radio Exitosa. Panama has two church-owned radio stations, Radio Hogar (Catholic) and La Voz del Istmo (Protestant). The U.S. Southern Command Network (SCN) operates AM and FM stations for the U.S. Armed Forces although the English-language broadcasts have a significant Panamanian audience.

Television

Television, a highly conservative communications media in Panama, is influential, especially in the Panama City area where an estimated 75 percent of homes have television sets.[48] Television programming has been limited in the past by the commercial and pragmatic views of its conservative owners. Stations have at times banned certain movies and creative programming dealing with social issues, calling them "noncommercial" and "subversive."

Panama's three main commercial stations—RPC Channel 4 (1961), Televisora Nacional Channel 2 (1964) and TeleMetro Channel 13 (1983)—carry a similar line of programs, primarily a mix of Mexican and Venezuelan soap operas and U.S. shows. The oldest station, RPC, owned by the Eleta family, supported the U.S. invasion and the Endara government, and it also threw its weight behind the Pérez Balladares administration. In previous years RPC was a strong supporter of the military regimes.

Televisora Nacional (Channel 2), was founded in 1963 by the Chiari family (President Roberto Chiari 1960-64) and sold to the PDF in 1983.[49] Telemetro (Channel 13), mainly a movie channel, is owned by a group of PRD members that includes Pérez Balladares. Channel 11, the educational station, is operated and owned by the Ministry of Education. While the commercial stations reach out to every corner of the country, Channel 11 is only seen in Panama City. Although Channel 11 originally belonged to the University of Panama, the Education Ministry assumed control of the station after the U.S. invasion. FETV (Channel 5) was founded by the Delvalle family in 1985 but was lost to debtors after President Eric A. Delvalle was politically disgraced. After the invasion the government passed the rights to the station on to the Catholic Church, which runs educational programs with some religious content.

Although commercial opinion polls are not always reliable, most agree that at present RPC commands almost 40 percent of Panama's TV viewers, Telemetro over 40 percent, and TVN over 10 percent. Channel 11 and Channel 5 together take in under 10 percent. English-language programming is run on U.S. Armed Forces SCN TV (Channels 8 and 10), which attracts a significant Panamanian audience.

The media revolution produced by VCRs and video entertainment has not passed by Panama, but rather produced a blossoming of video rental stores all over the major cities. Initially many of the stores rented out pirated versions of international and Hollywood films. Largely in response to U.S. claims on intellectual property and the requirements placed on Panama's bid to enter the World Trade Organization, the government enacted an author's copyright law in early 1995 that outlawed the rental of pirated videos.

U.S. Government Information Services

As in other countries, the U.S. government disseminates written and electronic news through USIS, the overseas branch of the U.S. Information Agency (USIA). In Panama, the U.S. government also coordinated clandestine broadcasting operations to prop up the Civic Crusade. The program began in 1988 with a secret FM station named Radio Constitucional, which soon went off the air.

Early in 1989 President Bush approved a $10 million covert operations plan for Panama that included a second attempt at clandestine broadcasting. These secret media operations were brought to a close by the Panamanian government in April 1989 when it arrested a U.S. businessman in charge of the clandestine broadcasting network and confiscated about $350,000 worth of radio and communications equipment from eight apartments around Panama City. The government charged that Washington was waging an "electronic war" as part of its destabilization campaign. The secret radio operation, however, represented no real threat since few Panamanians outside the government knew or cared about the clandestine station.[50]

Access to U.S. news is not a problem in Panama because radio listeners and TV viewers can easily tune into U.S. programs in Spanish on a daily basis. Three times a day, the major TV networks broadcast U.S. commercial news programs, most sent by satellite from Miami. This programming has replaced old formats in which local journalists covered international news stories by using tapes out of their archives. Cable TV makes available 24-hour news programs in Spanish and English (as well as in German and other languages). The U.S. Southern Command's radio and television stations also broadcast 24 hours a day in English.

During the Noriega crisis of the late 1980s, a host of U.S. journalists descended upon Panama in search of a scoop that would propel them into fame and fortune. Now that Noriega sits in a Miami jail, journalists visit Panama City with less frequency. President Endara never attracted much attention and the 1994 elections went largely unnoticed in the U.S. press. When the elections were covered, they focused on the candidacy of singer Rubén Blades and the resurrection of the "party of Noriega," the PRD.

A 1988 report in the *Columbia Journalism Review* concluded that U.S. journalists covering Panama typically follow the lead of the White House in their reporting. The article by Ken Silverstein noted that the U.S. press was largely silent about the fraudulent 1984 elections, paralleling the U.S. government's own "see-no-evil approach" at the time. "Recently—and only recently—coverage has focused on General Manuel Antonio Noriega, who has been portrayed as a thug presiding over a corrupt regime. Any reporter with even a minimum of initiative—or encouragement from an alert editor—could have written this story years ago."[51]

Religion

Panama, as well as the rest of Latin America, is the product of the Spanish Conqueror's sword and the missionary's Cross. The isthmus became the seat of the first diocese established on the Western Hemisphere's mainland, and its colonial churches are constant reminders of the influence of the Catholic church in Panama. The cathedral's tower in Panamá Viejo, which was ransacked and burned in 1671 by Welsh pirate Henry Morgan, remains the centerpiece of Panamá Viejo—a present-day tourist attraction. The oldest Catholic church in the Americas is in Natá in the Coclé province, some 100 miles west of Panama City.

Through the centuries the Roman Catholic Church has often served as an instrument in struggles for political domination. Political parties, businessmen, labor leaders, the military, and even the U.S. Embassy regularly pay homage to the bishop's robes in recognition of the powerful ideological force that the church represents, despite the state and church having been officially separated in Panama for almost a century.

Since the 1968 military coup both progressive and conservative forces (especially Christian Democrat politicians) have pushed for the church to play a more committed social and political role in Panamanian society. The church patriarch who stood at the center of these struggles from 1969 to 1994 was Archbishop Marcos McGrath, a Panamanian who before becoming archbishop presided over the Santiago diocese in Veraguas and was a theology professor at the Catholic University of Chile.

Before becoming archbishop, McGrath was known as a liberal within the church ranks because of his political work and his activism in poor peasant communities. McGrath left the archbishop's office amid controversy over his public support for the U.S. military intervention in December 1989. Only two weeks after the U.S. bombing had ceased, Archbishop McGrath organized a special outdoor mass with President Endara, dignitaries, and U.S. military officers. There he proclaimed: "Let the foreign military presence be remembered in the future as an act of liberation." The church since then has tried to downplay McGrath's statement.[52]

After 25 years as Archbishop of Panama, McGrath presented his resignation to Pope John Paul II, claiming painful illness as the cause. In early 1994 José Dimas Cedeño, a conservative bishop, was named to replace him. In contrast to McGrath's background as a Panamanian of Scottish parents who migrated to Panama in the early 1900s, Cedeño hails from a family with enduring ties to rural Panama.

The Institutional Church

Outside of the archdiocese of Panama, the balance of the country is divided into the dioceses of David (Chiriquí), Chitre (Herrera and Los Santos), Santiago (Veraguas) and Coclé. There are also the special jurisdictions of Colón, San Blas, Bocas del Toro, and Darién. Catholicism is taught in most public schools, although the instruction is not obligatory.

Despite having the vast majority of Panamanians identify themselves as Catholic and maintaining an important political influence, the church in Panama is a weak institution. In a series of surveys, 86 percent of Panamanians identified themselves as Catholic and 8 percent as Protestant.[53] Less than 20 percent of the country's self-identified Catholics regularly attend mass, however. This lack of a strong social base is reflected in the small number of local vocations. At least 75 percent of Catholic clergy are foreign missionaries.[54] In 1980 there was only one priest to serve 6300 Catholics.[55] Strong participation by the laity through such organizations as the Delegates of the Word partially compensates for the low number of clergy.

In the mid-1970s the U.S. bishops funded a study to determine how the Panamanian church could become more self-sufficient. One result of that study was a series of annual fundraising campaigns that by 1986 were providing the church with $800,000 in annual income. Contributions by church members began to fall dramatically in 1987, seriously endangering the institutional stability of the church. Lack of funds have also undermined its ambitious evangelizing campaign at a time when pentecostal churches have increased their own evangelization.[56]

Politics and the Church

The Catholic church has modernized relatively slowly in Panama. Prior to the 1960s clergy dedicated themselves almost exclusively to administering the sacraments, celebrating mass, and operating schools. Involvement in education, especially at the high school level, was regarded as the most effective way to maintain and extend the influence of the church, particularly among the society's dominant class.

Most rural towns in Panama receive a priest once a year for religious celebrations where baptisms take place and festivals are organized by local merchants. In the 1950s the church hierarchy created a Federation of Christian Farmers Leagues to counteract leftist influence among peasant communities. But it was not until after Vatican II that the church actively began defending and promoting the interests of the country's poor majority. This identification with the poor deepened after the Medellín Bishops' Conference in 1968, which advocated that the church assume a "preferential option for the poor." As part of the renovation process spurred by Vatican II and Medellín, the church placed more emphasis on the participation of the laity. As part of that effort the church hierarchy promoted the slogan, "Christian, you are the church."[57]

The church founded peasant training and popular education organizations such as the Center for Social Instruction (CCS) and the Center for Research, Promotion, and Social Assistance (CEPAS). Through the John XXIII Center, the church formed and trained community cooperatives.[58] A center for this new social role was in the Veraguas region, presided over by Bishop McGrath until 1968. McGrath spearheaded an economic development plan for the area called Plan Veraguas, which received government backing and was implemented in close cooperation with U.S. Alliance for Progress and Peace Corps projects.

This developmentalist orientation of the institutional church later paralleled and legitimized the populist politics of the Torrijos regime. The church's commitment to social causes was reaffirmed in 1969 with the appointment of Archbishop McGrath. For the first time the church began to speak out on social issues, denouncing injustices and circulating pastoral letters on such issues as the 1977 Canal Treaties and the controversial Cerro Colorado copper mine.

Encouraged by the church hierarchy, many poor urban and rural communities formed Christian Base Communities (CBCs) throughout the country. These CBCs, most of which adopted the precepts of the theology of liberation, soon formed a left flank within the church which was self-described as the Popular Church. Although rhetorically committed to "the preferential option for the poor," the institutional church led by McGrath took an increasingly defensive posture in the face of the growing independence and militancy of the CBCs. This discrepancy between rhetoric and activism led to the increased isolation of the CBCs within the institutional church, although elements within the church hierarchy remained fully committed to practicing "the preferential option for the poor."

Symptomatic of the move of the institutional church away from progressive reforms was its alliance with the oligarchy to oppose the educational reform proposed by the Torrijos government in the late 1970s. The church together with the APEDE businessmen's group opposed the measure because they felt that the introduction of social issues into the curriculum would facilitate the spread of communism.[59]

Several factors contributed to the radicalization of the CBCs and other socially committed elements of the church. One was the influence of an activist and politically progressive sector of the foreign clergy. Another was the failure of the developmentalism and populism of the church and government to resolve the structural causes of poverty. Yet another radicalizing factor was the development of a strong Central American solidarity movement within the church. The examples of Nicaraguan, Guatemalan, and Salvadoran church activists inspired Panamanian Catholics. In the early 1980s the assassination of Archbishop Romero of El Salvador was commemorated by large processions through downtown Panama City.

A local martyr revered by Panamanian church activists is Father Héctor Gallego, who was kidnapped and assassinated in 1971, presumably for his strong commitment to the struggles of the poor in his parish in Veraguas.[60] In 1994 a jury found three former National Guard officers guilty of kidnapping and murdering Gallego. One of the few parks in Panama City, Parque Omar, originally named in honor of General Torrijos, was renamed Parque Héctor Gallego for the murdered priest.

In 1983 the political right organized a campaign of defamation directed against those sectors of the church associated with liberation theology. A nationally publicized attempt by the right wing to discredit the CBCs in Chiriquí was directed against the Vicentian, Augustinian, and Jesuit priests working with the poor communities of the area. It was claimed in a letter to the bishop that the priests excluded people of other social classes, abused the liturgy, and constituted a national security threat because they backed the Nicaraguan Sandinistas. Shortly following this incident the Committee to Defend Democracy in Nicaragua, Panama, and Central America formed to continue the attacks against the socially committed church. Heading the Committee was Dulcidio González, president of the National Council of Private Business and chief of the Liberal Party.[61] The

Panamanian Bishops' Conference vigorously defended the priests under attack.

The popular church, while not as strong as it was in the late 1970s, remains an influential sector within the Catholic church. CBCs are especially active in Chiriquí, Darién, and San Miguelito near Panama City. The leader of the national human rights group COPODEHUPA is a practicing priest. Some Protestant churches, especially the Lutheran and Methodist churches, also support CBCs. A robust countervailing trend within the Catholic church that has the support of the archbishop is the spiritualist Charismatic movement which has more in common with the emotion-charged Christianity of groups such as the Full Gospel Businessmen's Fellowship than with the socially committed popular church.

The Catholic clergy had from the beginning thrown their support with the Civic Crusade. Archbishop McGrath invited the Civic Crusade leaders to stand by him while he delivered his May 29, 1988 sermon accusing the Noriega regime of being illegitimate and repressive. In response, the government-linked Radio Nacional called for the expulsion of all foreign priests. Church organizations also received U.S. funds to monitor the 1989 elections and circulated a pastoral letter condemning the election fraud.

In 1994 the church sponsored and acted as guarantor for an agreement to ethical conduct by most political parties during the national election campaign. The Catholic Church also served as a mediator in 1995 in talks between government and labor unions stemming from the conflict over reform of the Labor Code. For the most part, however, the church has backed away from popular pressures to use its influence to challenge the country's socioeconomic structures.[62]

Protestantism to Pentecostalism

Protestant missionaries were active in the territory that is now Panama since the early 1800s. In 1815 a mulatto Methodist preacher, Mother Abel, accompanied a group of Jamaican and English immigrants who settled at Careening Bay in western Panama (Bocas del Toro). Her mission was later passed to the Wesleyan Methodists.[63] The Panama Railroad, begun in 1850, attracted the Protestant Episcopal Church, which established Christ Church By-the-Sea, in 1864 in Colón. It is said that it is the second non-Catholic church built on the Central American Isthmus, the oldest being St. John's Cathedral, founded in 1825 in Belize City.

The construction of the Panama Canal marked the beginning of an era of Protestant evangelism. Originally limited to the West Indians and U.S. citizens working on the canal, since the 1970s Protestant missionaries have extended their mission to the rest of the country's population. Today more than two-thirds of the country's growing Protestant population are Spanish-speaking. Although missionaries have been evangelizing among the Indian community, especially the Kuna, since the early 1900s, it was not until the 1950s that serious outreach work began. Among the most active groups has been the New Tribes Mission, which has had as many as sixty U.S. missionaries working among Panama's indigenous communities.

Historically the largest Protestant church in Panama has been the Methodist Church, which started its work with the construction of the Panama Canal. In 1910 Methodists built a church in the heart of Panama City near the famous Flat Arch of St. Dominique. The church developed the Panamerican Institute (IPA) that primarily caters to students from middle class families. Methodist Bishop Secundino Morales was responsible for taking the church from a politically conservative position held in the 1960s to a socially active agenda beginning in the 1970s and continuing into the present.

In the 1920s the Church of the Foursquare Gospel and the Seventh Day Adventists arrived in Panama. Through the 1960s and 1970s the Church of the Foursquare Gospel was one of the country's largest Protestant denominations. The more traditional Protestant denominations (including Wesleyan Methodist, Southern Baptist Convention, Episcopal, Lutheran, and Church of Christ) have been largely eclipsed by the Pentecostal churches. Leading the way was the Foursquare Church, but since the early 1970s it has been newer Pentecostal churches like Assemblies of God and Church of God that have been the most dynamic forces in the evangelical movement. The first U.S.-sponsored evangelical crusade was that of T. L. Osborn in the early 1950s among the West Indian population of Colón. More recently, the healing campaigns of the Assemblies of God have found great resonance in Panama. Evangelical crusades have also been sponsored by the Alfa y Omega (Campus Crusade for Christ).

The political and economic crisis of the late 1980s proved a great boon to the evangelical churches, which preach a moral and political conservatism. Although still a small minority, the Protestant-evangelical community, with more than 2,000 congregations, is expanding quickly, challenging the traditional religious and cultural hold of the Catholic church.

The Protestant evangelical movement made its political debut in the May 1994 elections. The political party Mission for National Unity (MUN) was founded to organize the entrance into politics by the many evangelical churches established in Panama. One of the Mission's evangelical leaders, David Guerra, ran as a vice-presidential candidate in the 1994 elections.

Women and Feminism

Panama has a long and proud history of women's rights activism. The Feminist National Party (PNF), founded in 1923, was one of the first feminist parties in Latin America. The party spearheaded the women's suffrage campaign in Panama, and through its Women's Cultural School pushed for social reforms benefiting women and children. In the 1930s the PNF protested the government's issuing of citizenship identity cards only to men. The party's antigovernment positions made its leaders and members targets for government reprisals. All the PNF-associated university professors were terminated in 1938. In 1944 many former PNF members founded the National Women's Union, which renewed the struggle for women's right to vote. The long suffrage fight finally bore fruit in the 1941 Constitution which gave women limited suffrage rights. In the 1946 Constitution women were granted full citizenship.[64]

The UN declaration in 1975 establishing International Women's Year sparked a new era of feminist organizing and consciousness-raising. Having won the right to vote, Panamanian women had pushed aside the main legal impediment to their full participation in society and politics. But many other institutional and socio-cultural obstacles kept full equality for women an unrealized goal.

The government ratified the international convention calling for the elimination of all forms of discrimination against women. Yet sexist provisions in the country's laws and codes have maintained women as second-class citizens. Until recently, widows and divorcees were prohibited from remarrying until 300 days after the death of the husband or a divorce decree—prohibitions that do not apply to men. Prior to the recent approval of the Family and Children Code, legal justifications for divorce included a one-time extramarital affair on the part of the wife and "scandalous concubinity" (a permanent extramarital affair) on the part of the husband. Bills against domestic abuse and sexual harassment have also been introduced in the legislature.

Among Latin American countries, Panama has one of the highest levels of female participation in the work force. Nevertheless, women workers suffer widespread discrimination. Not uncommonly women are required to take a pregnancy test and preferential employment goes to single women who are then laid off if they become pregnant. To avoid having to pay the government-mandated severance payment, employers often have women workers sign three-month contracts.

Women constitute 52 percent of university enrollment, but higher education levels do not necessarily mean equal pay. The International Labor Office (ILO) found that while median monthly income of both men and women increases significantly with increased education, the disparity between the monthly incomes of men and women increases rather than diminishes with the level of education.[65] Furthermore, women's unpaid domestic work typically is overlooked in studies of sexual discrimination and the economic value of labor.

The economic crisis has hit poor women hard, forcing many mothers into the work force. The female labor force is growing much faster than the male labor force, and the number of woman-headed households also increased dramatically in the 1980s.[66] Many women from the lower income strata work as domestic laborers, an occupation not protected by the Labor Code and, as a result, one that does not specify free time or work-day length. Another common source of employment for working-class women is the export-oriented industrial sector. Laboring under sweatshop conditions, thousands of Panamanian women assemble clothes for export for such textile companies as Vanity Fair, Intimate, Gregor, and Durex.[67]

In the mid-1990s Panama had a strong sector of women's organizations. According to Teresita Arias of the Foundation for the Promotion of Women in Panama, the principal problems faced by Panamanian women are poverty, discrimination in the work force, and domestic violence. Other organizations active in pushing forward women's issues include the Center for Women's Development (CEDEM), an independent think-tank; CEASPA, a popular research and education organization; Ngobe Women's Association; Panamanian Women's Center (CEMP); Women's National Coordination (CNM); Center for Support for Abused Women (CAMM); National Forum for Women and Development; and the Women's Coordinator of Organizations of Integral Development (CODIM). The government sponsors several women's activities through the Labor Ministry's Women Department, the Legislative Assembly's Women Commission, and the Health Ministry's Women and Development Commission. In the past there also existed an anti-imperialist women's organization called the Women's Front Against Aggression (FUMCA). Numerous female professional associations, church groups, and wings of labor unions and political parties also exist.

A 1994-2000 National Plan for Women and Development was drawn up by the National Forum on Women and Development in which fifty institutions and organizations participated. The plan set out an agenda for improving women's participation in the political process, establishing legal gender equality, and promoting human and economic development programs for women.[68] Another sign of a strengthening women's movement was the announcement on March 8, 1995—International Women's Day—by the Center for Studies and Family Training (CEFAS) that it was beginning a two-year campaign to increase the recognition of gender equality. One indication that women's organizations are having an impact was the institution of a new Family Code in 1994 that gives women more benefits in divorce settlements. In mid-1995 assembly members were also considering bills aimed at reducing domestic abuse and sexual harassment.

Historically, the women's movement has been largely leftist and anti-imperialistic, but women played a major role in supporting the Civic Crusade. In an analysis of this phenomenon, a 1987 article in the Panamanian magazine *Diálogo Social* speculated that women were attracted to the anti-government, oligarchy-backed movement because of its tone of moral outrage. Politically inexperienced churchwomen and housewives provided an important activist base for this movement.[69]

Women played an important role in Panama's 1994 elections. Mireya Moscoso de Gruber, who ran television ads appealing to women but who refused to participate in any of the public debates, won 29 percent of the vote in the 1994 presidential campaign. Of the eighty-three women candidates for Legislative Assembly, six won, the same number of women elected in the 1989 elections. Balbina Herrera, former PRD mayor of the town of San Miguelito, became the first woman president of the Legislative Assembly. Three women were candidates for mayor of Panama City, including Isabel Corro, popular leader of the victims of the U.S. invasion, and the winner, Mayín Correa.[70]

Minorities and Native Peoples

Spanish-speaking *mestizos* account for about 70 percent of the population. Blacks compose the largest minority sector—divided between those of colonial/slave descent within Panama (about 8 percent) and those of West Indian origin (about 5 percent). A white *criollo* sector, about 10 percent of the population, dominates the society's economic elite. The indigenous population, divided among several different peoples, accounts for about 8 percent of the Panamanian population.

The first blacks came to the country as slaves from Africa, and their descendants are found in dispersed pockets of black communities along the country's Atlantic coast and in small isolated villages in Darién. The second group of Panama's blacks came from the Caribbean islands under contracts to work on the railroad or the canal. Other Caribbean blacks immigrated to seek work on the banana plantations in Chiriquí and Bocas del Toro. Because of their origin, the term *antillanos* (Antilleans) has long been associated with the country's black population, which is concentrated in the urban corridor of Panama City and Colón and in Puerto Armuelles.[71]

Although the black community is more integrated socially than in other Central American countries (with the exception of Belize), blacks are still widely considered second-class citizens. This treatment dates back to the early 1900s when during the construction of the Panama Canal white workers were paid in gold while the *antillanos* and many *mestizo* workers were compensated in silver.[72] White workers received as much as four times more than their black counterparts. In the Canal Zone, the housing, restaurants, hospitals, and other services all belonged to the U.S. government, and all practiced segregation.[73] In the 1950s the U.S. administrators of the canal pushed blacks out of the Canal Zone to avoid civil rights protests and the mandate, stemming from the 1955 Remón-Eisenhower Treaty, to end the different pay scales for black and white workers.[74]

The U.S. government was not the only perpetrator of racism; the Panamanian oligarchy and middle class also encouraged racist sentiments and practices. The Harvard-educated Arnulfo Arias fomented racist sentiments in the Communal Action movement of the 1920s. Arias and others regarded blacks as foreign competitors for the benefits of the Canal Zone. In the 1930s Arias organized a nationalist-populist coalition that launched him to the presidency in 1940. Although progressive in some respects, Arias was a confirmed racist and pushed through a new constitution that prohibited further immigration of blacks and denied them basic civil rights, such as the right to own property, unless they could demonstrate a familiarity with the Spanish language and Panamanian history.[75]

Although until the 1970s *antillanos* did not generally share the nationalist sentiments of the *mestizo* population, they integrated themselves into the country's labor and popular movements. They led strikes for higher wages and food, braved U.S. military repression of their union movement in 1920, and were active in the 1925 Renters' Movement.[76]

The advent of *torrijismo* in 1968 helped end the historical monopoly of power by white Panamanians. As a result of this new anti-oligarchic populism, blacks were more easily accepted into the government, security forces, and even business. Large numbers of blacks have become culturally Hispanicized and are now accepted as bona fide *panameños*. Even so, throughout Panama, especially in Colón, blacks have fewer work opportunities than whites and *mestizos*—in part for lack of good connections but also because of underlying racism.

Native Panamanians

Five different indigenous peoples exist in Panama. The Ngobe-Buglé (formerly known as the Guaymí), the most numerous with 123,000 tribal members, live in western Panama in Bocas del Toro on the Atlantic side and in the provinces of Chiriquí and Veraguas on the Pacific side. The Kuna, with an estimated 47,000 members, live mainly on the San Blas islands off the country's northeastern coast but are also found in settlements along the Gulf of Urabá (bordering Colombia), in the Darién province, and increasingly in Panama City. The Emberá indians (formerly known as the Chocó), with an estimated population of 15,000, live in the Darién lowlands, bordering the Caribbean and Pacific Oceans. The Wounaan people (2,600) also live in Darién and have a similar river basin culture. Small numbers of the Teribe (2,000) and Bokota (4,000) indians are neighbors of the Ngobe-Buglé in the Tabasara Sierra.

When the Spanish first explored the northwestern Caribbean coastline, they encountered several indian tribes. Besides the Guaymí people, the Térrabas, Talamancas, Cabégaras, Changuena, and Dorasque also inhabited this region. Colonization by the Spanish decimated the native populations, pushing them inland and into Costa Rica. Gold which local peoples acquired through trade with Colombian natives was confiscated, and many were kidnapped and sold as slaves.[77] In the seventeenth and eighteenth centuries the Guaymí were the target of raids by Nicaraguan Miskito indians organized by British colonizers.[78] The Ngobe-Buglé people and culture are presently menaced by the construction of highways, mining projects, and the invasion of their lands by cattle-ranching agribusinesses.

Over the past two decades the Ngobe-Buglé have organized to protect their land and culture. Through the Ngobe-Buglé General Congress they have demanded that the government establish an autonomous *comarca* (reserve)—a demand that was quashed in 1984 when the executive branch suspended talks and passed the problem to the Legislative Assembly. The Ngobe-Buglé continue to petition for the right to administer justice in their own language and based on their own laws. They have also asked for protection against the incursion of evangelical sects, which are further weakening their culture.[79]

The commercial exploitation and contamination of Ngobe-Buglé land by nonindians combined with the traditional slash-and-burn type agriculture practiced by the people have degraded the environment, causing severe erosion in many areas, particularly in Chiriquí and Veraguas.[80] This environmental crisis has become one more cause of Ngobe-Buglé poverty and unemployment. To make a living, most Ngobe-Buglé families leave their homes to join the country's migrant workforce. On the coffee and banana plantations, they are generally relegated to the lowest-paying jobs. They are specifically singled out to work with the most toxic chemicals. When burns, cancer, and poisoning disable the Ngobe-Buglé workers, they are laid off with little or no severance pay.[81]

Those formerly known as the Chocó consider themselves to be two distinct peoples—the Emberá and Wounaan. They are not natives of Panama but migrated to the eastern Pacific river basins in the late 18th century from northwestern Colombia where most are Wounaan and live in the Chocó province. Famous for their poison-tipped blowgun darts, bands of these Amerindians were brought in from Colombia by the Spanish to break the resistance of the Kuna indians who inhabited the Darién region.[82] Settlements previously inhabited by the Kuna were seized by these immigrant peoples, who later also moved into the areas abandoned by the Spanish.

In the 1960s the Emberá and Wounaan gradually began to organize themselves into self-governing communities and to demand government recognition of their land rights and access to public services.

In 1983 the government recognized the Comarca Emberá-Drua, a reserve of 300,000 hectares which overlaps with the area classified as the Darién National Park and Biosphere Reserve. This victory has been soured by the steady environmental degradation of the reserve. Much of the reserve, particularly the areas surrounding the recently established villages, are depleted of game animals and wild plants. Accustomed to a hunter-gatherer economy, the Emberá-Wounaan indians have turned increasingly to cash crops. Aggravating the environmental crisis is the steady encroachment of lumber companies and agricultural colonists from the western provinces.[83]

The Kuna have been the most successful in preserving their land and culture. It is not clear if the Kuna people inhabited the Darién region at the time of the Spanish conquest or if they migrated to the region from what is now Colombia. Descriptions by Spanish expeditions and pirates in the seventeenth century, however, establish their presence in the Darién province by that time.[84]

In the mid-nineteenth century the Kuna began relocating many of their communities on the San Blas islands. Strategic concerns and the abundance of pests and disease in the Pacific lowlands were probably among the reasons for this migration. Strong local hierarchies developed on the occupied islands, and an elaborately organized political infrastructure developed.[85] The local governments were eventually integrated into the Kuna General Congress, which meets twice annually and establishes the direction of Kuna national politics. Three national chiefs preside over the Congress and act as the Kuna spokespersons to the Panamanian government and society.[86]

The establishment of the Comarca of San Blas in 1938 resulted from a long history of Kuna efforts to protect their land and culture. The geographic isolation of the Kuna on the San Blas islands proved important to the preservation of their culture and the development of a self-directed economy. On occasion, the islanders violently repelled European traders who tried to come ashore. In the early 1900s the Kuna people repeatedly clashed with non-Kuna rubber traders and agricultural colonists who were encroaching on tribal land. The Kuna revolted in 1925 against government acculturation programs and attempted control by government police. The now-celebrated 1925 revolt was also the result of accumulated tensions between the Kuna people and Catholic missionaries and colonists.[87]

The successful revolt, in which the Kuna indians received assistance from North American adventurer Richard Marsh, led to a 1930 treaty reaffirming the partial autonomy of the San Blas region. Eight years later, the Kuna territory gained official status as a *comarca*.[88] The Kuna also signed an agreement with the U.S. Army in 1932 to employ Kuna men on military bases in the Canal Area; many kitchens on the bases were headed by Kuna chefs into the mid-1990s. The Kuna have maintained a strong cultural foundation and now survive on an economy based largely on tourism, crafts, coconuts, fishing, and cash transfers from Kunas employed in urban areas. In 1985 the Kuna were the first indian people to establish an internationally recognized forest reserve, covering 60,000 hectares of rainforest within the *comarca* along the Caribbean coast. The Kuna have founded a learning center in the reserve where non-Kuna are instructed in appropriate rainforest management techniques and scientists carry out rainforest research.[89]

Unfortunately, the outlook for the Kuna is not an entirely auspicious one. Child malnutrition on the islands of Kua Yala is the highest in the country. This is due largely to the monetization of the subsistence economy and the out-migration of able-bodied men, leaving only women, children, and old people behind. Increasing population is putting growing pressure on natural resources. Fish and lobster populations are declining and the native palm used for roofing has all but disappeared. The coral reef is also suffering from population pressures as community members cut blocks of coral from surrounding reefs to create foundations for new homes.

Overall, however, the Kuna have been exceptional among the Central American indians. Not only did they survive the Spanish conquest, but they also seemed to have emerged stronger and better organized from the regional turmoil during the centuries that followed. Partially due to the relative inaccessibility of their territory, they have kept outside influence to a minimum, enabling them to protect and promote their culture and lifestyle. Kuna traditions, such as the renowned mola (cloth art) of the Kuna women, are strongly anchored within Kuna society and Kunas are proud of their ethnic traditions—an attitude increasingly rare among most exploited and alienated American indians. Kuna workers were often more organized and prepared than their nonindigenous counterparts to make use of former military lands for community goals.

The Kuna and Emberá-Wounaan people in the Darién region have joined forces with environmental groups on both sides of the Panama-Colombia border to resist a planned extension of the Pan-American Highway through the jungle. Panama and Colombia have formed a binational commission to push for the road, heralded as a "dream come true" for business interests on either side of the border. Indigenous people fear the project will bring squatters and illegal loggers who will destroy their hunting, fishing, and forest resources as well as the rivers they depend upon for transport. As one tribal leader explained, "the fear here is that if the colonists cut down the forests, the rivers will dry up during the dry season and we will not be able to get our crops to market." In 1994 the road project was tabled indefinitely.

Refugees and the Internally Displaced

Panama did not experience the significant refugee influx that affected other Central American countries during the 1970s and 1980s. The UN High Commission on Refugees (UNHCR) reported in 1988 that it provided assistance in Panama to some two-hundred Nicaraguans, 750 Salvadorans, and a small number of Guatemalans.[90] Salvadoran refugees were eventually repatriated to El Salvador in 1990.

At least 17,000 Panamanians were displaced by the December 1989 U.S. invasion and its ensuing conflict. Displaced families, mainly from the poor neighborhoods where the fighting was most intense, found temporary refuge in schools and churches. When the firing stopped most of the displaced moved in with families and friends, although several thousand were sent to former U.S. air force hangars used by the PDF for temporary housing and were given rations by the U.S. Agency for International Development (AID) and U.S. private relief organizations. The U.S. government promised to rebuild the El Chorrillo neighborhood located next to the Panamanian military high command, which the U.S. invasion force destroyed. To provide new housing for the displaced, Washington allocated $42 million mostly for private sector construction programs.

In September 1994 the incoming Pérez Balladares government agreed to allow up to ten thousand Cuban "boat people" to be given "temporary refuge" in U.S. military bases along the Canal. The refugees were not permitted to leave the camps and the United States agreed they would leave the bases within six months of their arrival. The U.S. government covered the bill for resettlement, which nearly got out of control three months after the agreement, when hundreds of Cubans revolted and tried to break out of the camps by stoning U.S. soldiers and breaking down the fences. Two refugees died in attempts to swim across the Canal. The U.S. military beefed up security in the camps, but eventually airlifted the Cubans to Guantanamo Naval Base in February of the next year.

Ecology and Environmentalism

More of the original forest cover remains in Panama than in any other Central American country, with the exception of Belize. Located below the hurricane belt and bathed in heavy rains, Panama hosts an abundance of tropical flora and fauna. More than eight hundred species of birds are found in Panama—more than are found in the entire area of the northern portion of the Western Hemisphere. The country is aflutter with aviary life, with three of the four major migration routes between North and South America converging on Panama.[91] With coral reefs paralleling Panama and the most extensive mangrove area in Central America, Panama also hosts abundant sea life.[92]

Like other Central American countries, however, Panama faces severe environmental problems. Foremost among these are deforestation, soil degradation, overfishing, water availability and contamination, and an institutional weakness in addressing the protection of natural resources and public health. Urban life is increasingly plagued by air and noise pollution and the consequences of inadequate waste disposal systems. Most of the sewage from the two urban centers, Panama City and Colón, is discharged directly into coastal waters and ditches that flow through the cities.

Natural resource degradation is evident in rural areas throughout the country. One of the starkest examples is the deforestation evident along the Inter-American Highway to Darién. Along the coasts, large stretches of mangroves are being cut down to make room for new urban developments, shrimp farms, and resorts. Mangrove bark, useful in the tanning industry, is being exported to Costa Rica, where the harvesting of red mangrove bark is prohibited. Birds, especially brightly plumed macaws and yellow-crowned parrots, are also shipped out of the country as part of the international trade in exotic house pets.[93]

Deforestation and National Parks

Panama's low population density, the concentration of its population near the canal, and its diversified economic base have all contributed to the country's relatively large area of remaining tropical forest. Just under half of the country remains under some sort of forest cover. Only 28 percent of the land base is dedicated to annual cropping, compared to 40 percent for the rest of Latin America, but large areas are reserved for extensive livestock grazing.[94]

Deforestation, nonetheless, is a rising concern in Panama. In the 1980s Panama lost an average of 80,000 hectares of forest each year while only 2,000 hectares are reforested annually.[95] The deforestation rate in 1993 was estimated to be 1.5 percent of the nation's forest cover. Panamanian ecologist Stanley Heckadon Moreno warned that by the year 2000 Panama could be a "desert with jungle representing less than 10 percent of the country." He predicted that the last forest areas will be located in indian zones where production systems do not present an immediate threat to the environment (Figure 4b).[96]

Soil erosion is a rising concern in Panama where 50 percent of the soils are of poor quality and 75 percent of the land is hillside terrain. Recent deforestation is only one reason for eroding soils. Overexploitation or mismanagement of fragile lands—which may have been deforested for decades or even hundreds of years—are the more immediate cause of most soil erosion. Estimates of severe erosion range from 20 percent to 30 percent of the country's territory, and soil erosion rates in some of the country's prime agricultural areas are thought to be among the highest in all Latin America. The most critical soil erosion is taking place in the volcanic highlands of the Chiriquí province, especially around the Barú volcano.[97] The waterways that flow from this watershed are now filled with silt, causing severe losses to affected agricultural areas in the lowlands below the volcano. A leading culprit of deforestation and the escalating soil erosion in several parts of Panama, but especially in the Darién region, are cattle ranchers who encourage peasants to clear frontier lands for temporary cultivation and later convert the land into pastures.[98]

A major environmental concern for Panama and the United States alike is the effect of deforestation on the canal watershed. A 1986 report by the Panama Ministry of Planning found that urbanization, slash-and-burn agriculture, cattle ranching, and road construction had deforested 70 percent of the watershed that provides the 52 million gallons of fresh water required daily by the canal locks. It has been projected that erosion and siltation from deforestation may reduce the capacity of the lake reservoirs for the canal operations by as much as 10 percent by the year 2000.[99]

Figure 4b
Deforestation in Panama

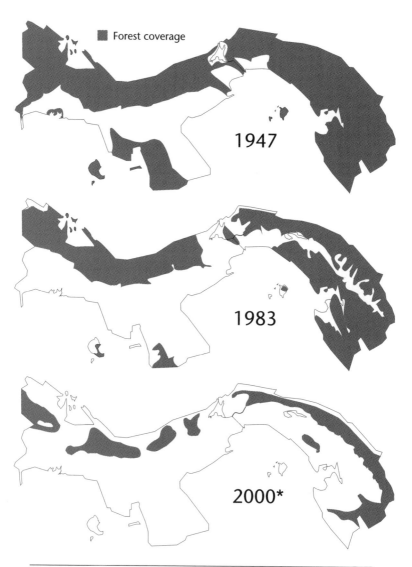

Forest coverage

1947

1983

2000*

*Projected

SOURCE: Stanley Heckadon and Jaime Espinoza, *Agonía de la Naturaleza* (Panama: IDIAP/STRI, 1985).

To avert this calamity, two national parks—Soberanía and Chagres—were created in the canal watershed. Together they account for almost half the watershed of the canal or some 600 square miles. As a result, the rate of deforestation in the canal watershed slowed from 1100 acres a year before 1976 to 540 acres a year between 1984 and 1987. Deforestation has also presented a threat to the country's drinking water and to the hydroelectric system which generates some 80 percent of the country's electricity, in the Bayano area and in Chiriquí.

International and local forces have combined to reserve a high percentage (17 percent) of the Panamanian land area as environmentally protected territory.[100] Most of this protected space is found within four large national parks. La Amistad covers the largest highland forest in Central America, extending into Costa Rica. Chagres Park covers the upper Chagres watershed of the Alajuela Lake which provides 40 percent of the water for the canal and is a major source of drinking water for Panama City. Coaba covers 270,000 hectares in Veraguas. The Darién national park encompasses a large stretch along the Darién border with Colombia, is the largest protected area in Central America, and has been declared a World Heritage Site by UNESCO.[101]

Environmentalists Organize

In the debates that unfolded during the 1994 presidential campaign, candidates almost unanimously voiced their support for initiatives to improve environmental conditions in Panama. Pérez Balladares, in particular, committed himself to working with environmental organizations. After the elections, however, word leaked out that the new president would probably appoint as Director of the Institute of Renewable Resources (INRENARE) an agribusinessman with investments in cattle raising and sugar exports. Perez Balladares' predecessor, Guillermo Endara had chosen a top executive of Delvalle's giant Santa Rosa sugar mill for the post.

Panama exhibits a strong environmental movement. The leading organization is the National Association for the Conservation of Nature (ANCON), which receives significant support from U.S. organizations (the Nature Conservancy and the John D. and Catherine T. MacArthur Foundation) and others, although the group has also been successful at local fundraising. Founded in 1985 ANCON's proclaimed mission is "exclusively to protect and conserve the natural resources and the biological diversity of Panama for the benefit of all the present and future generations of Panamanians."

ANCON has played a major role in supporting the creation and maintenance of the national park system. At the same time it has been sharply criticized within Panama as being a cover for large business interests attempting to gain control over new resources. According to its critics, investors associated with ANCON have gained control over areas of the national parks which they intend to use for mining and tourism projects.

Another activist group is the Student Association for the Conservation of the Environment (ACECAP), which successfully pressured the government to protect a couple of endangered coastal areas on the relatively pristine Atlantic coastal region, which is now being spoiled by increasing oil spills and development projects.[102]

Student and environmental organizations have also coalesced around a series of projected shipments of plutonium waste from France to Japan that could traverse the Panama Canal. A coalition that included university students and Greenpeace staged a die-in in January 1995 in front of Japan's consulate in Panama City to protest the possible shipments and the risk they pose to Panamanians living on the banks of the canal. The organizing led to a symbolic rejection of the shipments by the Panamanian Assembly's committees on the environment, the canal, and foreign relations.[103]

Along with organizations whose main objectives are environmental protection and conservation, there are many popular organizations and small communities whose organizing is focused around environmental issues. Quality of life issues, not strictly natural resource conservation concerns, are at the center of much popular organizing in Panama. Communities have organized to prevent the extraction of construction materials from rivers and beaches, to demand potable water, to protest careless use of agrochemicals, to halt contaminating mining practices, and, in the case of indian villages, to stop colonists from settling frontier lands.

The principal government organizations that involve themselves in environmental concerns are the Panamanian Institute of Renewable Resources (INRENARE) and the National Environmental Commission (CONAMA). An AID-funded natural resource management project called Fundación Natura has lent financial and technical support to the conservation and sustainable development efforts of INRENARE and nongovernmental organizations. The new Environmental Law (1994) and Forestry Law (1995) indicate increased governmental concern about Panama's deepening environmental crisis.

Part 5

U.S.-Panama Relations

© Eileen O'Leary/Escape Photos

Wealth, Power, and Nationalism

Panama's relations with the rest of the world have always been dominated by the isthmus' geographic position and its value as an international crossroads. From Spain to Colombia to France to the United States, one power after another has used Panama as the shortest route to transport wealth and to trade with other powers and dependencies. From Theodore Roosevelt's claim that "I took the Canal Zone, and let Congress debate," to former President Reagan's claim that, "We bought it, we paid for it, we built it...we are going to keep it," the characteristic U.S. attitude toward Panama has been one of arrogance.

For their part, Panamanians have had unequal relations with these successive powers and have seen tantalizing amounts of wealth pass through their country. The history of neocolonial relationships has given rise to strong, although sometimes latent, nationalist aspirations. The prospect of benefiting significantly from the riches that pass through has generated persistent demands for greater participation in commercial enterprises on the isthmus, and has also occasionally meant the mortgaging of popular nationalism.

U.S. interest in Panama dates from the 1840s, when steamships and railroads began to revolutionize transportation technology. In 1846 the United States and Colombia signed the Bidlack-Mallarino Treaty, which in exchange for a promise to defend Colombian sovereignty over Panama gave the United States unrestricted transit across Panama and removed discriminatory tariffs on U.S. goods. With the addition of California and New Mexico to U.S. territories and the discovery of gold in California in 1848, the forces bringing the United States and Panama into alliance were consolidated.[1]

After Colombia granted the New York Steamship Company a concession to build the trans-isthmus railroad, the construction of the railroad joining the Atlantic and the Pacific began in 1850 and brought thousands of Caribbean, Chinese, European, and North American workers into Panama, joining the many gold seekers passing through the isthmus. About 12,000 railroad laborers died during the five years it took to build the railway, including many Chinese who committed suicide because the U.S. managers forbade the use of opium.[2]

Following a rash of robberies of travelers, many carrying gold with them back from California, the U.S. railroad company hired a former indian-fighter named Ran Runnels to organize vigilante squads. Operating at night, the vigilantes rounded up men and on at least two occasions hung dozens of alleged robbers along the seawall in Panama City. Runnels and his squad also broke apart an attempt to organize railroad workers by beating up and threatening to kill the union's principal organizer.[3]

Once the North had won the Civil War and the internal obstacles to U.S. industrial development had been removed, U.S. economic expansion increasingly involved overseas trade and investment. At the same that U.S. business was looking for foreign markets for its new industrial goods, it was in search of new sources of raw materials. As the United States became more of an imperial power, the urgency for a quicker and less expensive sea route around the hemisphere increased.[4] The long voyage around the tip of South America taken by U.S. naval forces during the Spanish-American War presented further impetus for imperialists. Leading foreign policy strategists, including Theodore Roosevelt, proposed the expansion of U.S. naval forces as the primary means to further what they considered to be the destiny of the United States—control of Latin America.

Poor design and financial mismanagement, combined with the heavy toll of tropical diseases, put an end to French plans to build a transisthmian canal. Also spurring the U.S. ambitions in Panama was the struggle with the British for political and economic control in Central America. Plans were temporally obstructed in 1903 when Colombia rejected a treaty that would allow a U.S.-constructed canal across its Panamanian territory. At the time, the main competing route was across Nicaragua, a scheme favored by U.S. senators from the South.

The political obstacles to the Panamanian route were overcome in late 1903 when Philippe Bunau Varilla, a major stockholder from the indebted French company, together with a New York lawyer conspired to support an anti-Colombian uprising in Panama. Counting on the support of U.S. warships to prevent Colombian reinforcements from landing, Panama declared itself independent in November 1903. Washington moved quickly to sign a treaty with the new state of Panama, which was written and signed by Bunau Varilla and U.S. Secretary of State John Hay. Although the recently formed Panamanian government had rejected Bunau Varilla's credentials to represent Panama, the Panamanian legislature ratified the first U.S.-Panama canal treaty in early December 1903—immediately after the United

States had threatened to withdraw military protection and leave the Panamanians to contend with hostile Colombia on their own.

The Hay-Bunau Varilla Treaty, a source of tension between Panama and the United States for the next seventy-five years, did the following:

- Established a ten-mile wide canal zone across Panama for the construction of the canal where the United States would act "as if sovereign."
- Gave the United States rights to the Canal Zone "in perpetuity."
- Required the United States to protect Panama's "independence."
- Gave the United States judicial power in the Canal Zone.
- Gave the United States the right to build installations outside the Canal Zone that it might find "convenient" for the defense or maintenance of the Canal.
- Required the United States to pay Panama $250,000 a year for the right to use and develop the Canal Zone.[5]

The U.S. approach to the canal enterprise was dominated by military thinking. During his 1906 visit to Panama, President Roosevelt frequently compared canal workers to soldiers and the work of construction to a war.[6] The construction effort came under the direction of U.S. Army officers, most notably Colonel George Goethals, who was given complete control of the undertaking. When military officers and civilians were appointed to the Panama Canal Commission at the time Goethals was commissioned, in 1907, they were called singly into President Roosevelt's office and told that Goethals would "have complete authority. If at any time you do not agree with his policies, do not bother to tell me about it—your disagreement with him will constitute your resignation."[7]

Beginning in 1904, the canal became the central focus of U.S. policy in Panama, whether regarding labor relations with canal workers, police relations, immigration, or acquisition of supplies. According to one historian, relations were more tense than they had been with the French, in part perhaps because the French were more similar in culture, in part because North Americans were often arrogant and condescending.[8] The United States established an apartheid labor system in the Canal Zone, institutionalizing a two-tiered system of "gold" and "silver" rolls that corresponded to white and nonwhite workers and stipulated unequal rates of pay.[9]

Economically, the years of building the canal from 1904 to 1914 were a boom period in Panama much like the earlier period of railroad construction. During the final years of canal construction, the work force reached 45,000 to 50,000, more than the combined populations of Panama City and Colón. Most were imported by the United

States from Jamaica, Barbados, and other islands of the West Indies, while only 3,500 came from the United States.[10]

The Canal Zone was administered by an appointed Governor, traditionally a member of the Army Corps of Engineers and supervised by the Secretary of War. The State Department was less involved in Canal Zone governance than the military.[11] Panama itself became a protectorate of the United States, which successfully exerted pressure on Panama's constitutional assembly to include an article authorizing the United States to police Panama to maintain internal order (Figure 5a).[12] The U.S. military intervened during the elections in 1906, 1908, and 1910, and in 1916 the U.S. Navy confiscated rifles from the Panamanian police.

Panamanians soon became dissatisfied with various clauses of the 1903 treaty, first with U.S. control of customs in the zone, which deprived Panamanians of trade being generated by construction, and increasingly with such other issues as the U.S. annexation of lands

---

Figure 5a

U.S. Interventions in Panama

1856: "To protect U.S. interests during an insurrection."

1860: Local disturbance, with British participation, for 11 days.

1861: Political disturbance.

1865: "To protect U.S. interests during a revolution."

1868: "To protect the property and lives of U.S. residents during a revolution."

1873: (twice) "To protect U.S. interests during hostilities caused by the inauguration of the government of Panama."

1885: "To re-establish free transit during revolutionary activity."

1895: "To protect U.S. interests during an attack on the town of Bocas del Toro by a bandit leader."

1901: "To protect U.S. property in the Isthmus and maintain transit lines open during serious revolutionary disturbances." With French participation.

1902: "To place armed guards in all crossing trains and maintain the railway open."

1903: "To protect U.S. interests and lives during and following the revolution of independence from Colombia, due to the construction of the canal in the Isthmus. With short interruptions, the Marines were stationed in the Isthmus from November 4, 1903 until January 21, 1914 to safeguard U.S. interests."

1904: "To protect U.S. lives and property in Ancon, at the time of insurrectionary threat."

1908: "At the request of the political parties, U.S. troops supervised elections outside the Canal Zone."

---

outside the zone for military bases. In 1926 the United States and Panama signed a new agreement that fundamentally maintained the provisions of the 1903 arrangement but was rejected by both Panamanian public opinion and Panama's legislature.[13] In 1936 another treaty removed the U.S. right to intervene in Panama to maintain public order, ended the U.S. role as guarantor of Panamanian independence, and authorized the construction of a highway across the isthmus. However, the treaty did little to diminish popular resentment of U.S. control.

Spurred in the 1940s by maverick politician Arnulfo Arias, Panamanian nationalism continued to demand changes in the relationship with the United States but with scant success. During World War II the U.S. military presence in Panama grew to over one hundred installations and 68,000 troops. An agreement to extend leases on fourteen bases in 1947 was met with street riots, and the agreement was defeated unanimously in the national congress.[14]

1910: "At the request of the political parties, U.S. troops supervised elections outside the Canal Zone." U.S. charge Richard Marsh and Canal construction chief Colonel George Goethals pressured the popular incumbent to bow out of the presidential campaign because he is a mulatto.

1912: "At the request of the political parties, U.S. troops supervised elections outside the Canal Zone."

1918-1920: "For police duties, according to treaty stipulations, during electoral disturbances and subsequent agitation."

1921: "A U.S. Navy squadron held maneuvers on both sides of the Isthmus to prevent war between the two countries [Panama and Costa Rica] over a border dispute."

1925: "Strikes and riots by tenants obliged some 600 U.S. soldiers to disembark to maintain order and protect U.S. interests."

1964: Panamanian students attempted to raise the Panamanian flag in the Canal Zone. U.S. soldiers kill 21 and wound over 500.

1988: In an effort to overthrow the Panamanian government, the United States imposed devastating economic sanctions starting in March 1988 and lasting until the U.S. invasion.

1989: On December 20, U.S. invades with 25,000 troops to protect U.S. lives and the Canal, stop drug trafficking, and restore democracy.

1990: On December 5, U.S. troops intervene to put down a protest by police who call for higher wages and political reforms.

SOURCES: *Este Pais* #2, July 1986; *NACLA Report on the Americas*, July-August 1988; Michael Conniff, *Panama and the United States: The Forced Alliance* (Athens: University of Georgia, 1992), pp. 33-34, 76. Quotes extracted from a longer list of U.S. interventions in the hemisphere presented in Senate testimony by Secretary of State Dean Rusk in 1962 to justify the option of direct intervention in Cuba.

Responding to the growth of popular nationalism in Panama after World War II, the United States developed a tutelary relationship with the Panamanian National Guard. The National Guard was established to contain anti-U.S. sentiment and as part of the national security concept of U.S. foreign policy which regarded leftist insurgency as the main threat to political and economic security. In addition, President Eisenhower began to use economic aid to placate nationalist aspirations. In 1955 the Remón-Eisenhower Treaty was signed between the two governments restricting Panamanian employees in the Canal Zone from using commissary and import privileges and creating a single wage scale for both Panamanian and U.S. canal workers.

Riots in 1959 and 1964, however, signaled that economic aid and Guard repression would not be able to contain Panamanian resentment. The January 1964 riots followed a promise to allow the Panamanian flag to be flown at a high school in the zone and attempts by U.S. students to take down the flag, and were especially damaging. Twenty-one Panamanians were killed and more than 400 wounded. In the context of decolonization in other areas of the world and Panama's increasing use of competition between the superpowers to obtain concessions, the riots led to heightened concern among U.S. policymakers over the international image of continuing U.S. colonialism in Panama. Newly inaugurated President Johnson agreed to a fundamental restructuring of the relationship.

A Vision of Mutuality

Despite the dominance of the Teddy Roosevelt legacy and of the chauvinistic culture of U.S.-resident "Zonians" in U.S. policy toward Panama, there has long existed within the United States a counter-perspective on Panama and the canal. This dissenting opinion has opposed the paternalism and domination of most U.S. policy, advocating instead policies of mutual respect. In 1904 an array of U.S. newspapers condemned Roosevelt's action as "nefarious" and "a rough-riding assault upon another republic." [15] From those early years, when accounts of inhuman conditions for Caribbean canal workers led to widespread criticism of the project and its methods, to 1992, when the Oscar-winning film *The Panama Deception* exposed U.S. duplicity in the 1989 invasion, there have been U.S. critics of the policies of domination.

In 1969, during the Vietnam War and the reemergence of the anti-interventionist movement in the United States, U.S. Quakers organized a protest vigil at the Quarry Heights military base in Panama.[16] In the 1970s the National Council of Churches called for U.S. withdrawal from Panama and supported campaigns of the Washington Office on Latin America and the Ecumenical Program for Interamerican Communication and Action (EPICA), both of which published educational materials in favor of transferring the canal to Panama.[17] The U.S. Solidarity Committee with the Peoples of Panama also organized to put the canal in Panamanian hands.

In 1994 the interfaith pacifist organization Fellowship of Reconciliation (FOR) initiated a five-year campaign to support U.S. military withdrawal, environmental clean-up, and economic conversion of U.S. bases under the terms of the canal treaties. "As long as a single U.S. military facility operates in Panama, it will be a symbol of foreign occupation and dependence for all Latin America," read a statement circulated by the FOR and signed by forty U.S. religious and peace leaders.

Treaty Negotiations

In the wake of the Vietnam War and the Watergate scandal, the climate was ripe for President Carter's initiative to renegotiate the canal treaties. Carter did not, however, anticipate the depth of possessive feelings many U.S. citizens had about the canal. To salvage passage of the new Panama Canal Treaties, which were signed in September 1977, Carter reluctantly agreed to the DeConcini Reservation, which gave the United States the right to intervene militarily even after the year 2000.

At the signing ceremony for the accords, Torrijos said, "This treaty, which I shall sign and which repeals a treaty not signed by any Panamanian, does not enjoy the approval of all our people, because the 23 years agreed upon as a transition period are 8395 days, because during this time there will still be military bases which may make our country a strategic reprisal target, and because we are agreeing to a treaty of neutrality that places us under the protective umbrella of the Pentagon. This pact could, if it is not administered judiciously by future generations, become an instrument of permanent intervention."[18]

There were two treaties, known as the Panama Canal Treaty and the Neutrality Treaty. The Panama Canal Treaty, unless renegotiated, will be in effect until the year 2000 and provides for the following:

- Appropriation of territorial jurisdiction by Panama over the Canal Zone in 1979 and immediate reversion to Panama of several dozen buildings and housing units on the Pacific side of the canal.
- Administration of the canal until the year 2000 by the new Panama Canal Commission, a U.S. federal agency, whose board of directors would be composed of five U.S. citizens and four Panamanian citizens.

- Reversion of canal operations and properties to Panama at 12 o'clock noon on December 31, 1999.
- Primary responsibility by the United States for defense of the canal, with increasing responsibility for Panama.
- Increased cash payments to Panama for use of the canal.
- Gradually increasing percentage of workers on the canal who are Panamanian.

The Neutrality Treaty will be in effect both until and after the year 2000, and provides that:

- The canal be an international, neutral waterway.
- The United States and Panama have the right to defend the canal from threats against its neutrality.
- The right to defend the canal not be interpreted as the right to intervene in Panama's internal affairs.
- The U.S. military will withdraw by the year 2000, leaving Panama with primary responsibility for the defense of the canal.
- U.S. ships transiting the canal move to the head of the line in case of an emergency.

A reservation tacked onto the Neutrality Treaty during the Senate ratification process by Senator Sam Nunn—and consented to by Panama—stipulated that the two countries may make new agreements to station U.S. military forces in Panama after the scheduled departure date. Other nations can accede to the Neutrality Treaty as a means of supporting its provisions. Thirty-eight countries had done so by 1994.[19]

The 1977 Canal Treaties established a new framework for U.S.-Panamanian relations. By significantly modifying the imperial-colonial character of bilateral relations, the treaties served to improve the U.S. international image and ensure that canal operations would not be disrupted by anti-U.S. nationalism.

Post-treaty relations with Panama were dominated by the Reagan administration's intensifying obsession with insurgency and counterinsurgency in El Salvador and Nicaragua. Under Manuel Noriega's leadership, the National Guard, renamed the Panama Defense Forces in 1983, was made the vehicle for preparations to defend the canal after the year 2000 and for cooperation in the regional military effort against the Sandinista government in Nicaragua and FMLN guerrilla forces in El Salvador. Panama was the site for a series of large-scale military exercises, and the U.S. bases in Panama were used to ship weapons and supplies to Nicaraguan contra forces. Noriega thus helped deflect the political unpopularity of the contra cause. "It was feared that a left-leaning successor to Noriega might demand that the United States relinquish military installations that were a valuable asset for operations in the Central American region," concluded a study commissioned by the U.S. Air Force.[20]

The U.S.-Noriega relationship began to crack after the 1985 murder of Hugo Spadafora, a popular Panamanian active with the contras, and Noriega's dismissal of President Ardito Barletta, whose inauguration a year earlier Secretary of State George Shultz had attended. New opinions about Noriega's role began to emerge in Washington policymaking circles. These were reinforced by the emerging antinarcotics agenda.

In March and April 1986, Senator Jesse Helms convened hearings about Spadafora's murder and alleged drug trafficking by the PDF.[21] President Reagan signed a National Security Decision Directive in April 1986 that branded narcotics as a national security threat and provided a philosophical basis for involving the military and intelligence agencies in the fight against trafficking.[22] In June the *New York Times* and *Washington Post* published major stories on Noriega's involvement in trafficking and money laundering. After the Iran-Contra scandal broke later that year, Noriega's major defenders in the CIA and National Security Council, William Casey and Oliver North, left government. As an expression of changing U.S. foreign policy, the Senate passed a resolution in June 1987 calling for Noriega to step down.[23]

U.S. policy toward Panama in the Reagan years was largely decentralized, however, allowing agencies and congressional actors to work autonomously from each other and sometimes at cross-purposes. There was no coherent policy to bring together the various U.S.

Figure 5b
U.S. Military Aid to Panama

In millions of U.S. $

	IMET	FMF/ FMS	MAP	Total
1983	0.5	5.0	—	5.5
1984	0.5	5.0	8.0	13.5
1985	0.6	—	10.0	10.6
1986	0.6	3.8	3.8	8.2
1987	0.6	—	2.9	3.5
1988-present	no military aid			

IMET=International Military Education and Training
FMF/FMS=Foreign Military Financing/Foreign Military Sales
MAP=Military Assistance Program
SOURCE: *U.S. Overseas Loans and Grants and Assistance from International Organizations* July 1, 1945-Sept. 30, 1983, 1985, 1987, 1989, 1991, 1994.

strategies for dealing with Noriega. This was especially apparent in the operations of the Drug Enforcement Administration (DEA), which collaborated closely with the PDF in antinarcotics operations and which led to a letter of commendation from DEA chief Jack Lawn and a State Department certification that Panama was cooperating in the drug war.[24] For the Southern Command, it was believed Noriega "was first and foremost a fact of life in Panama." When U.S. military aid to Panama was cut off in 1987, Southern Command contended that this reduced its ability to influence the PDF (Figure 5b).[25]

Grand juries in Miami and Tampa operated independently of policymakers in Washington, partly because testimony was deliberately kept confidential. The separate aims at work in U.S. policy were brought home when the Justice Department moved to indict Noriega in January 1988. The State Department was informed of the indictments only a week before they were handed down.[26] The indictments, which accused Noriega of trafficking and money laundering, reduced the ability of policymakers to make a retirement deal with Noriega without losing face in the drug war. Instead, the indictments served to escalate the U.S. policy of forcing Noriega out, and were consistent with the U.S. low intensity conflict doctrine of using institutional pressures to achieve policy objectives. Absent was any discussion about whether the United States had the right to indict and try a foreign national for actions taken on foreign soil. However, several attempts to negotiate with Noriega were subsequently made. According to a RAND Corporation analyst, "Indicting Noriega was consistent with combating drug smuggling but not with easing Noriega out of his position in Panama." [27]

On a parallel track, a Washington interagency committee oversaw negotiations with José Blandón, the Panamanian Consul in New York who claimed to represent Noriega, and twice sent DOD officials "to convey a tough message" in December 1987. When these efforts failed to put Noriega back in line, Washington decided to implement sanctions designed to force Noriega out without resorting to military intervention. In February 1988 the U.S. suspended Canal Commission payments to Panama and in March froze $27 million of Panamanian assets being held in U.S. banks, followed in April with a prohibition on tax and other payments by U.S. companies operating in Panama.

Ironically, the U.S. strategy of freezing assets was thwarted by contradictory actions from within the U.S. government itself. Because no checks or credit cards could be used in Panama, the Panama Canal Commission and the Department of Defense paid their Panama employees their full salaries in American currency. Specially flown in from the United States, the fresh supply of cash helped keep the economy going. Continued Latin American and European trade with Panama also undermined U.S. measures. The sanctions did cause extensive damage to the Panamanian economy over the longer term, however, and also hurt U.S. investors and U.S. political allies within Panama. In the case of Latin American governments, regional resentment of U.S. interference was expressed by a resolution against the U.S. actions in Panama that passed seventeen to one (with eight abstentions) in the Organization of American States.[28]

After the May 1989 elections were denounced as fraudulent by former President Carter and the Catholic Church, President Bush urged the PDF to overthrow Noriega, in the belief that the PDF would not need help from the United States. An October 3 coup attempt failed, however, when troops loyal to Noriega used the one access road not blocked by U.S. forces in order to overcome the rebel officers. By this time, the U.S. had already moved toward using force on its own—a fact signaled a few days earlier by the appointment of General Maxwell Thurman to take charge of the Southern Command.[29]

The U.S. Invasion

Just after midnight on December 20, the United States launched its invasion in the largest U.S. military action since the Vietnam War. Simultaneously, President Endara and his two vice-presidents were sworn in during a videotaped ceremony on a U.S. military base.[30]

President Bush gave four reasons for the intervention: "to safeguard the lives of Americans, to defend democracy in Panama, to combat drug trafficking, and to protect the integrity of the Panama Canal Treaty." The first and last of these did not hold up to scrutiny. A U.S. soldier had been killed in an organized attempt to run a PDF roadblock during a time when tensions between the two militaries were already running high. In another incident a U.S. civilian woman was allegedly molested by PDF agents, but the report was never substantiated. The U.S. military and media portrayed the actions as unprovoked and unforgivable. However, only a month before, the Guatemalan military had abducted and tortured a U.S nun—an incident not even publicly acknowledged by Washington. Admiral Eugene Carroll termed the level of preinvasion violence in Panama "lower than exists in Washington, DC, every day."[31]

The Canal Treaties expressly forbid intervention in the internal affairs of Panama, and the invasion represented the first time in its history that the canal was closed due to human causes. The democratic legitimacy and strength of the Endara government was seriously undermined by its path to office. Moreover, drug trafficking in Panama was apparently undiminished by Noriega's arrest and imprisonment.

The invasion involved some 27,000 troops and new sophisticated weaponry, including the F-117 "Stealth" fighter. At the University of Panama's Geology Department, the seismic graph showed that 442 bombs had been dropped in the first thirteen hours of the invasion.[32] Within a short time the invading forces overcame the minimal organized resistance. With the police and defense forces in disarray, captured, or in hiding, looters raided supermarkets, malls, and warehouses.[33] Looting was reportedly spearheaded by the Dignity Battalions who broke into supermarkets to take provisions to supply the local defense against the invaders.

Noriega himself escaped capture, despite an all-out manhunt by U.S. troops. He did not appear again until December 24, in the papal nunciature, where he holed up for a week and a half while U.S. soldiers outside played rock music on loudspeakers in an attempt to harass him into surrendering. He was taken into custody by DEA agents on January 5.

The invasion was condemned as a violation of international law by the United Nations and Organization of American States in lopsided votes. Both resolutions called for the immediate withdrawal of U.S. troops.[34] In effect, George Bush resurrected Teddy Roosevelt's paean to coercion: "I took the Canal, and let the Congress debate" about the legalities.

Other policy objectives were served—consciously or not—by the invasion. Two were immediately served. The canal treaty stipulated the appointment of the first Panamanian administrator of the canal to take office on January 1, 1990. The administrator was to be nominated by Panama, but Noriega's selection, Tomás Altamirano Duque, owner of *La Estrella* newspaper, was rejected by the Bush administration. With the installation of a pro-U.S. government in Panama, the administration could be sure of a more like-minded nomination. Gilberto Guardia was nominated for the post in March 1990 and confirmed by the U.S. Senate in September of that year.[35]

A second objective of the invasion, initiated by the State Department in action planning several months before the invasion, was the elimination of the PDF—over which the U.S. had lost much influence—and its replacement by a police force, first under U.S. military and later Panamanian civilian control.[36] This went hand in hand with more long-term objectives: the expansion of policy options for the United States until and after the year 2000. Such long-term strategy was a bedrock of the conservative Santa Fe Committee, whose 1988 foreign policy blueprint, known as Santa Fe II, had largely been adopted by the Bush administration. Santa Fe II stated:

> Once a democratic regime is in place...discussions should begin on a realistic defense of the Canal after the year 2000. Those

talks should include the United States' retention of limited facilities in Panama (principally Howard air base and Rodman naval station) for proper force projection throughout the Western Hemisphere.[37]

The invasion shifted the balance of power and served to change the terms of negotiations on a series of issues, from debt conditionalities to who assumes responsibility for clean-up of military toxics.

In addition, the invasion served as a demonstration for U.S. policy in the region. Nicaraguans, whose presidential elections were less than two months away, could not have failed to notice what the United States might do if they did not vote for the "right" candidates. Furthermore, in the context of a renewed offensive against cocaine trafficking—inaugurated by President Bush in a national television address three months earlier—the invasion was also a demonstration to the Andean countries that the United States would not rule out military intervention in the war on illegal drugs. Less than a month after the invasion, two U.S. war ships steamed toward the Colombian coast with the announced intention of a "virtual air and sea blockade" of drugs leaving Colombia. The action was suspended after diplomatic protest from Colombia.[38] In the context of the ongoing disintegration of the Soviet bloc, the invasion also demonstrated the new U.S. willingness to assume an active, interventionist leadership in the post-cold war period.

Finally, the invasion served domestic purposes. President Bush had been attacked by both Democrats and Republicans during the 1988 presidential campaign for his history of relations with Noriega. After the failed PDF coup attempt against Noriega in October, congressional and media critics implied that Bush was a wimp for not taking more decisive military action in support of the attempted putsch.[39] The invasion also drew attention away from the administration's problems arising from revelations of its friendly relations with China in the wake of the repressive crackdown there earlier in the year.[40]

The Invasion's Aftermath

The invasion generated a lasting debate over its costs to Panamanians. It may never be known how many Panamanians perished in the action since the U.S. military gave a low priority to finding out. Its early public count was 314 PDF soldiers and 202 civilians killed, although an internal Army memo estimated as many as one thousand civilian casualties.[41] In March 1990 the Southern Command revised its estimate of Panamanian soldiers killed to 51, although it did not change its total figure, implying that some 465 civilians had been killed. Panamanian church and refugee sources, as well as a commission established by former Attorney General Ramsey Clark, estimated that the number of deaths reached more than two thousand.[42]

No matter what figure is used, the invasion was certainly a traumatic event for many Panamanians. About 18,000 lost their homes, mostly in El Chorrillo, the neighborhood of wooden tenements near the *comandancia* where Noriega had his office. El Chorrillo residents persistently protested the shabby construction of replacement apartment complexes built in 1991. Some buildings had no foundation, resulting in the repeated flooding of ground floor units.

Material damage from military attacks and from looting resulted in $670 million to $1.17 billion in losses to the private sector.[43] A lawsuit for damages against the United States by Panamanian businessmen was rejected by the U.S. Supreme Court in October 1992.[44] However, a suit before the Inter-American Human Rights Commission by Panamanians who lost family members in the invasion was more favorably considered, although neither the Endara nor Pérez Balladares governments supported it. The Commission ruled that victims of a military action could sue regardless of the position of their governments, and it heard the invasion victims' oral arguments for compensation in February 1995. But the commission's ruling, scheduled for late 1995, is not binding on the United States.[45] Manuel Noriega was tried and convicted in Florida on eight of ten counts of drug trafficking. In July 1992 the presiding judged sentenced the humbled general to forty years in prison, which are to be served as a prisoner of war.[46]

International Aid Steps In

In the wake of the invasion, the United States and international lending agencies entered the scene to assist reconstruction efforts and to reestablish Panama's good standing within the international financial system. In February 1990 the U.S. Congress authorized $42 million in urgent economic aid for housing, public works, small business rehabilitation, and technical assistance. Apartment complexes were constructed in El Chorrillo and vouchers provided to other displaced people who were unable to find housing elsewhere.

The U.S. government also ordered the release of $278 million in funds frozen by the 1988 sanctions, which allowed Panama to reduce its foreign debt arrears. Some of Panama's assets that had been embargoed by Washington were not released until 1994, however, after U.S. claimants had been given the opportunity to seek damages from Panama.[47]

The showcase of U.S. assistance was a $420 million package approved by Congress in May 1990, making Panama the largest recipient of U.S. aid in Latin America in 1990 (Figure 5c).[48] The package included:

- $130 million to international financial institutions for Panamanian debt relief.
- $108 million for bank liquidity and private sector loans.
- $114 million for projects in the public sector, including improvements in agriculture, health, education, justice, natural resources, infrastructure and other social sectors.
- $68 million in development programs.

Although Panama's GDP grew at dramatic rates in 1990-91, very little of this growth could be attributed to any "jump start" associated with U.S. economic aid. Each of the U.S. assistance programs was conditioned on enactment of a variety of reforms by Panama, thereby stalling disbursement of the funds. Less than ten percent of the aid had been disbursed by February 1991, more than fourteen months after the invasion.[49]

For the United States to release each portion of the aid, Panama was required to implement a series of reforms, which included:

Figure 5c
U.S. Economic Aid to Panama

In millions U.S. $

	DA	ESF	PL480 Tit. I	PL480 Tit. II	Peace Corps	Total
1983	6.3	—	—	1.1	—	7.4
1984	10.7	—	—	1.3	—	12.0
1985	24.3	50	—	0.1	—	74.4
1986	20.1	13.2	—	0.1	—	33.4
1987	12.1	—	—	—	—	12.1
1988	1.2	—	—	—	—	1.2
1989	—	—	—	0.3	—	0.3
1990	3.5	392.8	—	0.3	—	396.6
1991	—	39.5	—	—	0.5	40.0
1992	14.5	—	4.0	0.3	0.7	19.8
1993	6.4	—	—	0.5	1.0	7.9
1994	4.3	—	—	0.1	1.3	5.7

DA=Development Assistance

ESF=Economic Support Funds

PL480=Food for Peace Program

SOURCE: *U.S. Overseas Loans and Grants and Assistance from International Organizations* July 1, 1945-Sept. 30, 1983, 1985, 1987, 1989, 1991, 1994.

- Reaching agreements with the IMF, World Bank, and IDB for short- and medium-term "stabilization" plans.
- Implementing reforms which included management of public sector finance, identification of five state firms to be privatized, labor policy, lowering of tariffs, reduction in the number of products subject to price controls, and elimination of quantitative trade restrictions.
- Reaching agreement with the United States on a Mutual Legal Assistance Treaty and for exchanging records on dollar transactions larger than $10,000.

There was no attempt by AID to track cash transfers, which were a large component of the aid program, and a General Accounting Office draft report concluded that the program as a whole had "no significant impact on the economy." One reason was that several of the major aid recipients for development projects were U.S. companies or agencies, such as economic analysts ($3.1 million for economic policy reform), Internal Revenue Service ($1.6 million for tax administration), Georgetown University ($6 million for scholarships to "inspire positive attitudes toward the United States"), American Institute for Free Labor Development ($500,000 for labor organizing), and AID itself ($6 million for operating expenses).

With the Panamanian police force in disarray after the invasion, the United States directed $13.2 million in development funds toward training a new police force as part of a $60 million, five-year Justice Department program administered through AID.[50] The Endara government made a conscious decision to employ mostly PDF officers at first hoping "not so much to transform former members of the PDF as to restructure the entire law enforcement apparatus," in the words of one U.S. adviser. Two and half years after the invasion, former PDF soldiers still constituted more than 90 percent of the newly created National Police and 85 percent of the Judicial Technical Police. Although there has been some progress toward removing former PDF soldiers, the newly created National Police is still widely regarded as being corrupt and unresponsive to citizen concerns.

Following U.S. congressional criticism of the deplorable prison conditions in Panama, the aid program was expanded in 1992 to include prison reform.[51] Unlike most other U.S. overseas police training, the program in Panama included the training of police SWAT teams. "With the demise of the military," explained a State Department spokesperson, "Panama needed some special operational capability for situations that might arise." [52] The congressional authorization for the program excluded lethal aid, but it did not stop a Panamanian SWAT team from purchasing M-16s and other police equipment from the United States in 1993.[53]

Other U.S. aid programs dwindled by 1995 to only $3 million, largely as a result of budgetary pressures. "We have had successes in the democracy area, so those [other programs] are being phased down," according to AID's Bernadette Bundy. By 1994 most of AID's assistance was focused on environmental issues, including the conservation of the canal's watershed, creation of a conservation endowment comanaged by the Nature Conservancy, demarcation and management of national parks, and community education about environmental issues confronting peasant communities. AID also had plans to work with municipal governments to strengthen administration, reform local judiciaries, and extend municipal services. But such programs are likely to be cut as the foreign aid establishment adjusts to overall cuts in funding. In the future, the lead donor will likely be not AID but the IDB, with which AID works closely on a daily basis. Other donors likely to provide grants or loans to Panama in the future include the European Community, Spain, Taiwan, Japan, the World Bank, and the IMF.[54]

U.S. Investment and Trade Relations

Historically, the United States has been the country's single most important source of investment and trade. In the 1970s rightwing defenders of U.S. control of the canal and the Canal Zone predicted that Panamanian nationalism would adversely affect U.S. financial interests in the country. Those predictions, however, proved unfounded. Instead, U.S. investor confidence increased after the signing of the 1977 Canal Treaties.[55] In 1979 the American Society of Panama formed the first American Chamber of Commerce in the country, which within a few years had over 150 sponsoring members.

Unlike in most Central American countries, U.S. financial interest is considerable, even by U.S. terms. The book value of U.S. investment in the country was $12.5 billion in 1993—the third largest in Latin America, and up from $9.3 billion in 1990.[56] According to the American Chamber of Commerce, about half of all private sector business in Panama is U.S.-related.[57] The United States is Panama's single most important trading partner, with the United States supplying 36 percent of its imports and buying 35 percent of its exports (Figure 5d). Another factor determining strong U.S. government interest in Panama is the presence of some forty thousand U.S. citizens—both civilian and military—who live and work in the country.[58]

Many hundreds of U.S. businesses are registered in Panama, but most are only "paper" companies with no operations there. Nonetheless, U.S. productive investment still plays an important role in the economy. Six of the top ten U.S. oil companies are active in Panama, one of which, Texaco, owns the country's only oil refinery. United Brands dominates the banana business, and Ralston Purina is the major investor in the seafood industry. General Mills owns a flour mill, and Borden produces dairy products. Northville Terminal and CBI Industries own the transisthmus oil pipeline in a joint venture with the government.[59]

Panama formally requested entry into the General Agreement on Tariffs and Trade (now the World Trade Organization, or WTO) in February 1992, seen by all as a prerequisite for a free trade agreement with the United States through accession to NAFTA.[60] It became an observer in GATT, but its application for full membership was still under consideration in 1995.

Panama's entrance into the WTO depends on support mainly from the United States but also from the European Union and other industrialized nations. In 1993 Ambassador Deane Hinton made clear that Panama would have to reform its labor code and lower tariffs before the United States would support its full membership in the multilateral trade agreement.[61] The progress of bilateral trade negotiations between Panama and the United States will be a good indicator of whether Panama will be permitted to join the WTO.

In a first round of negotiations between Panama and Washington in November 1994, Panama resisted increased pressures by the U.S.

Figure 5d

Direction of Trade, 1993

In millions of U.S. $

Foreign Suppliers

United States	798.4	36.5%
Japan	170.6	7.8%
Ecuador	83.1	3.8%
Netherlands Antilles	65.6	3.0%
Costa Rica	61.2	2.8%
Total	2,187.3	

Foreign Markets

United States	175.6	34.6%
Germany	71.6	14.1%
Sweden	48.2	9.5%
Costa Rica	34.0	6.7%
Italy	27.9	5.5%
Total	507.6	

SOURCE: Economist Intelligence Unit, *EIU Country Report: Panama*, 1995.

to lower tariffs, in some cases from ninety percent to ten percent. Panamanian negotiators also fought against opening the economy to services—including sales, insurance, health, tourism, and transport—many of which are currently restricted to Panamanians.[62]

The Drug Card

Panama's reputation for drug trafficking and money laundering continues to be the card the United States plays against Panama to leverage policy concessions. Yet as long as Panama has such an open economy and relies for income on its international banking sector, it will be an easy mark for traffickers and thus for U.S. sanctions. Panama's economy historically has been extremely open for geographic reasons—a characteristic bolstered by neoliberal trends in the hemisphere. With or without Noriega or another centralized broker for contraband, Panama will be vulnerable to trafficking and money laundering.

This structural openness was made clear in the two years following the U.S. invasion, when police found an increasing amount of cocaine being shipped through the isthmus. After revelations in 1993 that President Endara's law firm had formed corporations that were used to launder drug money, Ambassador Hinton observed, "Constitutional government might not survive if widespread corruption or even uncertainty about the extent of corruption were slowly to eat away at public confidence in democracy." In response to Endara's assertion that he was unaware of the money laundering, Hinton went on, "Failing to check client credentials may not be illegal, but now that the corrupting criminal threat is widely perceived, such neglect is at best irresponsible and immoral." Secretary of State Warren Christopher also said that the situation in postinvasion Panama was "not much better" than under Noriega.[63]

The U.S. perception of Panama's lack of will to combat trafficking and money laundering was brought to bear in a number of ways. In the first year of the Endara government, the U.S. and Panama signed several bilateral agreements, which allowed the U.S. Coast Guard to patrol Panamanian waters and board ships suspected of carrying narcotics, and control precursor chemicals used in the production of cocaine and heroin. Another accord required the private sector to report every banking transaction greater than $10,000 to the central government.

The most controversial agreement was the Mutual Legal Assistance Treaty (MLAT), signed in April 1991, which gave U.S. officials access to banking records for money laundering and drug offenses, and upon which release of $84 million in aid was contingent. Bankers in Panama feared the agreement would damage Panama's image as a tax shelter, prompting Panamanian negotiators to eliminate provisions for investigating U.S. tax evasion from the agreement.[64] The MLAT was submitted to the U.S. Senate for ratification in October 1991, but it fell hostage to objections by Jesse Helms in the Senate Foreign Relations Committee. The treaty was finally ratified by the Senate in April 1995, with the condition that the United States not be required to pass information to Panamanian officials charged with trafficking themselves.[65]

Small aid programs also focused on drugs. The State Department's Bureau of International Narcotic Matters provided nearly $1.8 million in the 1990-92 period, mostly for boats, vehicles and other equipment.[66] The Coast Guard and Drug Enforcement Administration regularly participated in joint antinarcotics operations with the Panamanian navy and police.

Accusations by U.S. officials of Panamanian complicity in the drug problem persisted through the Endara administration. The State Department's 1994 international narcotics control report called Panama's performance "disappointing," particularly in the area of obstructing money laundering and the slowness of its judicial system. The State Department exempted Panama from sanctions, since "a cut-off of assistance could impair other [Panamanian] cooperation that is required more than ever as we move into the Canal Treaty's delicate transition period."[67]

In the U.S. Congress, Senator Robert Kerry contributed to the steady stream of criticism from the United States, saying at the height of Panama's 1994 election campaign that "Panama is again moving large amounts of cocaine to the United States" aided by "a system of disorganized crime under the current government." In response to these accusations, the incoming Pérez Balladares government reassured Washington that "to fight this enemy [drug trafficking] we must do everything possible, including joining with other countries in the hemisphere."[68]

In an apparent reward for Pérez Balladares' cooperation on a variety of issues, the State Department in 1995 qualified Panama as a "cooperating country" in the war on drugs. "The Pérez Balladares administration indicated clearly its intention to remedy Panama's institutional flaws," the State Department's 1995 drug control strategy report said. It cited close cooperation with the DEA, new border control agreements with Colombia and Costa Rica, a near record seizure of three and half tons of cocaine in 1994, and diminished charges of drug-related corruption. Yet the report also noted that cocaine addiction in Panama was believed to be the highest in Central America.

Only two days after the certification, Alberto Aleman, a PRD deputy in the Panama Assembly's narcotics control committee, called on Washington to explain the activities of DEA agents in the country.

"The Panamanian government has no information about the tasks of these agents, since the North Americans manage this information as ultra-secret," he said.[69]

U.S. Military Presence

U.S. Southern Command (SouthCom) based in Panama is responsible for U.S. military relations with all of Central and South America (not with Mexico or the Caribbean). Its stated missions are: prepare for combat and other operations; help other U.S. agencies and regional allies to attack illegal drug production and trafficking; help eliminate security threats against the region; help professionalize the region's militaries; maintain a neutral and open Panama Canal; help in implementation of the Canal Treaties; provide disaster relief when requested; and maintain a high quality of life for U.S. soldiers and dependents.[70]

During the 1980s U.S. planes hauled weapons and personnel from Howard Air Force Base in Panama to contra forces in Honduras.[71] Beginning in 1983, U.S. reconnaissance planes from Panama also flew at low altitudes over guerrilla held territory in El Salvador, taking infrared photos of people, fires, and concentrations of metal and beaming the photos to SouthCom. Technicians at SouthCom then processed the data before forwarding it to the Salvadoran Air Force, which used it in an air war to target peasants and combatants alike.[72] SouthCom has lobbied for strategies that will keep a strong role for militaries in the region, currently focusing on "nation-building" exercises such as construction of roads and schools and on anti-drug operations.[73] In 1989, of course, the bases were a staging area for the invasion of Panama.

SouthCom also coordinates:

- Requests for U.S. military aid to Central and South American and Mexican militaries.
- Selection of soldiers to attend the U.S. School of the Americas in Fort Benning, Georgia and other U.S. military training institutions.
- Combined exercises with Latin American militaries.
- Joint "civic action" programs with civilian agencies in Panama and with militaries in Guatemala, El Salvador, Colombia and other countries.
- "Mobile Training Teams" to train military forces in Colombia, Peru, and other nations.
- Intelligence flights over coca and cocaine producing areas of the Andes.

This assortment of SouthCom's activities illustrates the military approach to such essentially nonmilitary problems as coca production and the lack of infrastructure and medical care. Despite expressions of concern about human rights, SouthCom continues to collaborate with militaries known to be the worst human rights violators in the hemisphere, including Peru and Colombia. SouthCom Public Affairs Director Col. James Fetig said in 1993: "These people [Latin Americans] don't know what we mean when we talk about human rights." [74] Given the lack of respect during the invasion for the lives of Panamanians however, there are grounds for skepticism in Panama about the U.S. military's discourse on respect for human rights.

SouthCom's budget in Fiscal Year 1995 was $690.4 million. In 1991 41 percent of SouthCom's funds were dedicated to air surveillance and intelligence activities. When and if U.S. military functions are moved to the continental United States, some military activities—surveillance flights, for example—will mean undetermined additional costs. SouthCom's planning headquarters headquarters, with a staff of between 500 and 700 who coordinate regional military missions, will be moved to Miami, Florida in 1997. In May 1995 the United States still had 8,500 soldiers, mostly from the Army, stationed in Panama.[75]

SouthCom saw its major mission in the early 1990s in the anti-drug campaign. "For SouthCom," military officials wrote in 1993, "this war embraces the full geographic breadth of the command's area of responsibility—a landmass extending from the tip of Chile to the Guatemala-Belize border with Mexico."[76] Especially revealing was the metaphor used by SouthCom in describing cocaine production in an article on anti-drug strategy. The Andean countries were shown with a large beehive, larger than the countries themselves, with bees swarming out of it into neighboring countries and the United States. Other analysts, however, picture cocaine production more like a water balloon: when it is squeezed in one region by counter-measures, it simply pops out in another region.[77]

Increasingly, however, possibly because the Latin American drug war is perceived as a losing fight, SouthCom promotes its function of supporting democracy and materially assisting Latin American nations. In 1993 SouthCom temporarily deployed more than 60,000 troops (up from 19,000 in 1990), most of them National Guardsmen and reservists, to 18 countries for engineering and medical exercises, "Deployments for Training," and other missions.[78]

Any examination of the U.S. military presence in Panama must include the intelligence agencies long active there. In the 1960s, the CIA and Army 470th Intelligence Group, both based at Fort Amador, competed for preeminence in Panama. While the CIA saw Torrijos as a dangerous communist and supported a failed coup attempt against him that led to Noriega's promotion to intelligence chief, retired military officers from the 470th were drinking buddies with Torrijos and saw the corruption of those around him as a fact of life. They had recruited Noriega when he was a high school student. Only later did the CIA become the dominant intelligence agency in Panama, paying Noriega up to $110,000 a year for his cooperation.[79]

The Future of the U.S. Bases

The Endara administration publicly disavowed any intention to negotiate a U.S. military presence after the year 2000, and said that the U.S. had "not even informally" suggested anything but compliance with the Canal Treaty.[80] Both sides probably understood that such negotiations would severely damage the Endara government's credibility. One PRD leader observed that "proposing to renegotiate the bases in Panama is only possible with a democratically elected government, since any [other] arrangement would not be valid."[81]

A U.S. Army War College study released in 1991 argued that "retention of an advance base in Panama would strengthen the U.S. capability for timely projection of military power throughout the region."[82] Later the same year, the U.S. Congress included a resolution with its Defense Appropriations bill calling on the president to "begin negotiations with the Government of Panama, at a mutually acceptable time, to consider whether the two governments should allow the permanent stationing of United States military forces in Panama beyond December 31, 1999."[83]

The congressional resolution stemmed from the premise that "the presence of the United States Armed Forces offers a viable defense against sabotage or other threat to the Panama Canal." According to a SouthCom official, however, the U.S. defense of the canal has always been strategic, and "it's our assessment that we can do that from the States." This assessment implicitly acknowledged that the U.S. military presence has never been tactically necessary or sufficient to defend the Canal. The Panama Canal Commission has a police force already that defends the canal's locks against attacks, but "if some sapper decides to create a landslide at Culebra Cut, there's hardly anything we can do about it," said the officer, who contended that the most serious threats to the canal are internal, such as mismanagement.[84]

In any case, negotiation of a new base agreement would have to be a mutual affair. Opinion polls have shown consistently that 60-70 percent of Panamanians favor keeping the bases after the year 2000.[85] Their reasoning, however, does not have to do with defense of the canal—which President Pérez Balladares reasoned "can be protected by a specialized force, possibly even private, similar to those guarding any modern industrial facility."[86] Nor does this public support for the

Current U.S. Military Installations in Panama, 1995

Pacific Coast

— Quarry Heights (home of Southern Command Headquarters and U.S. Special Operations Command South)

— Fort Kobbe, west side of the Canal

— Howard Air Force Base, west side of the Canal (forward element of U.S. Southern Air Force)

— Rodman Naval Station (southern detachment of the Atlantic Fleet based in Norfolk, Virginia) and nearby Marine Barracks, west side of the Canal

— Fort Clayton, including the sub-post of Corozal (home of U.S. Army South)

— Albrook Air Force Station

— Fort Amador, Army (housing) and Navy sections

— Chiva Chiva Range (radio antenna site)

— Curundu (housing area)

Atlantic Coast

— Fort Davis (to have been reverted in 1995)

— Fort Sherman

— Fort Gulick (known as Fuerte Espinar, also to have been reverted in 1995)

— Galeta Island (communications facility)

Off-coast

— Balboa West (firing range)

— New Empire Range (firing range)

— Semaphore Hill (a radar station used for counternarcotics)

— U.S. Navy Trans-Isthmian Pipeline

Support facilities

— Gorgas Hospital

— Several schools and secondary housing areas

— Oil tank depository

— Office of the Military Traffic Management Command

SOURCE: U.S. Department of Defense, *Panama Canal Treaty Implementation Plan*, February 1992, obtained through Freedom of Information Act request.

presence of the U.S. bases emanate from support for U.S. regional policy objectives. Panama rejected, for example, a U.S. proposal in 1993 to locate a Drug Enforcement Administration interrogation center at one of the bases.[87] A poll in early 1994 showed that the first reason given for keeping the bases was the economic benefits they offer the country.[88]

The bases bring about $255 million into the Panamanian economy, including paychecks for 5100 Panamanian civilians.[89] A leading voice within Panama for keeping the bases has been Local 907, the AFL-CIO union representing base workers, whose wages, as federal employees, are based on U.S. pay scales, four or five times higher

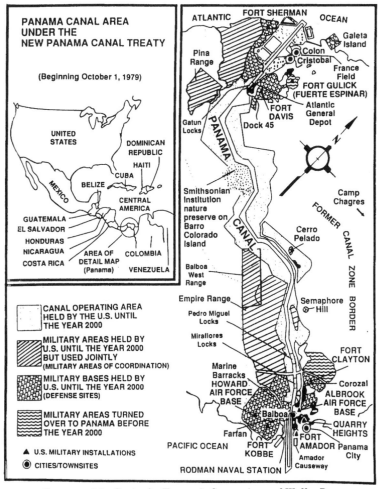

Courtesy of the Center for Economic Conversion and Waller Press

than salaries prevailing in Panama. Former Local 907 leader Ray Bishop even suggested that "the government's refusal to listen to base workers' proposals leaves the people only violent positions in order to defend their right to work."[90]

Future Uses of the Canal Area

Most areas—both military bases and canal operating areas—are likely to be transferred to Panama toward the end of the 1990s (Figure 5e). A wide range of ideas for use of these areas is under discussion, though few specific plans had been put forward by 1995.

The group with the most specific ideas, and the one most active in promoting them, is the business association APEDE, which with the help of Texaco and other corporate sponsors produced a 12-minute video about its vision of making Panama into a "maritime nation." APEDE's vision is based on the Singapore model, whose economic development is based on international commerce but without sacrificing public education or living wages.

"We believe Panama can take advantage of the infrastructure [offered by the bases] and we should be able to use it in a sustainable manner, promoting an international maritime strategy," according to APEDE. Such a maritime strategy would include rehabilitating the dry docks, an area for servicing and repairing containers, and supplying goods to the three dozen ships that daily pass through the canal.[91]

Figure 5e
Treaty-Mandated Transfers to Panama since 1979

1979: Buildings and housing units in Army section of Fort Amador
     Albrook Airfield hangars, buildings and airstrip
     Housing units at Curundu Heights and Quarry Heights
1979-82: Several buildings in the Panama Air Depot
     Remaining housing units at Curundu Heights
1984: Fort Gulick (retaken by U.S. during 1989 invasion)
     Housing units at France Field, Atlantic side
1991: Housing, barracks, and school complex at Coco Solo, Atlantic side
     Gatun underground storage tanks
1992: Officers quarters at Curundu Heights
1994: Coco Solo Hospital

Source: U.S. Department of Defense, *Treaty Implementation Plan.*

There are downsides to APEDE's strategy, however. According to Charlotte Elton, an economist and Director of the Panamanian Center for Research and Social Action (CEASPA), "This [APEDE] proposal enters directly in conflict with some of the environmental proposals for management of the canal area." She also believes that "even though on paper, it looks like Panama would be a good place to invest, we have not seen that international investors are interested in Panama."[92] The success of APEDE's proposal relies on a high level of such investment.

Another proposal related to the maritime strategy was articulated by Rafael Arosemena, former member of Panama's canal conversion commission and owner of a ship repair business in Colón. He suggested the use of extensive underground fuel tanks or "tank farms" on Rodman Naval Base for supplying ships. Other ideas offered by Arosemena included the development of agriculture and food processing plants to supply ships; low-wage assembly plants or *maquiladoras* along the banks of the canal; and the use of Fort Sherman, where there are four hundred species of birds, as a center for "ecotourism." The Chamber of Commerce has proposed using Panama Canal College and Balboa High School as sites for universities and research centers. Finally, there is a proposal to turn Fort Clayton over to the United Nations as a site for a UN agency.[93]

It is not clear what will happen to Gorgas Hospital, the major medical facility in the zone. Coco Solo, a medical clinic which was transferred to Panama in 1994, was purchased by Panama's Social Security agency and put into immediate operation as a public clinic. The clinic serves between 600 and 700 patients per day, according to its director.[94]

Development of reuse plans has been hampered by the kind of resistance experienced in communities everywhere when the United States announces closures of income-generating facilities. Another obstacle is the taboo associated with the bases in Panama. Most Panamanians have always perceived the bases as off-limits and as places where the laws and culture are determined by foreigners. Most have never seen the inside of a U.S. military base. The resistance to the loss of jobs and the ignorance about the bases have slowed enthusiasm for economic conversion, opening the way for heated conflict over how to conduct the transfer and conversion process.

Military Toxics: An Emerging Issue

For more than fifty years the U.S. has conducted exercises with live munitions on the New Empire, Balboa West, Piña, and Fort Sherman firing ranges—leaving behind hundreds or thousands of unexploded munitions. Like other military sites around the world, the bases in Panama are also the site of contaminants such as solvents used to clean airplanes, petrochemicals from underground storage tanks, and PCBs from electrical transformers. There are also reports of defoliated areas where the U.S. military may have tested chemical weapons or saturated the terrain with pesticides.[95]

Live munitions on the firing ranges in Panama have been picked up by children playing and by adults looking for metal to recycle, leading to explosions resulting in injuries and death.[96] The munitions also pose a hazard because of toxic substances such as lead that may leak from them into the water table or the Canal's waters. The canal is fed by fresh water that is used as a drinking source for more than a million Panamanians.

The U.S. military firing ranges fall within a mostly forested area in the canal watershed. Because conservation of the forested watershed is crucial both to protect its biologically diverse ecology and supply fresh water that keeps the canal flowing, Panama's natural resources agency has proposed making the area into a national park that would stretch all across the Panamanian isthmus. Although the project counted on AID support and was officially approved by President Endara, the project was later suspended by the government's base conversion agency Interoceanic Regional Authority (ARI) because of the potential danger posed by unexploded munitions.

A precedent of concern to Panamanians is the contamination of San José Island in the Gulf of Panama, which was used by the U.S. military to test chemical weapons in the 1940s, according to a study by CEASPA.[97] In 1972 the inventor of Tupperware proposed setting up on the island a center for scientists to create and improve patents. The U.S. government was asked for assurance that the island was not contaminated with threats to human health or safety. But this request languished in the State Department, which never supplied the necessary written certification, and the project was cancelled.[98]

The full extent of toxic contamination in Panama remains unknown. The Panamanian Foreign Ministry made a request to the Southern Command in 1993 for detailed information about the environmental condition of military facilities and lands, but the Pentagon did not respond.[99]

For Panama to be able to use transferred military areas for the benefit of civilians—whether for housing or for job creation—it will need access to information on pollution of the areas. The catch for Panama is that DOD policy says that "all host nation claims for damage will be challenged unless clearly substantiated." [100] Yet only the U.S. military and government have the full story of what toxics and unexploded munitions have been used and left in Panama during the last fifty years.

U.S. Policy for Clean-Up in Panama

DOD clean-up policy is governed by host nation environmental laws or by treaties and Status of Force Agreements, whichever is stronger.[101] According to the Panama Canal Treaties, the United States must remove "every hazard to human life, health and safety" from military sites "insofar as may be practicable" before turning them over to Panama.[102] The treaties also require the United States to consult with Panamanian officials on environmental problems.

But as a Southern Command official said, "Not just because [a site] requires remediation will we remediate." In 1994 the Pentagon developed a policy paper on clean-up in Panama as part of a larger interagency policy review toward Panama. The paper reportedly required DOD to turn over information on contamination a year before any given site is transferred. With only six months to go before the scheduled August 1995 transfer of two bases (scant information was turned over), the United States was not complying with that provision of its own policy.[103]

On the Panamanian side, the agency responsible for U.S. military areas being turned over to Panama announced in November 1994 that it would ask the United States to "decontaminate" the U.S. bases before they are turned over to Panama. Carlos Mendoza, president of the ARI, said that Panama does not have the hundreds of millions of dollars that will be required to clean up the bases.[104]

The ARI established an interagency technical committee of its own to gather information and address clean-up issues on the bases. The committee included mostly governmental representatives, with a few from citizen and academic groups, but none representing communities near contaminated areas.

U.S. Canal Policy

The Panama Canal continues to be the major strategic interest of the United States in Panama. Ambassador Hinton told the Isthmian Foundation for Economic and Social Studies in 1993, "The principal U.S. interest in Panama in the next century will be the efficient functioning of the canal under its new administrators."

More than 13 percent of all U.S. maritime traffic passes through the canal, and two thirds of canal traffic originates in or is destined for the United States. The comparable figure for Japan, the next largest user of the canal, is 23 percent—a percentage that appears to be in decline.[105]

In the 1960s the discovery of oil in Alaska and its planned shipment to Atlantic ports led the United States to contemplate a new canal, possibly at sea-level, to overcome the limitations of the existing canal. In 1982 the United States and Panama initiated a study for alternatives to the Canal and eventually invited Japan to participate.

The Tripartite Commission, as it was called, delayed by the political crisis in Panama and reportedly beset by friction between the United States and Japan, finally issued its recommendations in September 1993. It concluded that the broadening of the Gaillard Cut, undertaken by the United States before the Commission concluded its work, would enable the canal to handle maritime demand until the year 2020. It recommended construction of a third set of locks to handle traffic after 2020, preparations for which would need to begin well beforehand. The commission found that a sea-level canal would have unpredictable consequences for the sea ecology because of mixing of species from the two oceans, and it recommended new environmental impact studies before construction of a third set of locks begins.[106]

The Japanese remained interested in a sea-level canal, despite these considerations and the $10-20 billion estimated cost. Thomas Burke, chief U.S. delegate to the commission, said, "We in the U.S. delegation felt [a sea-level canal] would not be in the best interests of Panama." The commission estimated the third set of locks would cost $6 billion and generate 95,000 jobs during its construction.[107]

Administrative preparations for the transfer of the canal to Panamanian control have also gone forward. Based on a study by Arthur Anderson, Inc. commissioned by the Panama Canal Commission, President Clinton in April 1994 issued a ten-point proposal to reform the PCC and make it "more in accord with private sector practice in corporate governance." The proposal, which echoed a bill first submitted in 1991, would give greater say to commission members and terminate DOD's control over the appointment of the commission chairperson. It would also provide for two international commission advisers—neither of whom would be a Panamanian or U.S. national—and create a fund with canal revenues to pay for the transfer costs to Panama. Finally, the proposal would eliminate required representation of various sectors on the Commission, including a labor representative.[108]

The proposal was largely supported by Panamanian commission members, while Pentagon officials opposed taking the PCC chair away from U.S. military control.[109] The bill that was resubmitted in 1995 maintained the DOD representative's power to "direct" the vote of the other U.S. members, and thus the majority of the PCC.[110] Fernando Manfredo observed that the authority of the PCC military representative to direct the vote of U.S. members "is not the practice of any commercial company."[111]

Probably the most significant change introduced by what was known as the "corporation bill" would, according to a staff member of the former House Subcommittee on Coast Guard and Navigation, permit contracting to private companies for various canal services "so it can run similarly to a business." Regarding the passage by Panama of a reform that would require Panama to assume the current PCC structure at the moment of transfer, the congressional staffer said, "That's why we're trying to get this bill passed, and in 1999 all the Panamanians have to do is step into it."[112] The potential for partial privatization of canal operations is consistent with the Pérez Balladares government's approach to other national utilities such as telecommunications and water services.

Meanwhile, the shipping industry has expressed fear that Panama will not operate the canal adequately. "I don't think Panama will put in sufficient money to maintain the canal...It'll operate for awhile and then fall apart," the president of the American Institute of Merchant Shipping said in 1992. Shippers raised the same fears in January 1995 when routine maintenance and heavy maritime traffic caused a back-up that made some ships wait six days to pass through the canal, although it was under U.S. management at the time.[113] Some shippers also believe that if Panama raises tolls it could prompt more industry to use the "land bridge" across the continental United States. But Canal Administrator Gilberto Guardia contended that "even if the Canal eliminates tolls, that sector of container traffic would still utilize the U.S. land bridge."[114]

Impact of 1994 U.S. Elections

The Republican ascendance to a majority in the U.S. Congress following the November 1994 elections will likely create new friction in U.S.-Panama relations. A spokesperson for the American Chamber of Commerce in Panama (AMCHAM) said that "Panama could face difficulties, because the main relations of Pérez Balladares' government are with the Democratic Party." Another AMCHAM representative, however, said he was optimistic, asserting that Republicans "can do more for Panama than the Democrats" because of commitments made by President Bush when he ordered the invasion of Panama in 1989.[115]

The reorganization of the House of Representatives led to the elimination of the Subcommittee on Coast Guard and Navigation, which had oversight of the Panama Canal and its budget. Canal issues passed to the National Security (formerly Armed Services) Committee, but without the congressional representatives and staff who had monitored U.S. foreign policy with respect to the canal for many years. At least until the next elections in 1996 a hawkish Republican-led National Security Committee will be overseeing U.S. military strategy in Latin America and the details of the canal transfer.

But the most prominent change was the ascendance of arch-conservative Senator Jesse Helms from North Carolina to the chair of the Senate Foreign Relations Committee. Helms has been a long-time opponent of the treaty provisions that stipulate turning over the Panama Canal and U.S. military bases to Panama. A new Senate Foreign Relations staffer said that Helms "favors discussion being pursued for base rights" in Panama and that a U.S. military presence "is very important for the next ambassador to deal with." In 1995 Helms introduced a Senate resolution calling for negotiations for a new base agreement.

Days after the November 1994 election, the confirmation of Robert Pastor as U.S. ambassador to Panama became a casualty of the shift to a Republican majority. As ranking Republican on the pre-election Senate Foreign Relations Committee, Senator Helms had delayed Pastor's nomination through exhaustive requests for documents on Pastor's activities on President Carter's National Security Council and by filibustering during a key staff meeting shortly before the Senate recessed. Ever since 1980, when Pastor had supported a proposal for U.S. aid to Sandinista Nicaragua, Helms had been critical of him.

The defeat of Pastor's nomination meant that the United States had no ambassador in Panama for more than a year. During the absence of an ambassador, the United States asked Panama to accept Haitian refugees who were fleeing the dictatorship of General Raúl Cedras and in early July appeared to have reached an initial agreement with President Endara. Only three days later, however, Endara backed out of the agreement, apparently in response to heated domestic opposition to the refugees' presence. Some observers noted that the presence of a U.S. ambassador could have prevented what became an embarrassment to both Endara and the Clinton administration.[116]

Treaty Implementation: "Critical Point"

In the vacuum created by the ambassadorial vacancy and lack of a proactive U.S. policy, the Pentagon and Republican conservatives such as Helms appeared to be at least temporarily filling the gap. Shortly after the 1994 election, Clinton's National Security Council initiated an interagency review of Panama policy to formulate a U.S. negotiating position on the post-2000 presence of the U.S. military in Panama and other treaty-related issues. The other participating agencies included the Defense Department's Treaty implementation office, State Department, Joint Chiefs of Staff, Office of Management and Budget, Panama Canal Commission, and the "intelligence community."

But even before the review was completed, the U.S. military identified for the first time which U.S. bases in Panama it planned to consider keeping beyond the year 2000. In hearings convened in March 1995 by the hawkish Republican leadership of the House International Affairs Committee, the Pentagon's Frederick Smith identified Howard Air Force Base, for its use in the drug war, and training centers at Fort Sherman and Rodman Naval Station as the facilities in Panama the United States could use into the next century.[117] With respect to concerns that the U.S. military bases in Panama were needed to defend the canal, however, Smith testified that the United States "could defend the Panama Canal against external threats with forces based in the United States." Rep. Robert Torricelli (D-NJ), ranking Democrat on the International Affairs Committee, reportedly called Howard Air Base "indispensable."[118] But the Pentagon's Smith was less emphatic and said that "the primary impact of not having a[n air] base in Panama will be on our ability to stage aircraft for counterdrug operations."

Besides counternarcotic and combat-training goals, the State Department's Anne Patterson cited "search and rescue and other humanitarian missions" and instilling "confidence in canal users" as other potential reasons for a limited U.S. troop presence beyond 1999. But Patterson also identified "countervailing considerations" that affect the feasibility of a continued U.S. military presence, albeit reduced. These included U.S. domestic opinion about keeping bases open in Panama while closing domestic bases, the intensity of the current sector of Panamanians opposed to extending the U.S. military presence, and the uncertainty of whether Panamanians will in the future passively accept continued U.S. military presence.

Responses in Panama

The news of active U.S. interest in keeping some bases open immediately stirred new protest in Panama. Roberto Eisenmann, former owner of *La Prensa*, Panama's largest daily, editorialized against the U.S. keeping the bases, saying that Panama is prepared to cooperate fully in the drug war. But, Eisenmann continued, "this requires neither military bases nor the presence of a single U.S. soldier on our soil."[119] Eisenmann demanded that Panama's government state clearly that it will demand strict compliance with the Canal Treaties, and called on Panamanians to "free ourselves from the old tradition of hoping for everything from a power we think of as superior, abdicating our civil responsibility." Rolando Murgas, dean of the University of Panama's law school, said that if Panama negotiates a new base agreement, "we would renounce an historical commitment that several generations have adopted in the fight for national sovereignty. Such military sites have served to subjugate our identity."[120]

One Foreign Ministry official, who did not wish to be cited, said that Panama needs more time to absorb some of the bases into the national economy but that a long-term lease is out of the question.[121] In February 1995 Felipe Rodríguez, the president of Panama's association of business executives, called for delays in the transfer of bases to Panama, claiming that Panama did not have the administrative capacity and legislation to put them to the best use. Rodríguez said he agreed with SouthCom commander Barry McCaffrey that because of all the conflicting opinions the transfer process is at a "critical point."[122]

Rodríguez' declarations came in the wake of Foreign Minister Gabriel Lewis' visit to the United States, where he visited Jesse Helms. Helms reportedly suggested to Lewis that a base be maintained in Panama for the drug war, but Lewis asserted that Helms' view is not a majority opinion in the Congress.[123]

Others indicated that base negotiations may only await a decision by the United States to make the first move. Solidarity Party leader Samuel Lewis, the brother of Panama's foreign minister from the same party, said "Panama has to maintain a dignified stance and not offer what has not been requested."[124]

Rep. Philip Crane (R-IL), a longtime opponent of the canal treaties, took the hint and advocated making a proposal for keeping bases "before that option is overtaken by events."[125] Republican Representatives pursued the same line in budget authorization hearings for the Panama Canal Commission around the same time. Members of the House National Security (formerly Armed Services) Committee, which took over jurisdiction of the Panama Canal after the Merchant Marine Committee was abolished in January, took the Pentagon's Frederick Smith to task for not maintaining barracks that are due to revert to Panama.[126] The Canal Treaties require the U.S. to turn over barracks and other non-removable properties, together with lands on which installations are built.

Rep. Crane proposed leasing bases from Panama in a "business-like arrangement between two nations wherein the host country, Panama, is cast in the role of owner and landlord." The State Department's Patterson, however, rejected the idea of paying "large amounts of U.S. taxpayers money" for bases in Panama.[127]

Prospects for U.S. Policy

"The strategic United States interest in Panama is the efficient and secure operation of the canal," said the State Department's Patterson in March, 1995, and it seems unlikely the United States would place at risk the generally smooth canal operations to pursue other foreign policy goals.[128] Although counternarcotics operations have become key in U.S. policy toward Panama since the late 1980s, the efficiency of canal operations continue to be paramount in most U.S. planning.

This importance of the canal in U.S. foreign policy planning is reflected in the various strategic interests that the U.S. Agency for International Development articulates for its Panama program. Three of the interests relate directly to the canal: the nation's strategic geographic position and the consequent volume of U.S. trade that passes through the canal; Panama's political stability and democracy as essential prerequisites for efficient canal operation and the transfer of territories; and the deforestation and development that threaten the fresh water resources that feed the canal.[129]

The United States can employ a variety of methods to ensure that its interests in the canal are protected. These include demanding that U.S. citizens help administer the canal, influencing multilateral loans to Panama (such as for environmental protection of the watershed), and using its leverage to ensure that toll structures and labor regimes it established be maintained after the transfer. Panama's constitutional amendment to adopt U.S. canal arrangements at the time of transfer gave the United States a wide berth. The U.S. role in the Tripartite Commission is another vehicle for U.S. influence on future canal policy.

Since the mid-1980s counternarcotics has been a major component of U.S. policy in Panama. This interest is expressed in programs to stem the domestic use of drugs within Panama, use of Panama as a transshipment point, and money laundering. These programs involve the United States in the administration of justice, police training, coastal and border patrols, customs, banking laws, systems for fiscal management of public funds to counter corruption, and joint military operations with Panama's police and "air service" against coca fields in Central and South America.

Counternarcotics may become a primary rationale for the United States to attempt to maintain a military presence in Panama after the year 2000. Bureaucratic pressures within the Pentagon for a continued presence and for military training sites may also contribute to an effort to maintain a limited presence. But without a compelling mission, the DOD will be hard pressed to find the necessary political clout to keep bases only for military training or as a logistical center for U.S. civic action programs in Latin America. The U.S. military's civic action programs in Panama came under direct attack in a 1994 General Accounting Office report, which described the program as out of control and said that many of the U.S. soldiers were working on projects for which they had no experience. The results included half-built roads in Panama that could not withstand a single rainy season and some schools in Honduras with their roofs caving in.[130]

The drug war, which General Barry McCaffrey called a "chronic illness" that requires "a long-term vision," may provide the foundation for a more credible and sustainable mission, at least within U.S. political circles.[131] International counternarcotics programs have had sparse success, however, and have come under fire by a variety of congressional critics, leading the Clinton administration to abandon the strategy of interdiction and return to a "source country" fight. A focus on eradication of coca and poppy fields in the Central American and Andean nations leads directly to an interest in a forward base that could facilitate intelligence gathering more easily than an air base in Texas or Arizona. Yet the United States attempted the source country strategy in the 1980s without success. The production of coca and coca paste simply moved to other areas where peasants poor enough to assume the risks grew the adaptable plant.[132]

The role of U.S. private investment in productive investment in Panama is small relative to U.S. foreign policy interests related to the canal and counternarcotics, but Panama is nonetheless heavily dependent on U.S. trade and investment. Most of the investment is in tertiary services such as insurance or corporations that serve as tax shelters. As a crossroads for international trade, however, Panama will have a key role in the U.S. vision for a hemispheric trading block that is competitive with Europe and the Pacific Rim.

Since the mid-1800s the transit zone across the Central American isthmus has symbolized U.S. imperialism and resulting patterns of dependent development. The 1977 Canal Treaties seemed to signal the restructuring of U.S. relations with the third world. But in Panama, as in most other Latin American nations, the nation's political and economic structures suffered in the 1980s as a consequence of both domestic and international forces. Government corruption, mismanagement, and repression—combined with the failure of popular movements and opposition political parties—undermined domestic stability. Working with domestic elites, the United States together with such international financial institutions as the World Bank and IMF imposed neoliberal economic policies that weakened national capacities to respond to the demands of the poor majorities.

The 1989 invasion was a brutal reminder of just how little U.S. relations with Panama and Latin America had changed. Similarly, rising U.S. pressures for countries to conform to its free trade and neoliberal restructuring policies affirm and perpetuate the U.S. hegemonic position in the hemisphere. The scheduled U.S. withdrawal from Panama provides an opportunity for the United States and an important Latin American country to break with conventional patterns and develop relations that are built less on domination and dependence and more on mutual interests and exchange.

At the same time, Panamanian support for the invasion and current polls indicating that most Panamanians do not want the United States to withdraw its military bases point to continuing internalized dependence and the difficulty of forging solutions that bolster national sovereignty while constraining U.S. dominance of hemispheric affairs. To restructure U.S.-Panama relations to reflect mutual interests and more equal exchange is a challenge reflected throughout the western hemisphere. For the United States, this will require a foreign policy that reflects a more enlightened concept of U.S. national interests that goes beyond short- and medium-term economic and military objectives.

References

Introduction

1. "Panama: Ever the Crossroads," *National Geographic*, April 1986.

Part 1: Government and Politics

1. In 1904, 1908, 1912, and 1916, the head of government was chosen by an electoral college. From 1920 to 1968 there was direct popular vote every four years. In 1972 and 1978, the presidential elections were conducted by the National Assembly. In 1984 the country returned to direct presidential vote. Marco A. Gandásegui, "La Democracia en Panamá," *Estudios Sociales Centroamericanos*, May-August 1988.

2. There are 71 elected deputies plus one so-called "Lone Ranger" seat for parties that retain their legal status but fail to gain any elected seats.

3. "Interview with Xabier Gorostiaga," *CEPAD Report*, September-October 1989.

4. Information from George Priestley, *Military Government and Popular Participation in Panama: The Torrijos Regime, 1968-1975* (Boulder: Westview Press, 1986), p. 11.

5. Ibid.

6. Quoted in John Weeks, "Of Puppets and Heroes," *NACLA Report on the Americas*, July-August 1988, p. 13.

7. A Costa Rican judicial investigation concluded in a December 1989 report that a drug and arms trafficking network including CIA operatives working with Lt. Col. Oliver North, Costa Rican officials, and Gen. Noriega was responsible for the 1984 press conference bombing at La Penca, Nicaragua which killed three journalists. The report also recommended the indictment of Lt. Col. Luis Córdova, a close Noriega associate, for the 1985 murder of Dr. Hugo Spadafora, an associate of Eden Pastora, target of the 1984 bombing. Shortly before his murder, Spadafora told pilots working as part of this drug and arms network that he intended to expose Noriega's drug trafficking. *Public Prosecutor's Investigation of "La Penca" Case* (San José: Costa Rica Department of Justice, December 26, 1989).

8. In addition to the term *rabiblancos* Panamanians also use *rabiprietos* (*mestizos*) and *rabicolorados* (blacks).

9. For a revealing look at the overlap between the country's political parties and business organizations see: Juana Camargo, "Los Partidos Políticos y los Gremios Empresiarles en la Coyuntura Actual," *Revista Panameña de Sociología*, No. 5 (Universidad de Panamá, Departamento de Sociología, 1989).

10. Sharon Phillipps, "Labor Policy in an Inclusionary-Authoritarian Regime: Panama Under Torrijos," Dissertation (University of New Mexico, July 1987), pp. 26-28.

11. John Weeks, "Panama: The Roots of Current Political Instability," *Third World Quarterly*, July 1987, p. 769.

12. CONEP, *En Pocas Palabras, Esto Es CONEP*, cited by Phillipps, op. cit., p. 26.

13. Phillipps, "Labor Policy," p. 45.

14. Ibid., p. 47.

15. For a discussion of the crisis of hegemony in Panamanian politics between 1968 and 1984 see: Marco A. Gandásegui, "Militares y Crisis de los Partidos Políticos," *Tareas*, No. 66, June-September 1987.

16. The first National Guard commander, José Antonio Remón Cantera (1943-1952), was an impoverished cousin of the Chiari family. His successor, Bolívar Vallarino (1952-1968), was a member of an important pre-independence family.

17. Raúl Leís, "Cousins' Republic," *NACLA Report on the Americas*, July-August 1988, p. 24.

18. Phillipps, "Labor Policy," p. 63; Robert Howard Miller, "Military Government and Approaches to National Development," Dissertation (Miami: University of Miami, 1975).

19. Gandásegui, "Militares y Crisis."

20. Phillipps, "Labor Policy," p. 57.

21. José Sossa, *Imperialismos: Fuerzas Armadas y Partidos Políticos en Panamá* (Panama City: Ediciones Documentos, 1977), cited in Phillipps, "Labor Policy," p. 58.

22. Gandásegui, "Militares y Crisis," p. 30.

23. According to Panamanian law, a comptroller general stays on at least three months after a new government takes office. In this case, it meant that Rodríguez was the only "legal" official of the 1984 government.

24. While the 1972 National Assembly was elected, the 1989 assembly was appointed. Like the 1972-1978 period, Panama had both a president and head of government. Demetrio Lakas was president from 1972 to 1978.

25. Priestley, *Military Government*, p. 56.

26. Phillipps, "Labor Policy," p. 107.

27. Priestley, *Military Government*, pp. 36-50.

28. Ibid., p. 120.

29. Ibid.

30. Brook Larmer, "Noriega Pulls Election Strings," *Christian Science Monitor*, April 12, 1989.

31. *Central America Report*, April 12, 1991, p. 100.

32. Cruz was later released due to lack of evidence to support the charges against him.

33. Jorge Sarsanedas, "Panama in Brief," *Envío*, July 1994, p. 23.

34. For a good summary of election results see CELA's *Coyuntura 94*, May 1994.

35. Economist Intelligence Unit, *EIU Country Report: Panama*, 1995.

Part 2: Security Forces and Human Rights

1. See Steve Ropp, *Panamanian Politics: From Guarded Nation to National Guard* (New York: Praeger, 1982). Also see *Revista Panameña de Sociología*, No. 5: Marco A. Gandásegui, "Las PDF y el Año 2000;" Renato Pereira, "Fuerzas Armadas y Partidos Políticos;" Everardo Bósquez De León, "Fuerzas de Defensa y el Año 2000."

2. Marco A. Gandásegui, *Panamá: Crisis Política y Agresión Económica* (Panama City: CELA, 1989), p. 16.

3. Good sources for this period include Ropp, *Panamanian Politics*.

References

4. George Priestley, *Military Government and Popular Participation in Panama: The Torrijos Regime, 1968-1975* (Boulder: Westview Press, 1986).

5. Alfonso Villarreal, "Fuerzas Armadas de Panamá: Aspectos Históricos, Políticos, y Jurídicos de la Ley No. 20," in *Revista Panameña de Sociología*, No. 5 (Universidad de Panamá, Departamento de Sociología).

6. See Manuel A. Noriega, "Este pueblo tiene un nombre y su nombre es Panamá," *Lotería*, 1986.

7. Good sources include John Dinges, *Our Man in Panama* (New York: Random House, 1990) and Kevin Buckley, *Panama: The Whole Story* (New York: Simon & Schuster, 1991).

8. See Daniel Delgado, "La resistencia armada a la invasión de Panamá," *Tareas*, No. 81, 1992. Also see Clarence Briggs, *Operation Just Cause* (Harrisburg: Stackpole Books, 1990).

9. U.S. Embassy, *Panama Defense Forces*, Information handout (1989).

10. Kenneth Jones, ed., *Panama Now* (Panama City: Focus Publications, 1986), p. 21.

11. U.S. Embassy, *Panama Defense Forces*.

12. Ibid.

13. See Arnulfo Castrejón, "Las FDP asumirán la defensa del canal en el año 2000," *Partido Revolucionario Democrático*, No. 2, 1988 and Daniel Delgado, "Fundamentos para la estrategia de defensa de la República de Panamá," *La República*, 1988.

14. *Latin America Weekly Report*, October 26, 1989.

15. Council on Hemispheric Affairs, *Survey of Press Freedom in Latin America 1985-1986* (Washington: COHA, December 1986), p. 45.

16. Andres Oppenheimer, "Noriega's Next Move in Doubt," *Miami Herald*, May 12, 1989.

17. "Proytecto de Ley: La Ley Orgánica de la Fuerza Pública," April 1995.

18. Interview, Coalition of Canal Area Worker Unions, May 19, 1995.

19. *Derechos Humanos en Panama, 1992-1993* (Panama City: SERPAJ, 1994), pp. 244-5.

20. *Mesoamerica*, September 1994.

21. *Derechos Humanos en Panamá*, p. 23.

22. *Central America Report*, September 2, 1994.

23. *Derechos Humanos en Panamá*.

24. *Panamá América*, May 18, 1995.

Part 3: Economy

1. Raúl Leís, "Diez Ideas Sobre el Panamá de Hoy," *Este País Mes a Mes*, February 1990.

2. Panama's percapita GDP in 1993 was $2,381, compared to $1,144 in El Salvador, $825 in Honduras, $943 in Guatemala, $1,822 in Costa Rica, $512 in Nicaragua, and $2,255 in Belize. IDB, *Economic and Social Progress in Latin America, 1994 Report*. By comparison, Costa Rica ranked 42 and Honduras 116 in the UN Human Development Index.

3. *La Chiva*, No. 7, September 1994.

4. For a desription of the Panamanian oligarchy see: Marco A. Gandásegui, "La Concentración del Poder Económico en Panamá," *Tareas*, No. 18, 1967; William R. Hugh and Ivan A. Quintero, *¿Quiénes Son los Dueños de Panamá?* (Panama City: CEASPA, 1987).

5. Alfredo Castilero Calvo, "Subsistencia y Economía en la Sociedad Colonial," *Hombre y Cultura*, 1(2), 1991.

6. Hernán Porras, "Papel Histórico de las Grupos Humanos en Panamá," *Las Clases Sociales en Panamá* (Panama: CELA, 1993).

7. Ernesto Castillero Pimental, *Panamá y los Estados Unidos 1903-1953* (Panama: Universidad de Panamá, 1953).

8. Marco A. Gandásegui and George Priestley, "Panama: Political Crisis and Economic Aggression," *Central America Bulletin*, 8(3).

9. Ibid.

10. Omar Torrijos, *La Batalla de Panamá* (Buenos Aires, 1973), p. 111, as cited in George Priestley, *Military Government and Popular Participation in Panama: The Torrijos Regime, 1968-1975* (Boulder: Westview Press, 1986), p. 57.

11. Cited in Priestley, *Military Government,* p. 65.

12. Ibid., p. 119.

13. Rubén D. Herrera, *La Necesidad de Cambios Sociales en el Desarrollo Económico* (Panama: Asamblea de Representantes, 1974). See also Ramiro Vásquez Ch., *Panamá en la Linea de Omar* (Panama: Ed. Bayano, 1982).

14. IDEN, "Lineamientos para un programa mínimo de urgencia," in *Cuadernos Nacionales* (Universidad de Panamá), No. 2, 1989.

15. Rogelio Alvarado, "El refinanciamiento de la deuda pública en Panamá," in *Informativo Industrial,* No. 6, 1987. See also R. Alvarado, "Préstamo para el ajuste estructural," in *Análisis*, 6(7), 1984.

16. Rolando Armuelles, "Deuda Externa, Ajuste Estructural y el Sector Agropecuario," in *Memoria,* Congreso de Ingenieros Agrónomos, 1984.

17. MIPPE, *Estrategia a corto plazo para la recuperación económica de Panamá* (Panama: MIPPE, 1989), p. 183.

18. The month before, National Security Adviser John Poindexter had traveled to Panama to communicate U.S. policy concerning drug smuggling and internal politics. Some observers claim that Noriega tried to strike a deal to offer to do more to support U.S. foreign policy in Central America in return for an end to U.S. pressure. Others argue, however, that Noriega refused to do U.S. foreign policy bidding in Central America. See Dinges, *Our Man in Panama*, pp. 235-7.

19. AID, *U.S. Overseas Loans and Grants: Obligations and Loan Authorizations, July 1, 1945-September 30, 1987* (Washington: AID, 1989).

20. Mark Sullivan, "Panama: Dilemma for U.S. Policy," *CRS Review*, February 1989, p. 21.

21. Andrew Zimbalist and John Weeks, *Panama at the Crossroads: Economic Development and Political Change in the Twentieth Century* (Berkeley: University of California Press, 1991), p. 146.

22. The informal sector of the economy rose from 28.4 percent in 1987 to 35.6 percent a year later.

23. *Washington Report on the Hemisphere,* March 15, 1989 quoting Michael May, spokesperson of the American Chamber of Commerce.

24. Gary Clyde Hufbauer and Jeffrey Schott, *Economic Sanctions in Support of Foreign Policy Goals* (Washington: Institute for International Economics, 1983).

25. Inter-American Development Bank, *Economic and Social Progress in Latin America: 1991 Report.*

26. *Panama Update*, Winter 1995.

27. *Mesoamerica*, September 1994.

28. *Panama Update*, Spring 1995.

29. Inter-Press Service, "U.S. Increases Requirements for GATT Membership Bid," November 18, 1994.

30. *Central America Report*, December 2, 1994. The United States wanted tariffs lowered from as high as 90 percent to 15 percent or less, while Panamanian industrialists insisted that a 40 percent tariff ceiling should be as low as Panama should go as part of its liberalization initiatives.

References

31. In 1992 43 percent of the volume of trade that passed through the Panama Canal was en route to East Asia from the U.S. East Coast, 10 percent of trade was traveling from Europe to the U.S. West Coast, 6 percent from the U.S. East Coast to the West Coast of South America, and 5 percent from Europe to the South American West Coast. Other routes accounted for 35 percent of trade. *Canal de Panamá Hoy*, No. 11 (Panamá), 1993, p. 6.

32. House Subcommittee on Coast Guard and Navigation, Hearings, 103rd Congress, March 1, 1994, p. 43.

33. Panama recieved $384 million in 1993 from the Panama Canal, including $188 million in wages paid to Panamanians and $88 million in payments according to Panama Canal Treaties. For a continuing review of canal operations see *Canal de Panamá Hoy*, a bimonthly published by the Centro de Estudios Latinoamericanos (CELA) in Panama City.

34. Midori Iijima, "The Panama Crisis and Party Politics," in *International Relations*, Vol. 98, 1991.

35. Panama Canal Commission, information published by *Canal de Panamá Hoy*, No. 12, 1994. p. 3.

36. *Financial Audit: Panama Canal Commission's 1993 and 1994 Financial Statements*, GAO/AIMD-95-98, March 1995, p. 14.

37. *Panamá América*, May 24, 1995.

38. A proposal to impose a 1.5 percent tax on free zone transactions met stiff resistance from free zone companies.

39. Elton, "Serving Foreigners," *NACLA Report on the Americas*, 1988, p. 30. See also Kenneth Jones, ed., *Panama Now* (Panama City: Focus Publications, 1986) p. 62.

40. *Mesoamerica*, March 1995.

41. Zimbalist and Weeks, *Panama at the Crossroads*, p. 71.

42. Figure from the Panamanian Tourist Institute, 1982.

43. Stephen Labaton, "Panama Is Resisting U.S. Pressure," *New York Times,* February 6, 1990.

44. Elton, "Serving Foreigners," p. 28.

45. *El Boletín*, June 20, 1994, p. 4.

46. Panama Petroterminal is a joint venture with the government holding 40 percent, Northville Industries 38.75 percent, and Chicago Bridge and Iron 21.25 percent.

47. *Panama Now,* p. 28.

48. The average rates of tariff protection have been below those imposed by the members of the Central America Common Market, but Panama has also protected local industry with extensive import quotas. These quotas were often imposed by the government at the request of well-connected manufacturers. Andrew Zimbalist, "Panama," in *Struggle Against Dependence: Nontraditional Export Growth in Central America and the Caribbean* (Boulder: Westview Press, 1988), pp. 86-7.

49. Inter-Press Service, "Indigenas Demandan Suspender Concesiones Mineras," November 18, 1994.

50. "Indigenous Accuse Mining Company of Usurping Lands," *Panama Update*, No. 10, 1994.

51. *Este País Mes a Mes,* February 1989.

52. H. Jeffrey Leonard, *Natural Resources and Economic Development in Central America* (New Brunswick: Transaction Books, 1987) pp. 4, 16.

53. Leonard, ibid., pp. 18, 222.

54. Tom Barry, *Roots of Rebellion: Land and Hunger in Central America* (Boston: South End Press, 1987), p. 9; *Centro América 1988* (Guatemala City: Inforpress Centroamericana, 1989), pp. 235-6.

55. AID, *Panama: Country Development Strategy Statement FY1988-1992* (Washington: AID, 1986), p. 15.

56. George Priestley, *Military Government*, p. 55. The information for this section on Torrijos and the peasantry is taken largely from this study.

57. Ibid., p. 56.

58. Ibid., p. 63.

59. Ibid., p. 60.

60. Economist Intelligence Unit, *EIU Country Profile: Panama*, 1989.

61. AID, *Latin America and the Caribbean: Selected Economic and Social Data* (Washington, DC: May 1994), p. 138.

62. Silvio Hernandez, "Poverty and Unemployment Up Despite Growth," Inter-Press Service, November 21, 1994.

Part 4: Society and Environment

1. Didimo Castillo, "Movimientos Sociales Urbanos y Democracia: El Caso de Panamá," *Revista Panameña de Sociología,* No. 5 (Universidad de Panamá, Departamento de Sociología). The origins of the nationalist movement were the protests against the Filos-Hines treaty of 1947 that extended the U.S. lease on its military bases in Panama.

2. Raúl Leís, "Cuatro Ideas Sobre el Papel de Los Sectores Populares en la Coyuntura Actual," *Este País Mes a Mes,* October 1987.

3. Frederick Kempe, "Most Panamanians Stop Waiting for U.S. Godot," *Wall Street Journal,* October 13, 1989.

4. For a provocative analysis of the state of social movements see Briseida Allard, "Movimientos sociales y cuestión nacional en Panamá: Perspectivas al final del Siglo XX," *La Chiva*, April 1995.

5. Lucía Luna, "La Clara Intervención Estadounidense, Dirigida Contra el Grupo de Los Ocho," *Proceso*, March 7, 1988.

6. *Opinión Pública,* (a monthly journal published in Panama City by CELA), No. 22-45.

7. *Opinión Pública,* No. 35-6, January and February 1991.

8. Adela de Castro and Darinel Espino, ed., *El caloroso recibimiento a Bush* (Mexico: El Día, 1992).

9. James Aparicio, "Las Barriadas Brujas," *Diálogo Social*, October 1986.

10. "El Movimiento de Masas en Panamá Después de la Invasión," in *Revista Panameña de Sociología* No. 7, 1991, pp. 266-7.

11. Virgilio Hernández, "El Más Jóven Distrito," *Diálogo Social,* January 1986.

12. U.S. Department of Labor, *Foreign Labor Trends: Panama* (Panama City: U.S. Embassy, 1993).

13. Ibid.; UNICEF, *Tendencias y Desafíos del Desarrollo Social en Panamá*, April 1994.

14. Two important sources on labor movement history are: Andrés Achong, *Orígines del Movimiento Obrero Panameño* (Panama City: CELA, 1980), and Marco A. Gandásegui, et. al., *Las Luchas Obreras en Panamá: 1850-1978* (Panama City: CELA, 1980).

15. Sharon Phillipps, "Labor Policy," p. 79. Much of the information for this section on labor history is drawn from this study.

16. Gandásegui, *Las Luchas Obreras en Panamá*, p. 43.

17. Hernando Franco Muñoz, *Movimiento Obrero Panameño 1914-1921* (Panama City: 1979), p. 15.

18. Phillipps, "Labor Policy," p. 83.

19. Ibid., p. 86.

References

20. Renato Periera, *Panamá: Fuerzas Armadas y Política* (Panama City: Ediciones Nueva Universidad, 1979), pp. 22-3.

21. Carlos George, "La Conciliación y el Arbitraje en Materia Laboral y su Vigencia en Panamá," Thesis (Panama: Universidad de Panamá, 1972), p. 206, cited by Phillipps, "Labor Policy," p. 88.

22. César Pereira Burgos, "La Huelga Bananera de 1960," *Tareas* No. 4, 1961.

23. Walter LaFeber, *The Panama Canal: The Crisis in Historical Perspective* (New York: Oxford University Press, 1978), p. 171.

24. Jorge Fabrega, *Labor Code of the Republic of Panama* (Panama: Litho Impresora, 1974), cited in Phillipps, "Labor Policy," p. 88.

25. There is some discussion whether Torrijos favored the more progressive CNTP over the CTRP. After the formation of the confederation in 1970, CNTP grew rapidly, counting on as many affiliates as the CTRP by the end of the decade. The 1973 CNTP National Congress was held in the National Assembly building, and the large banana unions both affiliated with the CNTP during the 1970s. But the CTRP was not shut out by the Torrijos regime. Its officials were appointed to head the Labor Ministry and as the country's ambassador to Jamaica.

26. Al Weinrub, "Panama's Unions Oppose U.S. Intervention," *Labor Report on Central America,* May-June 1988.

27. *Boletín Mensual,* January/February 1993, p. 8.

28. *Inforpress Centroamericana,* September 2, 1993.

29. "Estrategia Lejos de Ser Viable," *Tareas,* No. 76, 1990, pp. 3-8.

30. AIFLD's description of operations in Panama for 1985, made available from AID's Latin American Regional Office.

31. Daphine Wysham, "Panama: Sovereignty Treaties," Distributed by CARNet, December 22, 1989.

32. The 1977 Panama Canal Treaties and their U.S. implementing legislation, Public Law 96-70 of 1979, established a special labor relations structure for U.S. military forces and the Panama Canal Commission which places all their civilian employees under U.S. federal labor law. U.S. Embassy, *Foreign Labor Trends* (Washington: Department of Labor, 1986), p. 10.

33. Lina Boza, "Posición de los trabajadores frente a la reversión del Canal de Panamá," in *Tareas,* No. 86, 1994.

34. U.S. Department of Labor, *Foreign Labor Trends: Panama,* 1993, p. 9.

35. Ibid., p. 215.

36. Otto S. Wald, "Condiciones Generales de Salud en la República de Panamá," *Revista Panameña de Sociología,* No. 3 (Universidad de Panamá, Departmento de Sociología, 1987); Bread for the World Institute, *Hunger 1994: Transforming the Politics of Hunger,* 1994.

37. Francisco Cedeño, *Salud y comunidad* (Panama: CELA, 1981).

38. Wald, "Condiciones Generales de Salud."

39. Interview at the Dirección de Estadísticas y Censo, 1994.

40. Ernesto A. and Carmelo Mesa Lago, *La Seguridad Social en Panamá: Avances y Problemas,* cited in Wald, "Condiciones Generales de Salud."

41. Wald, "Condiciones Generales de Salud."

42. Kenneth Jones, ed., *Panama Now* (Panama City: Focus Publications, 1986), p. 14.

43. Paik-Swan Low, "Contraception: Is it Just Say No?" *Links* (NCAHRN), Winter 1987.

44. Fundación para la Promoción de la Mujer, *Situación de la mujer rural en Panamá* (Panama: 1992), p. 14.

45. Silvio Hernandez, "El Rock Se Empina como Arma Contra el SIDA," Inter-Press Service, November 22, 1994.

46. U.S. Information Service, *Panamanian Media 1968-1989.*

47. A group within *La Estrella* split off to produce a new daily in mid-1995.

48. U.S. Embassy, "Country Data: Panama," January 1, 1989.

49. *Este País Mes a Mes,* April 1989, p. 5.

50. William Branigan, "U.S. Move in Panama Called Inept," *Washington Post,* April 29, 1989.

51. Ken Silverstein, "The Panama Story, or Here We Go Again," *Columbia Journalism Review,* May-June 1988, p. 20.

52. *La Estrella de Panamá,* January 10, 1990, p. 2A.

53. Clifton L. Holland, "Religion in Central America," *Mesoamerica*, February 1995. Holland is executive director of the Latin American Socio-Religious Studies Program (PRO-LADES), the organization that conducted the surveys.

54. Bertrand de la Grange, "Church Drops Neutral Façade," *Miami Herald,* May 21, 1989.

55. Holland, "Religion," p. 129. In the last decade, there has been an increase in native vocations, largely due to the expansion of the church from 23 parishes in the mid-1970s to 74 in the mid-1980s.

56. James C. Rauner, "The Church Suffers with the Poor," *America,* October 29, 1988.

57. Jones, *Panama Now,* p. 88.

58. For an excellent examination of the social and political role of the Catholic church see Andrés Opazo Bernales, *Panamá: La Iglesia y la Lucha de los Pobres* (San José: DEI, 1988).

59. Ibid., p. 48.

60. Ibid., p. 69.

61. Guillermo Meléndez, "Church Workers Unite Against Detractors," *Latinamerica Press,* June 16, 1983.

62. Holland, "Religion."

63. Ibid. This excellent overview of religion and churches was the source for most of this section on Protestantism in Panama.

64. Aida Libia de Rivera, *Perfil de la situación de la mujer en Panamá y lineamientos de acciones prioritarias* (Panama: CEDEM, 1992), p. 25.

65. International Labor Office, *Panamá: Situación y Perspectivas del Empleo Femenino* (Santiago, Chile: OIT, 1984), cited in International Center for Research on Women, "Integrating Women into Development Programs: A Guide for Implementation for Latin America and the Caribbean," *Gender Issues in Latin America and the Caribbean* (Washington: AID, 1986), p. 10.

66. United Nations, *La Mujer en el Sector Urbano* (Santiago: UN, 1985).

67. "La Situación y Luchas de la Mujer en Panamá," *Cuadernos Liberación de la Mujer* (Partido Socialista de Trabajadores, ca. 1984).

68. National Forum for Women and Development, *Plan Nacional Mujer y Desarrollo, 1994-2000,* Panama, 1993.

69. Urania Ungo, "La Mujer y La Cruzada Civilista," *Diálogo Social,* August-September 1987.

70. CELA, *Encuesta Elecciones 94,* No. 1-5, 1993-4.

71. For a discussion of blacks and black organizing in Panama see: Gerardo Maloney, "El Movimiento Negro en Panamá," *Revista Panameña de Sociología*, No.5 (Universidad de Panamá, Departamento de Sociología, 1989).

72. Michael L. Conniff, *Black Labor on a White Canal: Panama, 1904-1981* (Pittsburgh, University of Pittsburgh Press, 1985).

73. George Priestley, "Etnia, Clase, y Nación," *Tareas,* No. 67, October-December 1987. Also see Conniff, *Black Labor.*

74. Ibid., p. 40.

References

75. Ibid., p. 43. Arias was quickly deposed and the constitution annulled.

76. Ibid., p. 41.

77. Burton L. Gordon, *A Panama Forest and Shore: Natural History and Amerindian Culture in Bocas del Toro* (Boxwood Press, 1982).

78. "The History of the Guaymís: They Still Demand Their Land," *Barricada International,* February 25, 1988.

79. Gordon, *Forest and Shore.*

80. Slash-and-burn agriculture requires a fallow period of 25 years—something no longer possible as the country's agricultural frontier shrinks.

81. For a sobering examination of the workplace hazards facing the Ngobe-Buglé migratory workforce see: Phillipe Bourgois, "Hazardous Pesticides in Panama: Guaymí Laborers at Risk," *Cultural Survival Quarterly,* 9(4), 1985.

82. Peter H. Herlihy, "Chocó Indian Relocation in Darién, Panama," *Cultural Survival Quarterly,* 9(2), pp. 43, 44.

83. Peter H. Herlihy, "Indians and Rainforest Collide: The Cultural Parks of Darién," *Cultural Survival Quarterly,* 10(3), pp. 57-61.

84. Gloria Evelyn Garvin, "Kuna Psychotherapeutics: A Psychological, Social, and Theoretical Analysis," (UME Dissertation Service, degree date: 1983); James Howe, *The Kuna Gathering: Contemporary Village Politics in Panama* (Austin: University of Texas Press, 1986), p. 9.

85. Howe, *Kuna Gathering,* pp. 10-3.

86. Brian Houseal, Craig MacFarland, Guillermo Archibold, and Aurelio Chiari, "Indigenous Cultures and Protected Areas in Central America," *Cultural Survival Quarterly,* 9(1), 1985, pp. 15-8.

87. Howe, *Kuna Gathering,* pp. 24-8.

88. Ibid.

89. Jason Clay, "Indigenous People and Tropical Forests: Models of Land Use and Management from Latin America," *Cultural Survival Report 27,* 1988, pp. 66-7.

90. U.S. Government Accounting Office (GAO), *Central America: Conditions of Refugees and Displaced Persons* (Washington: 1989).

91. Leonard, *Natural Resources,* pp. 26, 27.

92. Ibid., p. 25; "Global Status of Mangrove Ecosystems," *Environmentalist,* 1983.

93. Leonard, *Natural Resources,* p. 156.

94. World Bank, *Social Indicators of Development 1993* (Baltimore: Johns Hopkins University Press, 1994).

95. AID, *Latin America and the Caribbean: Selected Economic and Social Data,* p. 115; Inter-Press Service, "Deforestation Threatens Water Supplies," April 25, 1995.

96. Stanley Heckadon and Jaime Espinoza, *Agonía de la Nauturaleza* (Panama City: IDIAP-STRI, 1985). The estimated forested area in 1947 was 70 percent, dropping to 38 percent by 1980.

97. Leonard, *Natural Resources,* pp. 130, 131.

98. *The Amicus Journal,* Fall 1988.

99. Panama Canal Commission, "Reports to Congress, 1986."

100. World Resources Institute, *World Resources Report 1994-95.*

101. *Ancon Boletín,* January 1989.

102. Gloria Batista, "The Campaign to Save the Atlantic Coast of Panama," *Earth Island Journal,* Winter 1988.

103. Inter-Press Service, January 27, 1995; interview by John Lindsay-Poland, February 1995.

Part 5: U.S.-Panama Relations

1. Michael L. Conniff, *Panama and the United States: The Forced Alliance* (Athens: University of Georgia, 1992), pp. 18-20.

2. Alex Perez-Venero, *Before the Five Frontiers: Panama from 1821-1903* (New York: AMS Press, 1978), pp. 67-8.

3. Conniff, *Panama and the United States*, p. 28.

4. Ernesto Castillero Pimentel, *Panama y los Estados Unidos*, pp. 16-7.

5. Walter LaFeber, *The Panama Canal: The Crisis in Historical Perspective* (New York: Oxford University Press, 1989), pp. 29-30.

6. J. Michael Hogan, *The Panama Canal in American Politics* (Carbondale: University of Illinois, 1986), pp. 44-5, 51.

7. David McCullough, *The Path Between the Seas: The Creation of the Panama Canal, 1870-1914* (New York: Simon & Schuster, 1977), p. 511. This is perhaps the most thorough work on the construction of the Canal.

8. See Conniff, *Panama and the United States*.

9. Excellent works on race relations during the construction years include Michael Conniff, *Black Labor*; Gerstle Mack, *The Land Divided* (New York: Knopf, 1944); and Velma Norton, *The Silver Men: West Indian Labour Migration in Panama, 1850-1914* (Kingston: University of the West Indies, 1984).

10. McCullough, *Path Between the Seas*, p. 559.

11. Conniff, *Panama and the United States*, pp. 74-6, 85.

12. LaFeber, *The Panama Canal*, p. 33.

13. Conniff, *Panama and the United States*, p. 86.

14. LaFeber, *The Panama Canal*, pp. 79-80; Leís, "Diez Ideas Sobre el Panamá de Hoy," p. 41.

15. LaFeber, *The Panama Canal*, p. 31.

16. Quaker Action Group, *Resistance in Latin America: The Pentagon, the Oligarchies & Nonviolent Action* (Philadelphia: AFSC, 1970).

17. Hogan, *Panama Canal in American Politics*.

18. Quoted in Richard F. Nyrop, ed., *Panama: A Country Study* (Washington: American University, 1981), p. 198.

19. University of Panama, Instituto del Canal de Panamá y Estudios Internacionales, *Libertad de Nevagación por el Canal de Panamá* (Panama: 1994), pp. 51-2.

20. Rebecca L. Grant, *A RAND Note: Operation Just Cause and the U.S. Policy Process* (Santa Monica: RAND, 1991), p. 17.

21. Dinges, *Our Man in Panama*, p. 238.

22. Peter Dale Scott and Jonathan Marshall, *Cocaine Politics: Drugs, Armies and the CIA in Central America* (Berkeley: University of California Press, 1991), pp. 2, 102.

23. Grant, *RAND Note*, p. 16.

24. Dinges, *Our Man in Panama*, pp. 258-9.

25. Grant, *RAND Note*, pp. 18-9.

26. Ibid., p. 20.

27. Ibid., p. 21.

28. John Weeks, "Of Puppets and Heroes," *NACLA Report on the Americas*, July-August 1988, pp. 18-9. The Latin American Economic System passed a similar resolution in March 1988—with 23 of 26 nations voting in favor.

29. Grant, *RAND Note*, pp. 33-4.

30. Conniff, *Panama and the United States*, p. 164.

References

31. Tom Wicker, "Panama and the Press," *New York Times*, April 20, 1990.

32. University of Panama, mimeo letter, January 1990; Raúl Leís, "Crisis, búsqueda y alternativas," *La Estrella*, December 18, 1993. This report was disputed by the new geology director at the University of Panama in a letter to U.S. Congressmen. See House Armed Services Committee, Investigations Subcommittee, *The Invasion of Panama: How Many Innocent Bystanders Perished?*, July 1992.

33. Interview, Nicolasa Terreros, SERPAJ-Panamá, March 1990.

34. U.S. General Accounting Office, *Panama: Issues Relating to the U.S. Invasion*, April 1991, pp. 2-3.

35. Mark P. Sullivan, *Panama-U.S. Relations: Continuing Policy Concerns*, Congressional Research Service Issue Brief, September 4, 1992, pp. 5-6.

36. John T. Fishel, *The Fog of Peace: Planning and Executing the Restoration of Panama* (Carlisle Barracks: Strategic Studies Institute, U.S. Army War College, 1992), p. 21.

37. Committee of Santa Fe, *A Strategy for Latin America in the Nineties*, 1988, p. 34. The Committee of Santa Fe was composed of radically conservative thinkers who assembled a policy blueprint, first for the incoming Reagan administration, then for what would be the Bush administration in 1988.

38. Washington Office on Latin America, *Clear and Present Dangers: The U.S. Military and the War on Drugs in the Andes*, Washington, 1991, p. 23.

39. Conniff, *Panama and the United States*, pp. 158, 162.

40. Noam Chomsky, *Year 501: The Conquest Continues* (Boston: South End Press, 1993), p. 89.

41. Memorandum from Maj. Joseph A. Goetzke, JA, reproduced in Investigations Subcommittee of the House Armed Services Committee, *The Invasion of Panama*, July 1992, p. 204.

42. John Weeks and Phil Gunson, *Panama: Made in the USA* (London: Latin America Bureau, 1991), p. 6.

43. Cámara de Comercio, *Estimación del monto total de las pérdidas ocasionadas por la acción bélica y por el saqueo a empresas comerciales e industriales*, December 29, 1989, cited in Roberto N. Méndez, *¿Liberación... o crimen de guerra?* (Panama: CELA, 1994), p. 219.

44. *La Estrella*, October 3, 1992.

45. Memorandum, Center for Constitutional Rights, December 1994.

46. Sullivan, *Panama-U.S. Relations*; Associated Press, December 15, 1992.

47. Leonard, *Natural Resources*, p. 112; President's message, "Development concerning the blocking of Panamanian government assets," October 3, 1994.

48. Sullivan, *Panama-U.S. Relations*, pp. 8-9.

49. GAO, *Foreign Assistance: U.S. Efforts to Spur Panama's Economy through Cash Transfers*, May 1993; GAO, *Aid to Panama: Status of Emergency Assistance to Revitalize the Economy*, April 1991; *Washington Post*, June 13, 1992.

50. *Washington Post*, June 13, 1992.

51. Senate Subcommittee on Terrorism, Narcotics and International Operations, May 6, 1992, pp. 18, 40.

52. Interview, Faye Armstrong, U.S. State Department, April 19, 1995.

53. *La Prensa*, July 7, 1993.

54. AID, *Congressional Presentation FY1996*, pp. 635-40.

55. EPICA, *Panama: Sovereignty for a Land Divided* (Washington: 1976), p. 11.

56. Department of Commerce, *Survey of Current Business*, August 1994, p. 137.

57. Charlotte Elton, "Serving Foreigners," *NACLA Report on the Americas*, July-August 1988.

58. Richard Millett, "Looking beyond Noriega," *Foreign Policy*, Summer 1988, p. 47.

59. Data from the Resource Center Compilation of Corporations, 1985; Tom Barry and Debra Preusch, *The Central America Fact Book*, New York: Grove Press, 1986, p. 310. U.S. investors in the oil pipeline were able to recoup their investment in just 18 months. See Elton, "Serving Foreigners," p. 28.

60. *Panamá América*, February 3, 1992.

61. See speech by Hinton to the American Chamber of Commerce, *La Prensa*, December 21, 1993.

62. Inter-Press Service, November 18 and 24, 1994.

63. *Washington Post*, January 31, 1993.

64. "Como en las Bahamas," *Este Pais*, June-August 1991.

65. Sullivan, *Panama-U.S. Relations*, p. 10; Interview, Panama Desk, U.S. State Dept., February 27, 1995; *La Prensa*, May 23, 1995.

66. Senate Subcommittee on Terrorism, Narcotics and International Operations, hearings, May 6, 1992, pp. 10, 32; *La Estrella*, August 15, 1992.

67. State Department, Bureau of International Narcotics Matters, *International Narcotics Control Strategy Report*, April 1994.

68. Inter-Press Service, April 21, 1994, July 28, 1994.

69. Inter-Press Service, March 3, 1995.

70. "Overview of the U.S. Southern Command," Headquarters, U.S. Southern Command, November 1994.

71. Dinges, *Our Man in Panama*, p. 149; "Panama Strongman Said to Trade in Drugs, Arms and Illicit Money," *New York Times*, June 12, 1986.

72. Raúl Leís, *Comando Sur: Poder Hostil* (Panama, CEASPA, 1985), pp. 55-6; "U.S. Pilots Fly Spotter Missions," *Los Angeles Times*, March 12, 1984.

73. See for example annual testimonies by SouthCom Commanders before the Senate Armed Services Committee.

74. Interview, U.S. Southern Command, December, 1993.

75. DOD Comptroller's Office, communiqué, May 1, 1995; House Appropriations Subcommittee on DOD, hearings, March 1, 1990; *New York Times*, March 31, 1995; *La Prensa*, May 25, 1995. The U.S. military presence was to be reduced to 7,500 by the end of 1995.

76. "Counterdrug Assistance: The Number One Priority," *Military Review*, March 1993, p. 26.

77. Washington Office on Latin America, *Clear and Present Dangers*, 1991, p. 105.

78. Senate Armed Services Committee, statement of Gen. George Joulwan, February 1991. "Overview of the U.S. Southern Command."

79. Seymour Hersh, "Our Man in Panama," *Life*, January 1990, pp. 81-93.

80. See declarations by President Endara and Foreign Minister Julio Linares, *La Prensa*, July 8 and 11, 1993; Linares in *La Prensa*, March 10, 1992; and Sullivan, *Panama-U.S. Relations*, p. 4.

81. Gerardo Gonzalez in *La Estrella*, May 1, 1993.

82. Munger, Brehm, Mendel and Ruhl, *U.S. Army South after Withdrawal from Panama (USARSO-2000)* (Carlisle Barracks: Strategic Studies Institute, U.S. Army War College, 1991), p. 33.

83. Public Law 102-190, Section 3505, December 5, 1991.

84. Interview, U.S. Southern Command, January 13, 1995.

85. See *La Prensa*, December 25, 1991; *Canal de Panamá Hoy*, CELA, February 1994.

86. *La Jornada*, January 18, 1994.

87. *Panamá América*, April 12, 1993.

88. *Canal de Panamá Hoy*, CELA, February 1994.

References

89. Panama Canal Treaty Implementation Plan briefing, U.S. Southern Command, December 1993. SouthCom broke down this amount as follows: $86.3 million on salaries to Panamanians; $84.5 million on local purchases of goods and services; $21.2 million on construction and repair contracts; $63 million on personal expenditures.

90. *Panamá América*, June 30, 1993.

91. Interview with Victoria Figge, Panama City, December 1993.

92. Interview with Charlotte Elton, Panama City, December 1993.

93. Rafael Arosemena, speech given to Colón Association of Business Executives, 1993.

94. Interview, May 25, 1995.

95. See Jaime Espinosa González, *La contaminación potencial en áreas militares del Canal de Panamá* (Panama: CEASPA, 1994).

96. Inter-Press Service, August 1, 1994; Leís, *Comando Sur*, p. 97.

97. Leís, ibid., p. 13.

98. Fernando Manfredo, *El Panamá América*, January 10, 1995, p. 2.

99. DEPAT, interview, January 1995.

100. Declassified memo, "DOD policy and procedures for the realignment of overseas sites," U.S. Secretary of Defense, January 1992.

101. OCONUS, "Defense Environmental Alert Qs and As Regarding DOD Environmental Restoration Policy," 1994.

102. Implementation Agreement for Article IV of the Panama Canal Treaty, Article IV, section (4).

103. Interviews, U.S. Southern Command, January 1995.

104. *La Prensa*, November 5, 1994.

105. "Comentarios al discurso del Embajador Estadounidense en Panamá," Instituto del Canal de Panamá y Estudios Internacionales, University of Panama, 1993; Masateru Ito, "¿Perdió interés Japón en un canal a nivel por el istmo de Panamá?" *Canal de Panamá Hoy*, August 1993, p. 3.

106. "Comisión Tripartita recomienda tercer juego de esclusas," *Canal de Panamá Hoy*, October 1993; Inter-Press Service, September 18, 1993.

107. Inter-Press Service, September 18, 1993; "Visita de Greenpeace e informe de Comisión Tripartita," *Canal de Panamá Hoy*, February 1994.

108. Presidential Message, "Recommendations for Changes to the Panama Canal Commission," April 12, 1994, p. 3.

109. "Pentagon official opposes shifting Panama Canal Commission control," *Journal of Commerce and Commercial*, February 19, 1992.

110. Interview, House National Security Committee professional staff, April 5, 1995.

111. *La Estrella de Panamá*, May 29, 1994.

112. Interview with Congressional staffer, December 1994.

113. "Panama Canal Gridlock Raises Questions About its Management," *Miami Herald*, January 31, 1995.

114. "Shipping firms concerned about Canal administration after 2000," *Christian Science Monitor*, April 23, 1992; House Subcommittee on Coast Guard and Navigation, Hearings, 103rd Congress, March 1, 1994, p. 12.

115. Inter-Press Service, November 23 and 25, 1994.

116. "Haitian and Cuban Refugee Controversy," *Panama Update*, Autumn 1994.

117. Testimony by Frederick C. Smith, Western Hemisphere Subcommittee, House International Affairs Committee, March 9, 1995, p. 5.

118. *La Prensa*, March 12, 1995.

119. *La Prensa*, March 15, 1995.

120. Inter-Press Service, March 15, 1995.

121. Interview, March 16, 1995.

122. Inter-Press Service, February 8, 1995.

123. Inter-Press Service, February 21, 1995.

124. Inter-Press Service, March 15, 1995.

125. Testimony of Philip M. Crane, Western Hemisphere Subcommittee, House International Relations Committee, March 9, 1995.

126. Interview, House National Security Committee staff, April 5, 1995.

127. Testimony by Anne Patterson, Deputy Assistant Secretary for Interamerican Affairs before Western Hemisphere Subcommittee, House National Security Committee, March 9, 1995.

128. Ibid.

129. AID, *Congressional Presentation FY1996*, p. 635. The fourth interest identified was a strong economy in order to provide markets for U.S. exports.

130. "US Army Role Questioned," *Latinamerica Press*, March 16, 1995.

131. Presentation by General Barry R. McCaffrey before the Senate Armed Services Committee, March 2, 1994.

132. For extended analyses of this phenomenon, see Washington Office on Latin America, *Clear and Present Dangers* and Diego García-Sayán (ed.), *Narcotráfico: Realidades y Alternativas* (Lima: Comisión Andina de Juristas, 1990).

Bibliography

The following periodicals are useful sources of information and analysis on Panama:

Análisis, Revistas Interamericanas.
Canal Panamá de Hoy, Centro de Estudios Latinoamericanos "Justo Arosemena," bimonthly.
Central America Report, Inforpress Centroamericana, weekly.
La Chiva, Centro de Estudios y Acción Social Panameño, monthly.
Panama Update, Fellowship of Reconcialition Task Force on Latin America and the Caribbean.
Premisas, Centro de Estudios Latinoamericanos "Justo Arosemena."
Revista Panameña de Sociología, Universidad de Panamá.
Tareas, Revista del Centro de Estudios Latinoamericanos, bimonthly.

The following reports, books and articles contain valuable background on many issues important to understanding Panama:

Clarence E. Briggs, *Operation Just Cause* (Harrisburg: Stackpole Books, 1990).
Kevin Buckley, *Panama: The Whole Story* (New York: Simon & Schuster, 1991).
Michael L. Conniff, *Black Labor on a White Canal: Panama, 1904-1981* (Pittsburgh: University of Pittsburgh Press, 1985).
John Dinges, *Our Man in Panama* (New York: Random House, 1990).
William Donnelly, M. Roth, and Linda Harrington, *Operation Just Cause* (New York: McMillan, 1991).

Marco A. Gandásegui, *La democracia en Panamá* (Mexico: Universidad Autónoma de México, 1989).

Carl Glenn, ed., *The US invasion of Panamá: The Truth Behind Operation Just Cause* (Boston: South End Press, 1991).

Simeón González H., *La crisis del torrijismo y las elecciones de 1984* (Panama: Ediciones Horizonte, 1985).

William R. Hughes and Ivan A. Quintero, *¿Quiénes son los dueños de Panamá?* (Panama: Centro de Estudios y Acción Social Panameño, 1987).

Christina Jacqueline Johns and P. Ward Johnson, *State Crime, the Media, and the Invasion of Panama* (London, Praeger, 1994).

Frederick Kempe, *Divorcing the Dictator* (New York: G.P. Putnam's Sons, 1990).

Walter LaFeber, *The Panama Canal: The Crisis in Historical Perspective* (New York: Oxford University Press, 1978).

José de Jesús Martínez, *La invasión* (Panamá: Ediciones Causadías, 1991).

José de Jesús Martínez, *Mi general Torrijos* (Havana: Casa de las Américas, 1987).

Sharon Phillipps, *Labor Policy in an Inclusionary-Authoritarian Regime: Panama Under Torrijos*, Dissertation (Albuquerque: University of New Mexico, 1987).

César Picón & Rodrigo Tarté, eds., *Ambiente y desarrollo: Panamá ante el desafío global* (Panama: NATURA/UNESCO/MinEd, 1994).

George Priestley, *Military Government and Popular Participation in Panama: The Torrijos Regime, 1968-1975* (Boulder: Westview Press, 1986).

Peter J. Schraeder, ed., *Intervention into the 1990s: US Foreign Policy in the 3rd World* (Boulder: Lynne Riener, 1992).

Giancarlo Soler T., *La invasión a Panamá: Estrategias y tácticas en el nuevo orden mundial* (Panamá: CELA, 1993).

Ricaurte Soler, *La invasión de EEUU a Panamá* (México: Siglo XXI, 1991).

Rolando Sterling, *La batalla de San Miguelito* (Panamá: CELA, 1991).

John Weeks and Phil Gunson, *Panama: Made in the USA* (London, Latin American Bureau, 1991).

Philip E. Wheaton, *Panama Invaded* (Trenton: The Red Sea Press, 1992).

Bibliography

Andrew Zimbalist and John Weeks, *Panama at the Crossroads: Economic Development and Political Change in the Twentieth Century* (Berkeley, University of California, 1994).

Chronology

1513	Balboa crosses Isthmus of Panama and claims Pacific Ocean basin for Crown of Spain.
1519	City of Our Lady of the Ascension of Panama founded looking into Pacific, foreshadowing Panama's future role in world trade.
1533	Pizarro sails south from Panama City; conquers Incan empire one of the richest American civilizations.
1534	Charles V of Spain orders territorial governor to study possibility of building canal to join Chagres River and South Sea.
1671	English pirate Henry Morgan attacks and destroys Panama City. City refounded at present site two years later.
1694	William Patterson, founder of Bank of England, tries to interest England in developing canal through Isthmus of Panama.
1789	Alexander Von Humbolt explores America and recommends nine possible routes for interoceanic canal, including passages through Nicaragua, Panama, and Colombia.
1821	Panama declares independence from Spain and joins Simon Bolívar's Great Colombia.
1826	Bolívar convenes first Conference of American Republics in Panama City.
1846	Mallarino-Bidlack Treaty gives U.S. government powers to guarantee neutrality and sovereign rights of New Granada on Isthmus.
1849	Gold rush makes Panama valuable transit route from U.S. Atlantic coast to California.
1850	U.S. businessmen finance construction of 48-mile (80 kilometer) Transcontinental Panama Railway, completed in 1855.
1865	U.S. troops intervene three times in next eight years to protect U.S. interests.
1878	Universal Interoceanic Canal Company (French stock) acquires exclusive right to build canal through Panama.

1902	U.S. Congress authorizes President Theodore Roosevelt to acquire strip of land in Panama from Colombia to build interoceanic canal.
1903	Secessionists declare Department of Panama an independent republic; new flag is raised by U.S. Army Corps of Engineers as three U.S. gunboats prevent landing of Colombian troops.
	U.S. Secretary of State John Hay and French entrepreneur Philippe Bunau Varilla formulate canal treaty very favorable to United States, authorizes United States to construct, maintain, operate, protect, and sanitize interoceanic canal through Panama "in perpetuity," allowing the U.S. to act "as if it were the sovereign of the territory." Panamanian signatory lacked full powers and credentials to sign treaty.
1904	U.S. troops intervene to quash protests against the Hay-Bunau Varilla Treaty.
	New constitution promulgated which grants United States right to intervene "in any part of Panama, to reestablish public peace and constitutional order." Panama informs the United States that the canal treaty does not entail a territorial grant or transfer of sovereignty.
	National army disbanded and Panama establishes monetary system based on U.S. dollar.
1906	Governor of Canal Zone, on instructions from President Theodore Roosevelt, opens zone to international trade, establishes duties on imported goods. U.S. Congress approves John Stephens' plan to build lock canal which raises vessels from sea level into artificial lake created for navigation.
1908	U.S. troops intervene in Panama for first of four times within next decade.
1914	Panama Canal opens for operation.
1918	U.S. troops intervene in Chiriquí province and remain for next two years surveying rich lowlands where United Fruit later expands its banana empire.
1920	United Brotherhood of Maintenance Way calls strike of over 17,000 canal workers.
1921	U.S. Navy intervenes in border conflict between Panama and Costa Rica set off by competing banana empires (Standard Fruit vs. United Fruit).
	Formation of Workers Federation of the Republic of Panama.
1925	Massive rent strike prompts arrival of U.S. troops in Panama City resulting in nine deaths.
1926	Panama and United States sign treaty designed to eliminate conflicts, but which legalizes many of them. Treaty is rejected by Panamanian Assembly.
1930	Government curtails labor organizing for next 15 years.
1932	Election of Harmodio Arias Madrid.
1936	Election of Justo Díaz Arosemena.

Panama and United States sign General Treaty of Friendship and Cooperation, which maintains all stipulations of 1903 treaty except the guarantee of Panama's independence and right of United States to intervene in Panama.

1939   After three year delay, revised treaty ratified by Washington.

Arosemena dies and is replaced by First Vice President Boyd.

1940   National Party candidate Arnulfo Arias Madrid elected.

1941   New constitution promulgated.

Arias toppled by U.S.-backed civilian coup and constitution declared void. Adolfo de la Guardia replaces Arias.

1942   Treaty with United States, to expire in six years, allows United States to build military installations and airfields outside Canal Zone.

1945   National Assembly refuses to grant de la Guardia an extension of his term.

Constitutional Assembly approves a new constitution with modern social and economic features.

Reemergence of labor movement.

Formation of Trade Union Federation of the Republic of Panama.

1946   U.S. Army opens School of the Americas ("the school of coups") in violation of 1903 treaty which only allows presence of U.S. troops for defense of canal.

1947   In response to popular pressure, National Assembly rejects new treaty to extend time allotted to U.S. military sites outside Canal Zone.

Colón Free Trade Zone created at Atlantic entrance to Panama Canal.

1948   Díaz Arosemena defeats Arnulfo Arias for presidency.

1949   Death of Díaz Arosemena creates political crisis resolved by Police Commander José A. Remón, who installs Arnulfo Arias after recounting year-old ballots.

1951   Panamanian police forces oust Arnulfo Arias.

1952   Police Commander Remón creates National Patriotic Coalition that carries him to victory in the presidential elections.

1953   With strong U.S. financing and backing, Panama creates National Guard modeled after Somoza's Nicaraguan National Guard.

Import-substitution law promotes industrial development.

1955   Remón assassinated; First Vice President José Guizado inaugurated and then impeached due to suspicion of his involvement in Remón's death; Second Vice President Ricardo Arias Espinoza installed as president.

Treaty of Mutual Understanding and Cooperation signed, granting Panama's growing manufacturing and cattle interests greater access to Canal Zone market.

1956   National Patriotic Coalition candidate Ernesto de la Guardia elected.

Formation of Confederation of Workers of the Republic of Panama with U.S. prompting and Panamanian government support.

1958	University students plant Panamanian flags in Canal Zone under "Operation Sovereignty."
1959	Anti-U.S. demonstrations over sovereignty of Canal Zone; Hunger and Desperation March sparks new renters' and minimum wage laws.
1960	National Opposition Union candidate Roberto Chiari elected president.
1963	Panamanian and U.S. governments issue joint statement advising that both national flags be flown side by side in Canal Zone.
1964	
Jan.	Panamanian students attacked by U.S. police after demanding flags of both countries be flown at Canal Zone high school. During subsequent civil protests, 21 Panamanians are killed, more than 400 wounded, and over 500 arrested; diplomatic relations with United States severed; OAS called in to mediate.
Apr.	Diplomatic relations with United States restored; negotiations begin to draft new treaties to resolve conflicts.
June	Study groups from University of Panama and National Bar Association object to draft treaties.
	Marco Aurelio Robles elected president.
1967	Set of three new treaties to replace 1903 agreements are signed by Presidents Robles and Johnson but are not ratified by U.S. Congress nor Panamanian Assembly.
1968	Arnulfo Arias elected for the third time, deposed by a military coup soon after being sworn in headed by Major Boris Martínez and Lt. Colonel Omar Torrijos. Junta is formed and power is assumed by the National Guard.
1969	Torrijos exiles Martínez. Torrijos survives abortive coup attempt after which he consolidates power.
1970	New banking legislation creates haven for international financial transactions in Panama. Soon Panama has over 100 banking establishments with over $40 billion in deposits.
1972	Panamanian government assumes control of Río Hato military base after refusing to renew agreement.
	Election of 505 member National Assembly of Community Representatives.
	New constitution promulgated; Torrijos named "Supreme Leader of the Panamanian Revolution" and Head of Government.
	New Labor Code becomes effective.
1973	UN Security Council meets in Panama and exhorts both countries to negotiate treaty returning Canal Zone to Panama. United States vetoes resolution.
1977	Torrijos and President Carter sign Panama Canal Treaties in Washington D.C. giving Panama control of canal at noon on December 31, 1999. Accords create Panama Canal Commission with binational board of directors to replace U.S. government's Panama Canal Company.

Canal treaties approved in Panama.

Comunbana becomes marketing arm of UPEB. United Brands refuses to load Comunbana ships in Panama, government threatens nationalization of United Brands acreage.

1978 Canal treaties ratified by U.S. Senate with provision that permits U.S. intervention if canal's operation is interrupted, though such action shall not be interpreted as a right of intervention in Panama's sovereignty or internal affairs.

National Assembly elects National Guard candidate Aristides Royo president.

Torrijos announces a "democratic opening," his return to barracks, and organization of Revolutionary Democratic Party (PRD).

1979 Canal treaties go into effect and U.S. control of Canal Zone officially ends.

Arrival of deposed Shah of Iran, triggering demonstrations and protests.

1981 Torrijos dies in unexplained plane crash; Col. Florencio Flores succeeds him as head of National Guard.

1982 President Royo resigns under pressure from national Guard; Ricardo De La Espriella becomes president.

Rubén Darío Paredes ousts Flores as head of National Guard.

1983 Paredes steps down as Commander and is replaced by Manuel Antonio Noriega who appears to support his bid for presidency.

National Guard is officially renamed Panamanian Defense Forces (PDF). Noriega becomes first PDF commander.

Jan. Contadora Group, composed of Colombia, Mexico, Panama, and Venezuela, meets for first time on Panamanian island of Contadora to develop peace accords to which Costa Rica, El Salvador, Guatemala, Honduras, and Nicaragua are parties.

Sept. Contadora peace plan unveiled; calls for policy of nonaggression in Caribbean Basin.

Oct. United States invades Grenada.

1984

Jan. Student immolates himself in front of U.S. embassy.

Feb. President De La Espriella resigns and is replaced by Jorge Illueca Sibuaste.

May Nicolás Ardito Barletta narrowly defeats Arnulfo Arias in fraudulent elections.

Sept. School of the Americas closes after training nearly 45,000 Latin American officers; relocates to Ft. Benning, Georgia.

Oct. New government inaugurated. Secretary of State George Shultz attends the ceremonies and calls Ardito Barletta "a longtime and respected friend."

1985 Hugo Spadafora, former vice minister of Health and heavily involved with contras, is assassinated upon his return from a visit to Costa Rica.

Inside Panama

Sept.	The military is accused of complicity in Spadafora's death; Ardito Barletta resigns; Noriega installs industrialist Eric Arturo Delvalle. Reagan administration shows its displeasure by canceling a performance by U.S. Air Force Thunderbirds.
Dec.	Admiral John Poindexter, Reagan's National Security chief, travels to Panama to confer with Noriega, allegedly on matters concerning contra campaign in Nicaragua.
1986	
Jan.	Blazing Trail and Kindle Liberty U.S. joint exercises in Honduras and Panama begin and continue for six months.
June	Seymour Hirsch alleges in *New York Times* that Noriega traffics in drugs and supplies arms to Colombian guerrillas.
	Oliver North plans to frame Sandinistas by "capturing" ship with arms in Panama Canal; plan bungled when military refuses to go along. Noriega seizes ship and exposes scheme.
1987	
June	Ousted second-in-command of Defense Forces accuses Noriega of rigging 1984 elections and murdering Hugo Spadafora; anti-government rioting results; ten-day "state of emergency" declared; constitutional guarantees suspended.
	Panamanian government informs United States and other creditor nations that it is stopping all principal and interest payments. Rumors of printing Panamanian currency lead to heavy bank withdrawals.
	U.S. Senate calls for Noriega to step down and calls for new elections. U.S. embassy attacked by a hundred protesters; United States demands payment for damages to building.
Sept.	Secretary of State George Shultz formally approves freeze of U.S. economic and military aid to Panama.
Dec.	All U.S. military aid suspended; sugar quota suspended.
	Panamanian government fails to pay Christmas bonuses to government employees.
1988	
Feb.	U.S. Justice Department seals indictments charging Noriega and others with international drug trafficking.
	After meeting with Elliott Abrams, President Delvalle attempts to fire Noriega. Delvalle himself is ousted by National Assembly, which then appoints Manuel Solís Palma. Delvalle goes into hiding but United States recognizes him as Panama's president.
	Run begins on national banks by depositors, strikes by opposition occur.
Mar.	U.S. government freezes Panama's assets abroad and Delvalle urges boycott of Panama.
	Government closes nation's banks which remain closed for nine weeks.
	Coup attempt shuts down economy; massive power outages shut down oil pipeline; transportation disrupted; two week lockout strike.

Chronology

	Dignity Battalions, PDF paramilitary groups, are formed and begin training to resist possible U.S. invasion.
Apr.	President Reagan bars U.S. companies and individuals from making payments to Panamanian government, instead asking them to make payments to Delvalle-controlled federal reserve account.
May	Secret bargaining collapses between Reagan administration and Noriega.
July	CIA develops coup plan which might result in Noriega's assassination by dissident officers; plan nixed by Senate Select Committee on Intelligence and opposition is given mobile transmitter instead.
Aug.	United States charges more than 240 cases of harassment against U.S. military personnel by Panamanian authorities.
Nov.	George Bush is elected president.
1989	U.S. supports opposition efforts to win scheduled general elections with a broad alliance (ADOC) of conservative and business interests led by Christian Democrats and *Arnulfistas*.
May	ADOC presidential candidate Guillermo Endara wins by a broad margin but Electoral Tribunal nullifies election.
	President Bush recalls U.S. ambassador, dispatches additional 2,000 troops to Panama, tells Pentagon to stage series of aggressive maneuvers.
	OAS forms a mediation commission with foreign ministers of Ecuador, Guatemala, and Trinidad-Tobago.
July	OAS ministers propose that Noriega step down, government of transition take power, and elections be held at later date; they also call for end to U.S. military and economic aggression, compliance with 1977 Canal Treaties, and OAS mediation during negotiation process.
	Estimated 75,000 civil servants protest U.S. army maneuvers along canal banks.
	U.S. commander in Panama, critical of Bush's escalating policies, is replaced by aggressive Gen. Maxwell R. Thurman who is told to prepare for invasion.
Aug.	Panama calls for urgent meeting of UN Security Council because of U.S. maneuvers.
	United States rejects calls from OAS to lift sanctions and presents alleged proof of Noriega's involvement in drug trafficking.
Sept.	General Council of State names provisional government led by Francisco Rodríguez and announces elections will be called within six months after sanctions are lifted. United States withdraws its ambassador; many Latin American ambassadors called home for consultations.
Oct.	Failed coup attempt against Noriega.
Nov.	Bush administration bans Panamanian flagged ships from U.S. ports.

Dec.	Noriega elected head of government with unlimited powers by National Assembly.
	U.S. invasion with 26,000 troops; United States installs Endara as president; after two weeks in hiding and sanctuary in the papal nunciature, Noriega turns himself over to U.S. officials.
1990	Noriega is arrested by DEA agents in Panama City and flown out of country to be arraigned in Miami Court on drug charges.
	United States recognizes 500 dead as consequence of December invasion. Others claim death toll in thousands.
	Vice-president Arias Calderón reorganizes PDF and changes name back to National Police.
	U.S. military puts down police uprising against President Endara.
1991	U.S. military occupation continues throughout country although signs of withdrawal are evident.
	Common graves are opened by nongovernmental organizations seeking to identify bodies hastily buried after invasion.
	Christian Democrats (PDC) abandon government alliance but continue cooperating in Assembly.
1992	Popular referendum rejects government proposed constitutional reforms including banning armed forces.
1993	Panama creates Interoceanic Regional Authority (ARI) to plan use of lands and properties formerly under U.S. jurisdiction.
	U.S. contends President Endara's government has not done enough to stop money laundering.
	U.S. invites Panamanian Police to U.S. Army School of Americas for special military training.
	Panamanian press releases story implicating Panamanian consular officials in Spain in international arms trafficking ring.
Sept. 1994	Jury acquits seven of ten soldiers implicated in Spadafora murder.
Jan.	Ruling government alliance (ADOC) among PLA, MOLIRENA, and *Arnulfistas* collapses.
May	Ernesto Pérez Balladares, PRD candidate and former Noriega political ally, wins presidential election with U.S. blessings.
June	First group of U.S Southern Command troops stationed in Panama leaves country, beginning all-out withdrawal to be completed by December 31, 1999.

SOURCES: Tom Barry and Debra Preusch, *Central America Fact Book* (Grove Press, 1986); *Conflict in Central America* (U.K.: Longman Group Limited, 1987); U.S. Embassy in Panama (1975); *Encyclopedia of the Third World* (1987); Gerald Greenfield and Sheldon Maran, eds., *Labor Organizations in Latin America* (Greenwood Press, 1987); *The Washington Post* (May 10, 1989); Central America Education Project (Summer 1987); Regionews from Managua, *Pensamiento Propio*, September 1989; *Albuquerque Journal* (October 4, 1989); *The Nation* (March 12, 1988); *Central America Report*.

For More Information

Resources

Centro de Capacitación Social (CCS)
Apartado Postal 9A-192
Panamá, República de Panamá

Centro de Estudios y Acción Social Panameño (CEASPA)
Apartado Postal 6-133, El Dorado
Panamá, República de Panamá
(507)26-6602   fax: (507)26-5320   e-mail: ceaspa@nicarao.apc.org

Centro de Estudios Latinoamericanos (CELA)
Apartado Postal 6-3093, El Dorado
Panamá, República de Panamá
(507)23-0028   fax: (507)69-2032   e-mail: cela@nicarao.apc.org

Fellowship of Reconciliation
515 Broadway
Santa Cruz, CA 95060
(408)423-1626   fax: (408)423-8716   e-mail: fornatl@igc.apc.org
Organizes campaign for U.S. military withdrawal from Panama, including regular delegations to Panama, advocacy, urgent action appeals, speaking tours.

Instituto del Canal de Panamá y Estudios Internacionales
Universidad de Panamá
Estafeta Universitaria
Panamá, República de Panamá
(507)69-9962   fax: (507)69-9963

Human Rights

Americas Watch
1522 K Street NW, Suite 910
Washington DC 20005

Amnesty International
322 8th Avenue
New York, NY 10001

Center for Constitutional Rights
666 Broadway
New York, NY
Handles the suit of victims of the 1989 U.S. invasion before the
Inter-American Human Rights Commission.

Coordinadora Popular de Derechos Humanos en Panamá
(COPODEHUPA)
Apartado Postal 1151, Zona 1
Panamá, República de Panamá
Works directly with invasion victims who are suing the United
States before the Inter-American Human Rights Commission.

Servicio Paz y Justicia (SERPAJ) Panama
Apartado Postal 87-2518
Panamá, República de Panamá
(507)24-0618   fax: (507)24-0782

Official

Embassy of Panama
2862 McGill Terrace NW
Washington DC 20008-2748

U.S. State Department
Citizen's Emergency Center/Travel Information
Main State Building
Washington DC 20520
(202) 647-5225

The Resource Center

The Interhemispheric Resource Center is a private, nonprofit, research and policy institute located in New Mexico. Founded in 1979, the Resource Center produces books, policy reports, and other educational materials about U.S. foreign policy, as well as sponsoring popular education projects. For more information and a catalog of publications, please write to the Resource Center, Box 4506, Albuquerque, New Mexico 87196.

Board of Directors

Become an RC member!

Yes! 1 want to support your efforts to make the U.S. a responsible member of the world community.

☐ **$25 Basic Membership:** You receive one year (four issues) of our quarterly *Resource Center Bulletin*.

☐ **$50 Amiga/Amigo Membership:** You receive subscriptions to the *Bulletin*, bimonthly *Democracy Backgrounder*, monthly *BorderLines*, and all our special reports.

☐ **$100 Compañera/Compañero Membership:** You receive all our periodicals, special reports, and a 33% discount on RC books.

☐ **$250 Comadre/Compadre Membership:** You receive all the benefits of a compañera/o membership as well as all new RC materials free.

☐ **$1,000 RC Sustainer:** You receive all new publications, and you may take your pick of existing materials from our catalog.

Charge my ☐ VISA ☐ MasterCard

Account # _____

Expiration date _____ Daytime Phone ( ) _____

Name_____

Street Address_____

City_____ State_____ Zip_____

The Interhemispheric Resource Center is a 501(c)3 nonprofit organization. All donations are tax deductible to the extent allowable by law.

☐ Please do not trade my name with other organizations.

To receive our catalog, write us or give us a call:

Interhemispheric Resource Center
P.O. Box 4506
Albuquerque, NM 87196
phone: (505) 842-8288
fax: (505) 246-1601

Central America

GUATEMALA
1992   307 pp.
ISBN 0-911213-40-6
$11.95

BELIZE
1995   181 pp.
ISBN 0-911213-54-6
$11.95

HONDURAS
1994   208 pp.
ISBN 0-911213-49-X
$11.95

COSTA RICA
1995   176 pp.
ISBN 0-911213-51-1
$11.95

EL SALVADOR
1995   283 pp.
ISBN 0-911213-53-8
$11.95

PANAMA
1995   196 pp.
ISBN 0-911213-50-3
$11.95

NICARAGUA
1990   226 pp.
ISBN 0-911213-29-5
$9.95

Everything you need to know about each nation's economy, politics, environment, and society.

ZAPATA'S REVENGE

Free Trade and the Farm Crisis in Mexico

by Tom Barry

The past and future collide in this compelling account of the drama unfolding in the Mexican countryside. Visions of a modernized and industrialized nation competing in the global market clash with the sobering reality of a desperate peasantry and falling agricultural production. These crises in Chiapas are the same ones confronting most of Mexico and the third world.

Barry views the crisis that confronts Mexico as alarming evidence of the incapacity of today's neoliberal and free trade policies to foster broad economic development. He explains that such strategies have resulted in reduced food security, environmental destruction, increased rural-urban polarization, depopulation of peasant communities and social and political instability.

This book offers personal interviews, investigative research, and analysis that goes to the heart of the development challenge faced by Mexico and other Latin American nations.

South End Press, 1995
ISBN 089608-499-X

250 PAGES
$16.00 paper

$35.00 cloth